FOURTH EDITION

CULTURES AND SOCIETIES IN A CHANGING WORLD

Other titles for your consideration from the Sociology for a New Century Series

SOCIOLOGY FOR A NEW CENTURY

FOURTH EDITION

CULTURES AND SOCIETIES IN A CHANGING WORLD

◆

WENDY GRISWOLD

Northwestern University

WITH

Christopher Carroll

Gemma Mangione

Michelle Naffziger

Talia Schiff

Los Angeles | London | New Delhi
Singapore | Washington DC

Los Angeles | London | New Delhi
Singapore | Washington DC

FOR INFORMATION:

SAGE Publications, Inc.
2455 Teller Road
Thousand Oaks, California 91320
E-mail: order@sagepub.com

SAGE Publications Ltd.
1 Oliver's Yard
55 City Road
London EC1Y 1SP
United Kingdom

SAGE Publications India Pvt. Ltd.
B 1/I 1 Mohan Cooperative Industrial Area
Mathura Road, New Delhi 110 044
India

SAGE Publications Asia-Pacific Pte. Ltd.
33 Pekin Street #02-01
Far East Square
Singapore 048763

Acquisitions Editor: David Repetto
Editorial Assistant: Lydia Balian
Production Editor: Astrid Virding
Copy Editor: Kristin Bergstad
Typesetter: C&M Digitals (P) Ltd.
Proofreader: Dennis W. Webb
Indexer: Molly Hall
Cover Designers: Anupama Krishnan and Candice Harman
Marketing Manager: Erica DeLuca
Permissions Editor: Adele Hutchinson

Printed in the United States of America

Library of Congress Cataloging-in-Publication Data

Griswold, Wendy.

Cultures and societies in a changing world / Wendy Griswold. — 4th ed.

p. cm. — (Sociology for a new century series)
Includes bibliographical references and index.

ISBN 978-1-4129-9054-7 (pbk.)

1. Culture. 2. Social change. I. Title.

HM621.G75 2013
306—dc23   2011040896

This book is printed on acid-free paper.

12 13 14 15 16 10 9 8 7 6 5 4 3 2 1

Contents

List of Figures

Foreword

Sociology for a New Century offers the best of current sociological thinking to today's students. The goal of the series is to prepare students, and—in the long run—the informed public, for a world that has changed dramatically in the last three decades and one that continues to astonish. These goals reflect important changes that have taken place in sociology. The discipline has become broader in orientation, with an ever-growing interest in research that is comparative, historical, or transnational in orientation. Sociologists are less focused on "American" society as the pinnacle of human achievement and more sensitive to global processes and trends. They also have become less insulated from surrounding social forces. In the 1970s and 1980s sociologists were so obsessed with constructing a science of society that they saw impenetrability as a sign of success. Today, there is a greater effort to connect sociology to the ongoing concerns and experiences of the informed public. Each book in this series offers a comparative, historical, transnational, or global perspective in some way, to help broaden students' vision. Students need to be sensitized to diversity in today's world and to the sources of diversity. Knowledge of diversity challenges the limitations of conventional ways of thinking about social life. At the same time, students need to be sensitized to the fact that issues that may seem specifically "American" (for example, struggles over gender equality, an aging population bringing a strained social security and health care system, racial conflict, national chauvinism, the interplay of religion and politics, and so on) are shared by many other countries. Awareness of commonalities undercuts the tendency to view social issues and questions in narrowly American terms and encourages students to seek out the experiences of others for the lessons they offer. Finally, students also need to be sensitized to phenomena that transcend national boundaries—trends and processes that are supranational (for example, environmental degradation). Recognition of global processes stimulates student awareness of causal forces that transcend national boundaries, economies, and politics. Using classical and contemporary sociological theory to analyze both traditional topics—such as culture and stratification, culture and identity, sociological approaches to arts and literature—and newer ones including global cultural flows, religious terrorism, and the profound impact of the Internet, *Cultures and Societies in a Changing World* explores the complex interplay between cultures—idea systems, artworks, popular culture, religious beliefs, common sense—and social structures. Within the framework of the "cultural diamond" this book uses a comparative analysis of cultural objects and practices in Nigeria, China, the United States, and other locations around the world to demonstrate how cultural producers and consumers express a changing world through culture and how culture itself contributes to social changes. Chapter-long examinations of the culture construction of social problems and organizational transactions reveal how the application of a culturally informed approach can illuminate seemingly non-cultural issues ranging from those involving social justice to those entailed in practical business operations.

Preface

Culture fascinates sociologists nowadays, but this was not always the case. When I began teaching, in the early 1980s, material outcomes and structural explanations for social phenomena—such things as income, education, fertility changes, and economic pressures—were under the sociological big top; culture and cultural explanations were a sideshow. True, there were always sociologists who studied religion, values, arts, and the like, and there were always anthropologists whose study of culture influenced sociological thinking. But as a whole, sociology did not pay much attention to culture. As any teacher or student of sociology will know, times have changed. The past several years have witnessed an explosion of cultural studies in sociology, as well as in the adjacent social sciences of political science, psychology, and even economics. This rise of cultural sociology has a number of causes, most generally the inherent limitations of strictly material factors to explain human behavior or to capture human experience. Therefore, most sociologists now view people as meaning makers as well as rational actors, symbol users as well as class representatives, and storytellers as well as points in a demographic trend. Moreover, sociology largely has escaped its former either/or way of thinking. The discipline now seeks to understand how people's meaning making shapes their rational action, how their class position molds their stories—in short, how social structure and culture mutually influence one another. Although all of this is very satisfying to cultural sociologists who no longer have to think of themselves as laboring in the wilderness, problems bedevil teachers and students in the classroom. Everyone wants to talk about symbols, discourse, meaning, and cultural practices, but systematic guides to such discussions are rare. Needed are concise introductions to cultural sociology to help students (1) explore the concept of culture and the nature of its linkages with the social world, (2) enhance their understanding of seemingly structural issues such as poverty or ethnicity by applying cultural analysis to these issues, and (3) broaden their cultural and social horizons so that they may operate effectively in the global economy and international culture of the twenty-first century. These are the goals of this book.

The Cultural Diamond

Cultures and Societies in a Changing World will enable students taking broad-ranging courses in sociology or social problems and students taking specialized courses in cultural sociology to think more clearly about the role culture plays in shaping our social world. The book introduces the sociology of culture, the branch of sociology that looks at cultural phenomena—including stories, beliefs, media, ideas, works of art, religious practices, fashions, rituals, specialized knowledge, and common sense—from a sociological perspective. At the same time, it suggests how such cultural phenomena operate in more general social processes. Finally, looking at the culture-society relationship from the other direction, it shows how social forces influence culture. In the book, I use the device of the "cultural diamond" to investigate the connections among four elements: *cultural objects*—symbols, beliefs, values, and practices; *cultural creators,* including the organizations and systems that produce and distribute cultural objects; *cultural receivers,* the people who experience culture and specific cultural objects; and the *social world,* the context in which culture is created and experienced. We examine these elements and connections in Chapters 1 through 4. Then, in Chapters 5 and 6, we discuss how the cultural diamond operates in two specific cases: social problems and business transactions. In Chapter 7, we look at culture and community in the dawning age of global electronic culture. In Chapter 8, we tackle the ever-more-pressing subject of power—political, social, domestic—and examine the role culture plays in exerting or resisting regimes of dominance.

A Global Approach

An international or global outlook is indispensable to any sociological study in today's world, and cultural studies are no exception. This study of culture is global in at least three ways.

Cross-National Cases

First, we consider examples of cultural phenomena and processes from a wide variety of countries and periods. The world has always contained a bewildering assortment of cultures, of course, but lately Americans have become increasingly concerned with the implications of this fact for their internal social policies and external economic and political relationships. Although we examine aspects of the Western cultural tradition in general and American culture in particular, we draw on materials from different traditions and cultures as well, including numerous examples from cultures of special interest to Americans, such as Israel and Japan. Four places— Nigeria, China, the Middle East, and the United States—serve repeatedly to demonstrate problems and issues in cultural analysis, because they constitute dramatically different starting points for societies entering the twenty-first century. Nigeria contains an extraordinary mixture of languages, ethnicities, and religions, with no one group in the majority. Under British colonial rule for more than half of the twentieth century, Nigeria struggles to reconcile political unity and cultural diversity while achieving greater economic development. China has had an advanced culture and centralized political control for millennia, but revolutionary political change in the mid-twentieth century has brought about massive social and cultural dislocations. Now China has embarked on an experiment with hitherto unheard of dimensions: to see whether economic freedom can flourish while tight political and cultural controls remain. The Middle East has dominated the headlines, hopes, and fears of the twenty-first century as pressures for social and cultural change collide with authoritarian regimes and strongly held traditions. Finally, the United States, along with its Western European allies, dominated the bipolar Cold War era of the mid-twentieth century. It seemed to represent the pinnacle of advanced, industrial society, complete with a modern culture, toward which all societies presumably were converging. Now the fracturing of former political alliances and the new complexity of international relations, along with the increasingly undeniable claims made by culturally diverse groups internally, challenge the validity of a specifically American culture and the applicability of American values in a troubled and rapidly changing world. For these reasons, Nigeria, China, and the United States offer thought-provoking running examples of some of the most perplexing culture problems facing the new century.

Global Culture

The second way in which this book is global in scope is that we consider how globalization processes themselves are affecting culture and cultures. From transnational media to tourist art to the immigration of peoples to international production of manufactured goods, processes taking place at the global level have all but obliterated pockets of cultural purity and have made parochialism increasingly costly as well as naive. Technological advances in communications have leaped cultural boundaries, just as global markets have transcended national differences; indeed, these two factors are closely related. The Internet seems to be both fostering a world culture without boundaries and encouraging a renewed sense of cultural particularism— new boundaries, rooted in ethnicity, religion, and geography. The point is neither to celebrate nor to bemoan these inexorable processes of globalization and differentiation but to understand them.

Cultural Conflicts

Third, many of the most intractable conflicts taking place in the post– Cold War era involve culture. Struggles over ethnic homogeneity and religious fundamentalism, to take just two examples particularly costly in human blood, clearly involve meanings and passions that go far beyond the merely economic or political. Similarly, negotiations between international business partners or heads of state, and more generally relations among people from different cultural backgrounds, can be smoother and more productive if the parties recognize the influences of different cultures. Understanding the cultural bases of past and current struggles and misunderstandings may help avoid repetition of costly mistakes. Such understanding will equip students to live their professional and personal lives as effective and wise citizens of a world where both cultures and societies are changing more quickly than ever before in human history.

About the Author

Wendy Griswold has a background in both social science and the humanities. She received her doctorate in sociology from Harvard University in 1980 and has a master's degree in English from Duke University. She taught at the University of Chicago from 1981 to 1997. She is the Bergen Evans Professor in the Humanities and Professor of Sociology at Northwestern University. She has been associate editor and book review editor of the *American Journal of Sociology* and has been on the editorial boards of *Contexts*, *Poetics*, and *Acta Sociologica*. She is on the Advisory Board for the Centro per lo Studio della Moda e della Produzione Culturale, Università Cattolica del Sacro Cuore, Milan and she is associate editor for *Contexts* and *Poetics*. She has received research support from the National Science Foundation, the National Endowment for the Humanities, support from the Guggenheim Foundation, the National Science Foundation, the American Council of Learned Societies, the Center for Advanced Studies in the Behavioral Sciences, and the European University Institute in Florence. Her research on culture has been international in scope. Her most recent book is *Regionalism and the Reading Class* (2008); she is currently completing a book on the WPA Federal Writers' Project and its impact on American culture. *Bearing Witness: Readers, Writers, and the Novel in Nigeria* (2000) won the "Best Book" award for the Sociology of Culture section of the American Sociological Association. Her first book was on the English theater (*Renaissance Revivals: City Comedy and Revenge Tragedy in the London Theatre 1576–1980* [1986]). In addition, she coedited a book on the sociology of literature (*Literature and Social Practice* [1989]) and has written on the sociology of religion, specifically on conflict within churches. Her current research explores cultural regionalism; she is also studying the relationship between the Internet and reading in Africa. She has written an influential paper on sociological methods for cultural analysis ("A Methodological Framework for the Sociology of Culture," *Sociological Methodology* 17 [1987]:1–35); much of her methodological thinking is incorporated in the present book.

1

Culture and the Cultural Diamond

Culture is one of those words that people use all the time but have trouble defining. Consider the following stories about some of the wildly different things we envision when we talk about culture.

In September 2010 France's Senate voted 246 to 1 to ban women from wearing a full-face veil (niqab or burqa) in public. Many Muslims argue that veiling, which they regard as defending female modesty from intrusive male eyes, is intrinsic to their culture. The minister of justice, on the other hand, says that the ban affirms French cultural values of dignity and equality. Girls growing up under these two cultures may feel torn by the incompatible rules for being a good French citizen and a good Muslim.

On a Friday evening in the college dining hall, a half-dozen students discuss their plans for the weekend. One says she's going to a basketball game, another says he's checking out a hip-hop group playing at a local club, and a third says she's staying in to download some music and watch videos. A fourth mutters, "Study and sleep, just like always, no life," while a fifth counters with "Party!" Then the sixth announces, "Well, guys, you may be wasting the weekend, but *I'm* going to get some culture. Tonight, I'm meeting friends at an art exhibit opening in a gallery downtown, and my girlfriend and I have symphony tickets for tomorrow." His friends start making cracks about him being a culture vulture, while he jokes back about *some people* having more *taste* than other people.

An American conducting business in Tokyo hopes to land a lucrative contract for her firm. When her Japanese counterpart presents his card, she takes it casually with one hand, glances at it, and sticks it in her pocket. Subsequent relations with her Japanese prospect prove frosty, and her firm loses the contract. "Ah," says an experienced friend, "you lost out because of a cultural misunderstanding. In Japan, the business card is considered an extension of the person; one treats the card with great respect, holding it with two hands and carefully putting it in a safe place. Americans don't think of it that way; for them, the card is just a convenience. You insulted the very person you were trying to court."

Fitness demands hours in the gym and years of self-denial pursuing the six-pack abs and lean musculature of the cultural ideal. The fit body carries a wealth of meanings—sexual attractiveness, discipline, health—but at the same time advertisers urge consumers to purchase this body, in effect, by spending both time and money (e.g., gym membership, personal trainers). One result is that fitness is more available to the affluent than to the poor. As both cultural ideal and cultural commodity, it helps reproduce class and gender inequalities (Dworkin and Wachs 2009).

In an urban mixed-race neighborhood, sociologist Elijah Anderson (1990) observes casual street encounters in which African Americans appear uncomfortable when they pass Caucasians walking their dogs, despite the dog walkers' assurances that their pets are friendly. This results from a cultural difference, he concludes:

> In the working-class black subculture, "dogs" does not mean "dogs in the house," but usually connotes dogs tied up outside, guarding the backyard, biting trespassers bent on trouble. Middle-class and white working-class people may keep dogs in their homes, allowing them the run of the house, but many black working-class people I interviewed failed to understand such behavior. When they see a white adult on his knees kissing a dog, the sight may turn their stomachs—one more piece of evidence attesting to the peculiarities of their white neighbors. (222)

All five stories involve culture, but each seems to talk about very different things: national customs (handling business cards), activities considered elitist (attending the symphony), personal practices (going to the gym), and local variations in symbolic meanings (what dogs or veils represent). Together they suggest that culture, though rather hard to pin down, is important to understand. Cultural ignorance or misunderstanding, it seems, can lead to highly undesirable outcomes: lost business, interethnic tension, or an inability to participate in either the comic or the transcendent moments in human experience.

What is this concept called culture that can apply to such a wide variety of situations? Why do notions of culture inflame such intense passions that huge numbers of people—from sectarians in Mumbai to gang members in Chicago—regularly kill and die for their symbols, their beliefs, and their cultures? Moreover, how can we gain a better understanding of the connections between the concept of culture and the social world? This chapter addresses these questions.

Two Ways of Looking at Culture

When sociologists talk about culture, Richard Peterson (1979) observed, they usually mean one of four things: *norms, values, beliefs,* or *expressive symbols.* Roughly, norms are the way people behave in a given society, values are what they hold dear, beliefs are how they think the universe operates, and expressive symbols are representations, often of social norms, values, and beliefs themselves. In the last decades of the twentieth century, sociologists added a fifth item to the list: *practices.* Culture in this recent view describes people's behavior patterns, not necessarily connected to any particular values or beliefs. We discuss these various meanings later, but for now the point is that even such specialists as cultural sociologists use the word *culture* to stand for a whole range of ideas and objects.

The academic perspectives on culture can be sorted into two schools of thought. It is fair to say that most notions of culture stem from assumptions rooted in either the humanities or the social sciences, particularly anthropology. Although this book presents the social scientific perspective by and large, the distinctiveness of this stance emerges only in comparison with its counterpart in the humanities.

Before we begin, however, we must clarify one thing: Neither "culture" nor "society" exists out there in the real world—only people who work, joke, raise children, love, think, worship, fight, and behave in a wide variety of ways. To speak of culture as one thing and society as another is to make an analytical distinction between two different aspects of human experience. Think of the distinction as such that culture designates the expressive aspect of human existence, whereas society designates the relational (and often practical) aspect. Hugging dogs, paying respect to business cards, working out—these all describe methods for expressing our lives as social beings. The same object or behavior may be analyzed as social (a business card communicates information necessary for economic transactions) or cultural (a business card means something different to a Japanese than to an American). Now, oriented with this rough distinction between the expressive and the relational and with the recognition that both culture and society are abstractions, we may explore the two most influential seedbeds for contemporary thinking about the culture/society relationship.

"The Best That Has Been Thought and Known"

In common usage, the term *culture* often refers to the fine and performing arts or to serious literature, as in the facetious statement of the art-gallery- and symphony-goer, "*I'm* going to get some culture." Culture in this sense, sometimes called "high culture"—as opposed to popular culture, folk cul- ture, or mass culture—carries implications of high social status. The unthinking equation of culture with the arts results from a line of thinking, prominent in those disciplines collectively known as the humanities, whereby culture signifies a locus of superior and universal worth.

In the nineteenth century, many European intellectuals posited an opposi- tion between culture and society or, as they often put it, between culture and civilization. As they used the term, *civilization* referred to the technological advances of the Industrial Revolution and the accompanying social upheav- als. Contrasting culture with civilization was, therefore, a protest against Enlightenment thinking, against the belief in progress as an invariable ben- efit, against the ugly aspects of industrialization, and against what Marx called the "cash nexus" of capitalism whereby everyone and everything seemed evaluated on an economic basis. If civilization meant filthy tene- ments, factories spewing smoke into the air, and people treated as nothing more than so many replaceable parts, many thoughtful men and women wanted no part of it. They saw culture—entailing the wisest and most beau- tiful expressions of human effort—as its contrasting pole and the salvation of over-civilized human beings. This dichotomy set the alienating, dehumani- zing effects of industrial civilization against the healing, life-enhancing capacities of culture. Typical of this polarizing tendency was the English social philosopher John Stuart Mill's account, in his autobiography, of how his highly rationalized training in logic and economics brought him to a nervous breakdown. Only by reading Wordsworth's poetry, he testified, could he restore his sanity.

The automatic question that arises today occurred to nineteenth-century thinkers as well: How can we believe in culture's extraordinary, redeeming value without this belief turning into a narrow ethnocentrism, a hymn of praise to Western European culture as the summit of human achievement? Matthew Arnold (1822–1888), a British educator and man of letters, answered this question by formulating a universal theory of cultural value ([1869] 1949). Emphasizing culture's potential influence in the social world, he harshly criticized Victorian England for its mindless materialism and its worship of machines and freedom (in other words, industrialization and democracy) without considering the ends to which either should be put. He feared a result of either dull, middle-class Philistinism or social anarchy produced by rioting workers. The aristocrats, whom Arnold dismissed as "barbarians" too busy hunting foxes to bother defending culture, would provide no help. Only culture could save modern society.

What constituted this salvation of humankind? Culture, Arnold asserted, was "a study of perfection." Culture could make civilization more human by restoring "sweetness and light." Although it is now used pejoratively to convey superficial amiability, Arnold intended the expression *sweetness and light* to refer to beauty and wisdom, respectively. He took the idea of sweetness and light from Jonathan Swift's parable about the spiders versus the bees. Everyone thinks spiders are very industrious, Swift observed, but, in fact, spiders work only for themselves; they spin all those webs just to catch their own dinners. Bees, on the other hand, more properly admirable, unselfishly produce benefits for others: honey and the wax used in making candles or, in other words, sweetness and light. Arnold appropriated the more socially productive of Swift's two creatures in his definition of culture. Like the honey and candles that come from bees, the beauty and wisdom that culture provides come from (1) awareness of and sensitivity to "the best that has been thought and known" in art, literature, history, and philosophy and (2) "a right reason" (an open-minded, flexible, tolerant intelligence).

How does culture work? Arnold, the educator, saw culture in terms of its educational potential. He maintained that culture enables people to relate knowledge, including science and technology, to conduct and beauty. Civilization potentially relates harmoniously with knowledge, beauty, conduct, and social relations—a Greco-Roman view—and culture can bring about this harmony. Culture is not an end in itself but a means to an end. It can cure the social ills of unrestrained materialism and self-satisfied Philistinism by teaching people how to live and conveying moral ideas. In a sense, Arnold believed, culture can be the humanizing agent that moderates the more destructive impacts of modernization.

Arnold's conception of culture holds that it addresses a different set of issues from those addressed by logic or science. Surprisingly, German sociologist Max Weber (1864–1920), whom we shall encounter often in this book, took the same view. In his essay "Science as a Vocation," Weber laid out the limits of what science *cannot* do to set up his arguments about what science *can* do. The limits are what interest us here. What meaning for our lives can science offer? Weber suggested none (1946:143, 153):

> Tolstoi has given the simplest answer, with the words: "Science is meaningless because it gives no answer to our question, the only question important for us: 'What shall we do and how shall we live?'" . . . Science today is a "vocation" organized in special disciplines in the service of self-clarification and

knowledge of interrelated facts. It is not the gift of grace of seers and prophets
dispensing sacred values and revelations, nor does it partake of the contem-
plation of sages and philosophers about the meaning of the universe.

To answer Tolstoi's question and find a meaning for their lives, Weber
asserted, human beings must look to prophets and philosophers, to religion
and ideas. Most generally, they must turn to culture.

Weber was a scientist and Arnold a man of letters, but both emphasized
the separation of culture from everyday life in modern society and its ability
to influence human behavior. This way of looking at culture is traditionally
associated with the humanities (although contemporary humanities disciplines are more critical). The traditional humanities viewpoint

- evaluates some cultures and cultural works as better than others; it believes
  culture has to do with perfection. Deriving from a root word meaning "cultivation," as in agriculture, this sense of culture entails the cultivation of the
  human mind and sensibility.
- assumes that culture opposes the prevailing norms of the social order, or
  "civilization." Harmony between culture and society is possible but rarely
  achieved.
- fears that culture is fragile, that it can be "lost" or debilitated or estranged
  from socioeconomic life. Culture must be carefully preserved, through educational institutions, for example, and in cultural archives such as libraries and
  museums.
- invests culture with the aura of the sacred and ineffable, thus removing it from
  everyday existence. This separation is often symbolically accentuated: Bronze
  lions, for example, guard the entrance to the Art Institute of Chicago (and
  many libraries and museums elsewhere). Because of its extraordinary quality,
  culture makes no sense if we consider only its economic, political, or social
  dimensions.

It is important to recognize this "traditional humanities viewpoint" as an
ideal type, with contradictions and complexities smoothed away for the sake
of comparison. Moreover, it describes a rarified "high culture" definition
that few contemporary humanities departments would endorse. Nevertheless,
this understanding of culture lies deep in most people's thinking. Consider,
for example, the revulsion much of the world feels over looters ransacking
treasures from the art museums and archeological digs of Iraq. Observers are
horrified that looting, and the illicit market for rarities that supports it,
reduces something precious and sacred to a mere commodity and in so doing
decimates the cultural heritage—"the best that has been thought and
known"—of the Iraqi people. Such a value-laden view of culture can often
be seen as elitist, but at the same time it is widely held.

"That Complex Whole"

During the nineteenth century, the new disciplines of anthropology and sociology simultaneously advocated a very different way of thinking about culture than that put forth by Matthew Arnold. An early statement of this position came from the German philosopher Johann Gottfried Herder (1744–1803), who reacted strongly against the smugness of European culture at the end of the eighteenth century. Fascinated by traditional folk verse and the poetry of the Old Testament, Herder regarded such oral literature as spontaneous products of innate human creativity that sharply contrasted with the more artificial literary output of an educated elite. If all humanity comprised natural poets, how absurd to think that the European educated classes had somehow cornered the market on the "best that has been thought and known." Or, as Herder put it:

> Men of all the quarters of the globe, who have perished over the ages, you have not lived solely to manure the earth with your ashes, so that at the end of time your posterity should be made happy by European culture. The very thought of a superior European culture is a blatant insult to the majesty of Nature. (Williams 1976:79)

Herder argued that we must speak of cultures, not simply culture, for the obvious reason that nations, and communities within or across nations, have their own, equally meritorious cultures.

This view of culture as a given society's way of life was introduced to English anthropology by E. B. Tylor, who dismissed the whole culture-versus-civilization debate out of hand in his book *Primitive Culture* ([1871] 1958:1): "Culture or Civilization, taken in its wide ethnographic sense, is that complex whole which includes knowledge, belief, art, morals, law, custom, and any other capabilities and habits acquired by man as a member of society." This wide-ranging anthropological definition of culture has dominated the social sciences, including contemporary sociology, ever since. Sociologist Peter Berger (1969), for example, defines culture as "the totality of man's products," both material and immaterial. Indeed, Berger argued that even society itself is "nothing but part and parcel of non-material culture" (6–7). Although social scientists don't all agree to quite so expansive a definition, they don't agree on much else about culture either. Back in the 1950s when two anthropologists counted the different definitions of culture used in the social sciences, they came up with more than 160 distinct meanings (Kroeber and Kluckhohn 1952).

Viewing culture as a people's entire way of life avoids the ethnocentrism and elitism that the humanities-based definition falls prey to, but such an all-encompassing definition lacks the precision desired in the social sciences. A recent trend leans toward cutting the culture concept down to size and characterizing the object of analysis. Wuthnow and Witten (1988), for example, suggest that sociologists should distinguish between implicit and explicit culture. Sometimes, we regard culture as a tangible social construction, "a kind of symbolic good or commodity that is explicitly produced" (50), as in the case of a fit body or a veil worn by a Muslim woman. At other times, we see culture more abstractly as an "implicit feature of social life . . . a prefiguration or ground of social relations" (50), as in the cultural ground whereby Japanese and Americans handle business cards in different ways or American blacks and whites act differently around dogs. This distinction proves useful, not because either kind of culture is conceptually superior but because it can act as a preliminary classification in sorting out the many definitions of culture with which sociologists must deal. Implicit culture is hard to study, of course; in fact, it's hard to spot in the first place. We will consider ways for sociologists to pin down this elusive concept, but, for now, the point is to recognize these two sorts of culture: explicit, expressive, symbolic forms on the one hand and implicit grounding for action on the other. (Sometimes, the former is seen as the domain of "the sociology of culture," whereas the latter falls under "cultural sociology," but this terminological distinction is not uniformly adopted.)

Unlike the old-school humanists, social scientists of various schools of thought tend to see harmony, not opposition, between culture and society. The two most influential social scientific theories of the twentieth century—functionalism and Marxism—regard the fit as a close one. Functionalism, the branch of social theory that assumes a social institution usually serves some specific function necessary for the well-being of the collectivity, identifies culture with the values that direct the social, political, and economic levels of a social system. In the functionalist perspective, a fit exists between culture and society because any misfit would be dysfunctional. Robert Merton (1938), for example, once suggested that American culture places a high value on economic success. When people lack the practical means to attain the goal of success, he said, they experience severe strain, often turning to criminal behavior as a result. For most people in America and in any culture that functions smoothly, the goals given by the culture and the means for attaining these goals work in harmony. Coming from the opposite direction politically, Marxists also see a close fit between social structure and culture, but they reverse the direction of influence—from social structure to culture, not the other way around. In their view, cultural products, implicit or explicit, rest on an economic foundation. Both functionalism and Marxism are discussed in Chapter 2; for now, note that they share what we might call the "close-fit assumption."

As an example of this assumption, consider Peter Berger's (1969) analysis of culture as formed through externalization, objectification, and internalization. Berger suggests that human beings project their own experience onto the outside world (externalization), then regard these projections as independent (objectification), and finally incorporate these projections into their psychological consciousness (internalization). We can easily think of cases that seem to illustrate Berger's model. Let's take the fact that human reproduction involves two sexes. Many religious belief systems might be said to externalize the dualism of biological reproduction into dual powers, such as the Manichean worldview of an eternal war between good and evil or the Chinese dualities of yin and yang. Such dualities, based on direct experience, become objectified and exist in the culture independent of any human thinker. Entire cosmologies of contending forces of good and evil thereby grow around the male/female dichotomy. These cosmologies, in turn, become internalized, influencing human thought and practice. Thus, Christians imagine good and evil fighting within the soul—an angel whispering in one ear, a devil in the other—whereas Chinese medicine centers on the perceived need for a yin and yang balance in the body itself.

Anthropologist Clifford Geertz (1973:89) defined culture as "an historically transmitted pattern of meanings embodied in symbols, a system of inherited conceptions expressed in symbolic forms by means of which men communicate, perpetuate, and develop their knowledge about and attitudes toward life." Geertz's influential formulation is more precise than the entire-way-of-life social science definitions because it focuses on symbols and the behavior that derives from symbolically expressed ways of thinking and feeling. This definition captures what most sociologists currently mean when they use the term *culture*. To recapitulate, the social science standpoint

- avoids evaluation in favor of relativism. As two sociologists once put it, "The scientific rhetoric, tight-lipped and non-normative, brooks no invidious distinctions" (Jaeger and Selznick 1964:654). We may make evaluations in terms of culture's impact on the social order but not of the cultural phenomenon itself.
- assumes a close linkage between culture and society. In some schools of thought, one tends to determine the other, whereas others stress the mutual adjustments that take place between culture and social structure.
- emphasizes the persistence and durability of culture, rather than its fragility. Culture, seen more as an activity than as something that needs preserving in an archive, is not what lies in the museum guarded by those bronze lions; instead, it is the ways museum-goers (and everyone else) live their lives.
- assumes that culture can be studied empirically like anything else. Social scientists do not regard culture as sacred or fundamentally different from other human products and activities.

Again, this is a simplification to emphasize the contrast between the two standpoints. And again, many twenty-first-century social scientists would reject such aspects of this view as the close-fit assumption (Swidler 2001). If we go back to the example of looting in the Middle East, the social science approach would focus less on the "treasures" being destroyed and more on the practices of the people in the area. It would posit that in a time of upheaval, people respond in ways consistent with their cultural grounding. Thus, in Iraq they would point out that (1) virtually all looters are men (in Middle Eastern cultures, women appear less in public); (2) they wear the same checked masks as the Palestinian fighters (a style distinctive to this part of the world); (3) they openly offer the looted objects for sale (practices common to a trading bazaar culture); and (4) the armed guards stand by (the demands of locality and possible kinship outweigh those of job description). In such an analysis, the social scientist takes no moral position on the activity in question but instead attempts to understand the behavior on its own cultural terms.

One might well respond to the distinction we have been setting between the traditional humanities and the social scientific approaches, saying, "Look, there are advantages to both points of view. In the case of radical Islam, for instance, to understand why some Muslims are eager to die for their religion, it helps to see that their adherents regard their religious beliefs as 'the best that has been thought and known' and thus extraordinarily valuable. At the same time, an understanding of the political and economic contexts—the links between religion on the one hand and Middle Eastern social structure on the other—is necessary to comprehend and explain the recurring explosions of sectarian violence. So, why not try to understand culture by approaching it from both directions?"

Why not, indeed? In this book, although our object is a specifically sociological understanding of culture, we try to incorporate the insights of both traditions. We begin to do so by envisioning the culture/society connection in terms of "cultural objects" located in a "cultural diamond."

Connections: The Links Between Culture and Society

We have been looking at various definitions of culture, from the most restrictive (high art; "the best that has been thought and known") to the most expansive (the totality of humanity's material and nonmaterial products). We have seen that the word and the concept, especially as employed in the social sciences, take many shapes and that, therefore, any discussion of culture must begin with a definition. Here, then, is our working definition: Culture refers to the expressive side of human life—in other words, to behavior, objects, and ideas that appear to express, or to stand for, something else. This is the case whether we are talking about explicit or implicit culture. Such a working definition is not evaluative or focused on "the best"; nor is it the most expansive definition, for it restricts culture to the meaningful.

Geertz, and Weber before him, took culture to involve meaning, and in this book, we follow their example. Thus, we could talk about a community in terms of its culture: its jokes and slang; its conventions, stereotypes, typical practices, and common knowledge; and its symbols that represent and guide the thinking, feeling, and behavior of its members. Or, we could talk about that community in terms of social structure: its network of relationships among members, its institutions, and its economic and political life. The community's culture influences its social structure, and vice versa; indeed, the two are intertwined and have been separated only for purposes of analysis. To understand the community, the sociologist must understand both.

We need to do more, however, than simply define culture and indicate how to distinguish it analytically from social structure. We need a way to conceptualize how culture and the social world come together or, in other words, how people in social contexts create meaning. To draw on both the humanities and social science views for our analysis of culture and to examine cultural phenomena and their relation to social life, we need a conceptual framework and conceptual tools, such as the cultural object.

The Cultural Object

A cultural object may be defined as shared significance embodied in form (Griswold 1986). In other words, it is a socially meaningful expression that is audible, visible, or tangible or that can be articulated. A cultural object, moreover, tells a story, and that story may be sung, told, set in stone, enacted, or painted on the body. Examples range widely. A religious doctrine, a YouTube video, a belief that women are more sensitive than men, a Shakespearean sonnet, a hairstyle such as Rastafarian dreadlocks or the Manchu queue, a habit of saying "God bless you" when somebody sneezes, or a quilt made by hand or by robots—any and all of these can be cultural objects. Each tells a story. Notice that the status of the cultural object results from an analytic decision that we make as observers; it is not built into the object itself. If we think of the quilt as a product in a department store's inventory or something to warm our feet in bed and not in terms of its meaning, the quilt is not a cultural object. But when we consider it in terms of its story—how it expresses women collectively piecing together scraps to produce an object of beauty and utility—the quilt becomes a meaningful cultural object and may be analyzed as such.

In this book, we talk equally of "cultural objects" and "culture," so it is important to keep the terms straight. Specifying a cultural object is a way of grasping some part of the broader system we refer to as culture and holding up that part for analysis. One might compare this distinction to how we would go about studying a marsh. We would need to analyze the soil, the water, the climate, and the specific forms of animal and plant life found there (e.g., the leopard frog) in order to understand how the ecosystem works as a whole. On the other hand, if we were primarily interested in a particular species of frog, our study would concentrate on it, with the marsh as a biological context. Analogizing to our terms, the cultural object is the leopard frog, and the culture is the marsh.

In attempting to understand the connections between a society and its culture, it seems to make sense to start the analysis with a close examination of cultural objects, those smaller parts of the interrelated, larger system. Here, we follow the lead of the humanities: Culture *is* in a world apart, at least for analytical purposes. Literary critics, art historians, and others in the humanities usually focus on a work of art as a self-referential universe possessing structure and meaning. This practice seems sound for examining cultural objects in our wider social sciences definition. We start, therefore, by paying close attention to the cultural object itself. This does not imply an "art for art's sake" (or culture for culture's sake) rejection of the external world and how it impinges on the cultural object but simply means we first take the cultural object as evidence about itself. In other words, we start with the cultural object, though we certainly don't end there.

Consider the homely case of bread. Plain old bread, traditionally the food of subsistence for people who can afford nothing better, has lately taken on a certain élan. Bakers in upscale communities have worked on improving the quality of American bread by introducing international baking techniques and new ingredients. Boutique bakeries have become so successful that they have forced industry giants such as Pepperidge Farm to compete on their level. Americans raised on plain white bread now munch on Italian focaccia, seven-grain pita, and sourdough baguettes that would amaze the French. New types of bread incorporating nine different stone-ground grains or hand-wrought into breadsticks receive fulsome tribute as being "first rate, handsomely crisp of crust and, yes, downright sexy" (Fabricant 1992). Bread, sexy?

Think of bread not simply as food or a commodity but as a cultural object. Americans and Europeans eat a lot of bread, but they don't pay a great deal of attention to it. Bread is basic, fundamental, at the foundation of the nutrition pyramid (yawn). Practical and boring though it may be, bread can be expressive as well. The post–World War II baby boom generation, for example, grew up on soft, spongy white bread like Wonder Bread. The "wonder" lay in the technology—Wonder Bread was infused with vitamins to "grow strong bodies in 12 ways"—and although it didn't have an especially memorable flavor, baby boomers who spread it with concoctions such as peanut butter and Marshmallow Fluff thought it tasted just fine. It seemed to express a child's view of the good life. Later, in the 1960s and 1970s, that same baby boom generation rejected white bread, just as it rejected much else from mainstream American culture; defying the conventions they grew up with, these young people turned eating whole-grain bread into a political statement, one that expressed a repudiation of American capitalism, technology, and homogeneity.

Not only can bread be expressive; a moment's reflection reminds us that it is steeped in tradition. The Bible abounds in references to bread: It is the staff of life, it is unleavened during Passover, it is miraculously multiplied along with the fishes, and it should be cast upon the waters. In the Christian communion, it even embodies the Divine. During the first centuries of Islam, white bread symbolized a lack of discipline to the Arabs; a manuscript illustration shows a man enjoying a self-indulgent meal of roast kid, wine, and white bread (Tannahill 1973:173). In the European ethnic heritage that shaped many American institutions, bread connotes security, love, frugality, and family—even life itself.

We further recognize that bread, though ubiquitous in American kitchens, is by no means universal. Human beings eat different grains in different places: Many Chinese depend on rice, Senegalese on millet, and Mexicans on corn. In some of these countries, eating bread signifies being Westernized or modern, and it can become a political issue. In Nigeria, which enjoyed a period of oil-based wealth during the 1970s, the middle class developed a taste for bread made from imported flour and a distaste for local starches, such as yam and cassava. White bread connotes affluence and modernity for twentieth-century Nigerians just as it did for eighteenth-century Europeans. In the poorer "oil bust" years beginning in the 1980s, however, taxes on imports plus government advocacy of using locally produced foods attempted to shift Nigerian consumer tastes back to West African traditional starches. The battle has not been altogether successful, however, and the streets of Lagos teem with young hawkers of high-priced spongy white bread, something like our old friend Wonder Bread.

So, bread is basic, fundamental, and boring—but it is also biblically sanctioned, expressive, symbolic of European heritage or the good life, and even sexy. It is as much a part of a cultural system—whether we think of the local cultural system (the latest gustatory trends) or the global cultural system (the meaning of white bread in Nigeria)—as the more obviously "cultural" artifacts, such as television or ballet. Bread, then, is clearly a cultural object. Cultural objects compose part of a larger cultural system that we may want to analyze. How do the myriad components in this system mesh together? To look at the bigger picture of culture in society, we need one more analytical tool.

The Cultural Diamond

Cultural objects are made by human beings, a fact intrinsic to all of the various definitions—culture is "the best that has been thought and known" *by human beings* (Arnold); culture is the "meanings embodied in symbols" *through which human beings* communicate and pass on knowledge and attitudes (Geertz); culture is the externalization, objectification, and internalization *of human experience* (Berger)—and is the basis for the familiar distinction between culture and nature. Therefore, we may regard all cultural objects as having creators. These creators may be the people who first articulate and communicate an idea, the artists who fashion a form, or the inventors of a new game or new lingo. Any particular object may have a single creator, such as the author of a novel, or multiple creators, such as all of the people listed in the credits at the beginning of a movie.

Other people besides their creators experience cultural objects, of course. If a poet sings her odes in the wilderness with no one to hear or record, if a hermit invents a revolutionary new theology but keeps it to himself, if a radio program is broadcast but a technical malfunction prevents anyone from hearing it, these present potential but not actual cultural objects. Only when such objects become public, when they enter the circuit of human discourse, do they enter the culture and become cultural objects. Therefore, all cultural objects must have people who receive them, people who hear, read, understand, think about, enact, participate in, and remember them. We might call these people the object's audience, although that term is a bit misleading; the people who actually experience the object may differ from the intended or original audience, and far from being a passive audience, cultural receivers are active meaning makers.

Both cultural objects and the people who create and receive them are not floating freely but are anchored in a particular context. We can call this the social world, by which we mean the economic, political, social, and cultural patterns and exigencies that occur at any particular point in time. Cultural sociology centers, first and foremost, on the relationship between cultural objects and the social world. This even-handed attention to both the cultural and the social is one of the things that differentiate cultural sociology from cultural studies, which focuses more heavily on the cultural side. A second difference is methodological: cultural sociology, as a social science, depends more heavily on empirical methods and the analysis of evidence, whereas cultural studies is more purely interpretive. That said, there is considerable overlap between the two fields. (A good discussion of this distinction is in Inglis, Blaikie, and Wagner-Pacifici (2007).

We have identified four elements: creators, cultural objects, recipients, and the social world. Let us first arrange these four in the shape of a diamond and then draw a line connecting each element to every other one. Doing this creates what I call a cultural diamond (a diamond in the two-dimensional sense of a baseball diamond), which looks like Figure 1.1.

Our cultural diamond features four points and six links. We cannot call it a *theory* of culture, because it says nothing about how the points relate. Nor can we call it a *model* of culture in the strict sense, because it does not indicate cause and effect; in the cultural diamond, violence in the popular culture (e.g., gangsta rap) could be seen as "causing" violence in the social world, but the reverse could equally be the case. Instead, the

Figure 1.1   The Cultural Diamond

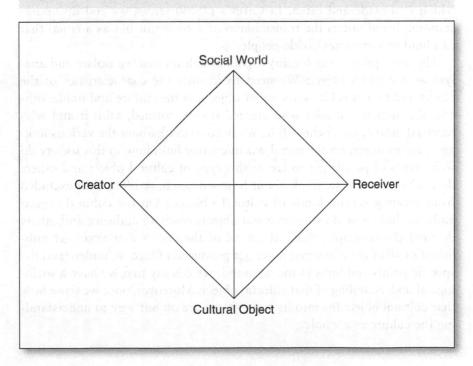

cultural diamond is an accounting device intended to encourage a fuller understanding of any cultural object's relationship to the social world. It does not say what the relationship between any of the points should be, only that there *is* a relationship. Moreover, the texture of that relationship lies as much in the links as in the four points.

Therefore, a complete understanding of a given cultural object requires understanding all four points and six links. Return to the example of bread, a cultural object of widespread but not universal meaningfulness. To understand bread in West Hollywood and Lagos, we would have to know about the producers (the growers, bakers, importers, trendsetting chefs and restaurant owners, and government bureaucrats setting import controls) and the consumers (the population and its demographic characteristics—how many children pack lunches, how many working couples eat out, how an aging and increasingly thrifty population gratifies its tastes for luxury, and how the African public has come to associate white bread with prosperity). We would need to understand linkages—the media connections advertising products to consumers, for example, or the system of distribution whereby Nigerian teenage boys acquire fresh bread to hawk on the highways. Only after investigating such points and connections can we feel confident that we understand the relationship—a specifically cultural relationship—that exists between bread and the society in which it is made and eaten. In Carey's (1989) terms, we end up understanding bread not as the transmission of a foodstuff but as a ritual that can bind or sometimes divide people.

The same proves true for any aspect of culture that we isolate and analyze as a cultural object: We need to identify the characteristics of the object and how it is like some other objects in the culture and unlike others. We need to consider who created (made, formed, said) it and who received (heard, saw, believed) it. We need to think about the various linkages; for example, on the social world/creator link, how in this society do some types of people get to create this type of cultural object and others do not? (For example, think about how women have often been excluded from creating certain kinds of cultural objects.) On the cultural object/audience link, how do some cultural objects reach an audience and others do not? (For example, think about all of the poems that never get published or all of the plays that never get produced.) Once we understand the specific points and links in the diamond, we can say that we have a sociological understanding of that cultural object. Moreover, once we sense how that cultural object fits into its context, we are on our way to understanding the culture as a whole.

SUMMARY

In this chapter, we learned the variety of uses for the term *culture* and how the term applies to ephemeral, even trivial, aspects of experience and to deeply held values for which people are willing to die. We compared the humanities' approach to culture with that of the social sciences and suggested that a full understanding of the relationship between culture and society must employ the insights of both perspectives. We suggested an approach to the sociological analysis of culture that uses the conceptual tools of the cultural object and the cultural diamond as a schema for organizing our thinking and investigation.

In the following chapters, we apply the cultural diamond schema to the complex web of connections between cultures and societies. The chapters are organized following the diamond: In Chapter 2, we concentrate on the meanings found in cultural objects (the social world/cultural object link); in Chapter 3, we examine creators of cultural objects (the diamond's left point); and in Chapter 4, we focus on systems of production (the links between creators, receivers, and cultural objects) and receivers or audiences themselves (the right point). In Chapters 5 and 6, we turn to two applications of sociologically informed cultural analysis: social problems and organizational transactions. In Chapter 7, we look at culture and politics, and in Chapter 8 we consider the relationship of culture and community in the global, postmodern, wired world of the new millennium.

QUESTIONS FOR STUDY AND DISCUSSION

1. Find an example of the word *culture* used in a magazine or newspaper. What are the cultural objects at issue? Is the writer using an implicit definition of culture more in line with the traditional humanities approach or the social science approach? What are the consequences of this definition for what the text is saying, and how would the message vary with a different definition?

2. Ask your friends and family what culture means to them. What are the significant similarities and differences in their understanding(s) of the word? Does age, gender, race, class, or place of residence shape their answers?

3. The cultural diamond was developed for the analysis of cultural objects such as works of literature or art. How well does it work for other types of objects such as religious beliefs, laws, customs, or rituals? Think of an example of such a cultural object; how could you apply the diamond? What insights might be gained from this type of analysis?

RECOMMENDED FOR FURTHER READING

Grazian, David. 2010. *Mix It Up: Popular Culture, Mass Media, and Society*. New York: Norton. Grazian takes a lively yet intellectually sophisticated look at the cultural world we live in, especially the urban, young, media-saturated world. His analyses of twenty-first century popular culture will provoke both debate and a surge of new examples of the sociological principles they illustrate.

Spillman, Lyn, ed. 2002. *Cultural Sociology*. Malden, MA, & Oxford, UK: Blackwell. This wide-ranging reader offers samples of some of the most important theoretical statements and empirical work in the field.

Williams, Raymond. 1976. *Keywords: A Vocabulary of Culture and Society*. New York: Oxford University Press. A Marxian literary critic, Williams gives the history of a number of terms that are important in the social sciences, including *culture*, and shows how such terms are by no means innocent of class-based assumptions.

The following are three books on the relationship between culture and community. You might read any of these with such questions in mind as "What has shaped the culture of this particular community?" and "What impact does this community's culture have on its residents?"

Anderson, Elijah. 2011. *The Cosmopolitan Canopy: Race and Civility in Everyday Life*. New York: Norton. Anderson offers a vivid and sociologically penetrating ethnographic tour of Center City, Philadelphia, and the public spaces—zones the streetwise urbanites recognize to be under a "cosmopolitan canopy"—where different races mingle under a (temporary and fragile) respite from racial tensions.

Bell, Michael Mayerfield. 1995. *Childerley: Nature and Morality in a Country Village*. Chicago: University of Chicago Press. Bell dissected the culture of an English village, whose residents work actively and self-consciously to maintain their rural culture even as they get drawn into the urban economy.

Klinenberg, Eric. 2002. *Heat Wave: A Social Autopsy of Disaster in Chicago*. Chicago: University of Chicago Press. Klinenberg compared two Chicago neighborhoods' responses to a heat wave, showing that despite their comparable poverty, one had a robust culture that enabled its residents to care for each other during a crisis while the other did not.

2

Cultural Meaning

They said, "You have a blue guitar,
You do not play things as they are."
The man replied, "Things as they are
Are changed upon the blue guitar."
And they said then, "But play, you must,
A tune beyond us, yet ourselves,
A tune upon the blue guitar
Of things exactly as they are."

(Stevens [1936] 1954:165)

W allace Stevens, a Connecticut insurance executive who also happened
to be one of the most important American poets of the twentieth
century, wrote "The Man With the Blue Guitar" as a commentary on the
ambiguous relationship between poetry and what most people regard as the
"real world." What he said about poetry applies more generally to culture
and cultural objects. We sense that culture is "beyond us, yet ourselves," and
we look for a simple relationship between cultural objects and "things
exactly as they are." But no simple relationship exists, for when something
becomes a cultural object—when, as it were, it is played upon the blue guitar—
that something indeed changes. And the change involves meaning.

19

By definition, a cultural object has shared significance; it has been given a meaning shared by members of the culture. In the aggregate, as Geertz's (1973) definition in Chapter 1 emphasizes, a culture comprises a "pattern of meanings" passed down over time. Meaning or significance (we use the two terms interchangeably) refers to the object's capacity—in addition to whatever practical or direct properties it may possess—to suggest or point to something else. Thus, the sound of a fire alarm "means" that everyone should clear the building, or an A on a test "means" that the student has mastered the material. Each of the stories that opened Chapter 1 is a parable about meaning. The Japanese businessman attached personal honor to his business card, whereas the same card meant nothing to the American beyond its practical function. A schoolgirl's veil means modesty to local Muslims, but it means a religious intrusion into the secular state's domain to non-Muslim French. Dogs, though significant cultural objects to both middle-class whites and working-class blacks in the neighborhood Anderson (1990) studied, meant different things to each group.

We can identify two types of meaning: simple and complex. Simple meaning denotes one-to-one correspondence. We express this type of meaning when we talk about signs and what they stand for. Algebra uses signs in this manner; in the equation $a^2 + b^2 = c^2$ we know that a "means" the length of one leg of a right triangle, b "means" the length of the other leg, and c "means" the length of the hypotenuse. Likewise, a flashing red light "means" stop and then go. All of these signs have a single referent.

Look for complex meaning in the signs typically called symbols. Rather than standing for a single referent, symbols evoke a variety of meanings, some of which may be ambiguous. Symbols do not denote; they connote, suggest, or imply. They evoke powerful emotions—think how many people have died for a flag—and can often both unite and disrupt social groups. A few years ago, for example, a Christian student association erected a giant cross at the University of Ibadan, the most prestigious university in Nigeria. Now, the cross symbol draws up a variety of deep-seated images, attitudes, and beliefs in Christians. This cross, however, happened to cast a long shadow over the Islamic student mosque in the afternoon sun. To the Muslim students, this accident of position symbolized the (literal) overshadowing of Islam by Christianity, an implied meaning they vehemently rejected. They retaliated by building a wall symbolizing their Islamic religious pride that blocked the shadow.

Because of its complexity, culture comprises complex rather than simple meanings, or meanings "embodied in symbols," to continue with Geertz's definition. To understand culture, we must be able to unravel these tangled webs of meanings. In other words, we must be able to analyze the relationship that may exist between a symbol, the "tune upon the blue guitar" on the one hand, and "things exactly as they are" on the other. This relationship, of course, can prove highly personal and individual, as when a psychoanalyst analyzes a patient's dreams for their symbolic content. The sociology of culture, however, looks for social meanings. And in our cultural diamond, meaning links cultural objects with the social world.

In this chapter, we consider why the need for meaning is fundamental to human existence. We then consider an influential theoretical model that suggests that cultural meaning comes from culture's capacity to mirror social life. We investigate the classical roots of this "reflection" model and two contemporary sociological versions of it: functionalist and Marxist cultural theories. Then, we look at Max Weber's striking reversal of the mirror model in his assertion that the social world actually reflects culture, not the other way around. We look at some contemporary sociological applications of reflection theory. Finally, we consider the "clash of civilizations" debate, in which some see different meaning systems as constituting a global threat.

Why Do We Need Meaning?

We all know that living beings grow and act according to instructions encoded in their genes. In animals, we call this genetic prompting of behavior instinct; for example, a hare instinctively knows to run from the scent of a fox but not from the scent of a chipmunk. Most of what animals do and know is genetically given—hardwired, so to speak. Human beings differ. In the first place, they are physiologically incomplete at birth. The large size of the human head requires a baby's birth to occur before all of its internal systems fully develop; some say that human "life" independent of the mother doesn't really begin until the child turns several months old. More to the point, human genetic encodings do not provide sufficient information for survival. A kitten, once weaned, could survive in the woods without other members of its species to show it what to do, but a one-year-old child could not. Humans must learn to live. And learning in humans is a social process of interaction and socialization whereby culture is transmitted.

Anthropologists stress how the total of such human interactions transmits patterns of meanings and behaviors and that these patterns are called culture. Consider Geertz's (1973:45–46) summary of how human culture compensates for genetic incompleteness:

> Man is so in need of . . . symbolic sources of illumination to find his bearings in the world because the nonsymbolic sort that are constitutionally ingrained

in his body cast so diffused a light. The behavior patterns of lower animals are, at least to a much greater extent, given to them with their physical structure; genetic sources of information order their actions within much narrower ranges of variation, the narrower and more thoroughgoing the lower the animal. For man, what are innately given are extremely general response capacities. . . . Undirected by culture patterns—organized systems of significant symbols—man's behavior would be virtually ungovernable, a mere chaos of pointless acts and exploding emotions, his experience virtually shapeless. Culture, the accumulated totality of such patterns, is not just an ornament of human existence but . . . an essential condition for it.

Peter Berger (1969) suggested, along similar lines, the ultimate human terror as not evil but chaos. A total absence of order, a world without structure or meaning, is so horrifying as to be unthinkable. As a bulwark against chaos, human beings create cultures through the externalization/objectification/internalization process we examined earlier, thereby constructing the worlds in which they operate. Ideals of order and stability—under Communism, capitalism, autocracies, liberal democracies—dominated the twentieth century, and ongoing fluctuations and upheavals may be dominating the twenty-first in a condition Zygmunt Bauman has memorably called "liquid modernity" (2000). The "Arab Spring" and its aftermath exemplify this new fluidity to which cultural meaning systems must respond.

Thus, the sociological analysis of culture begins at the premise that culture provides orientation, wards off chaos, and directs behavior toward certain lines of action and away from others. Culture provides meaning and order through the use of symbols, whereby certain things designated as cultural objects are endowed with significance over and above their material utility. We can most easily see this in the case of tangible or visible objects—business cards, dogs, or works of art—but the same holds true for ideas or bits of behavior. The attributes of a desirable husband, for example, or the social script in which a young woman looks at a man, lowers her eyes for a moment, and then looks at him again describe cultural objects that carry meaning. Some cultures—rural Italy perhaps—would consider the aforementioned young woman's behavior appropriate; others would see a coy, irritating display of pseudo-innocence; still others would consider it immodest and even whorish. Likewise, in West African cultures, such as that of the Yoruba, patterned facial scars mean that a man's kinship affiliations make him either desirable or off-limits as a suitor. Other societies would consider these scars either irrelevant or disfiguring. Neither scars nor lowering the eyes has meaning in and of itself, but both become intensely meaningful insofar as they are embedded in a culture that produces or interprets them.

Culture and Meaning in Reflection Theory

If culture involves meanings, and if meanings are social, again we must ask: What types of relationships exist between the social world and cultural objects or patterns? The basic questions include "Where does meaning come from?" and "What difference do meanings make?" Two of the most important sociological answers to these questions—those provided by functionalism and Marxism—we can consider versions of reflection theory, whereby culture is seen as a faithful reflection of social life. The third answer, offered by Max Weber, emphasizes the degree to which social life reflects culture. We need to take a careful look at the whole idea of reflection and the implications of this model for how we think about culture. We start by considering the background of the reflection model in classical Greek thought. Equipped with this background, we explore the forms that reflection theory takes in functionalism, Marxism, and Weberian analysis.

Culture as Mirror

The assumption behind the idea of culture as reflection is a simple one: Culture mirrors social reality. Therefore, the meaning of a particular cultural object lies in the social structures and social patterns it reflects. The sociologically informed analyst, it follows, should look for direct, one-to-one correspondences between culture and society.

The reflection model has much to recommend it, including common sense. Most people believe, for example, that the violence and mayhem depicted on television reflect the violence and mayhem in our society. Without denying that television violence may itself contribute to social violence, these simply present two different connections on the cultural diamond that may or may not vary together but that are conceptually distinct, as indicated in Figure 2.1. In one conceptualization, television violence reflects the social world; in the other, the social world reflects television violence. Traditionally, cultural sociology prefers the former way of describing the connection, asking how culture reflects society and admitting the latter way—how society reflects culture—only as a secondary consideration.

Putting this simple reflection model on our cultural diamond, as in Figure 2.1, shows how we might go about testing common beliefs about the connection between television and violence. If the question is "Does television reflect changes in the social world?" we would measure incidents of violence in a given society at some starting point (T1) until some later point (T2). We similarly would measure changes in violent episodes on television

Figure 2.1   Reflection Model of Television and Violence

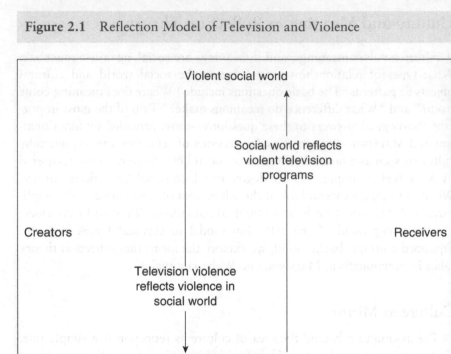

over the same time. We would expect, following reflection theory, that television violence, allowing for a certain time lag, would rise and fall along with the rates of real-life violence. That does not mean social violence *causes* television violence, only that the two correlate. If, on the other hand, the two rates rise and fall together but the ups and downs in television violence *precede* corresponding changes in the rate of social violence, this would support the social-world-reflects-culture argument.

Besides, according with our common-sense observations of the way the world works, reflection theory gains credibility from the fact that artists, writers, and other cultural creators often describe their creativity in these terms. As the nineteenth-century French writer Stendhal responded to critics who accused him of portraying sordid materials ([1830] 1958:363),

A novel, gentlemen, is a mirror carried along a highway. Sometimes it reflects to your view the azure of the sky, sometimes the mire of the puddles in the road. And the man who carries the mirror on his back will be accused by you of immorality! His mirror shows the mire and you blame the mirror!

As well as both a great deal of plausibility and the endorsement of modern culture creators, reflection theories of culture also have a long history. Like so much else, they go back to Plato. A brief review of the history of the reflection model will show how certain assumptions about the relationship between culture and the "real world" entered into sociological models.

The Greek Background to Reflection Theory

We begin our consideration of the classical origins of reflection theory with Plato (ca. 430–347 BC), Athenian philosopher and student of Socrates. According to Plato's theory of forms, advanced in book 10 of the *Republic,* behind all appearances lies an idea or a form. For example, although we sleep on a physical bed, the physical piece of furniture is mere appearance. Reality is a preexisting form, bed. The physical bed reflects this ideal bed, although imperfectly. Human beings, however, confuse appearance for reality, just as when people in a cave take as reality the flickering shadows a fire throws on the wall.

Even appearances come from somewhere, and Plato suggested that they come from reflection. He asked, How could someone—a cultural creator, we would say—make all of the works of the universe, all of nature, all of the heavens, and all of the gods? "Impossible," said a student, but Plato replied:

> There are many ways in which the feat might be quickly and easily accomplished, none quicker than that of turning a *mirror* round and round—you would soon enough make the sun and the heavens, and the earth and yourself, and other animals and plants, and all the other things of which we were just now speaking, in the mirror.

Plato thus envisioned three types of creators: (1) God, the creative being, who makes the one real bed in its ideal form, (2) the carpenter who makes a physical bed, and (3) the painter who makes a picture of the physical bed. Thus, art, such as that produced by the painter, is an imperfect copy of an imperfect copy. All art—hence all mimesis or imitation—is a long way from truth; the artist can imitate so many things because he or she only superficially understands any of them. Plato views human life as a pilgrimage from appearance to reality. Art presents an obstacle to this journey because it seduces people into a mistaken understanding of the real.

Note some features of this argument: Plato links his objection to art based on the theory of forms with his objection based on the educational function of culture. Of course, the two need not go together. As we have seen, Matthew Arnold made the liberal argument that art, like all culture, widens experience, thus making people more sensitive and selective. Notice as well the religious basis of Plato's objections. Good art does not imitate divine patterns but participates in them. This view compares to the Islamic injunction against representing humans or animals; according to Islamic aesthetic theory, art should not compete with Allah's creation. Such religious objections to the representation of living things are common, as in the Judeo-Christian second commandment: "You shall not make for yourself a graven image, or any likeness of anything that is in heaven above, or that is in the earth beneath, or that is in the water under the earth" (Exod. 21:4 [RSV]).

Thus, Plato's theory of forms contains three components: the form, the appearance, and the art. Translating into our terminology, we could say that the idea, the material embodiment of the idea, and the symbolic or cultural expression of the idea form a double-diamond, as in Figure 2.2. However, the consequence of this three-part structure, for Plato, downgraded the third term as doubly removed from reality.

Aristotle (384–322 BC), a younger contemporary of Plato and a member of his academy, suggested a way to defend art (and, by extension, culture): Redefine the middle term. He argued that art imitates not the ideal realm but universal truths about human existence. Aristotle's redefinition—art imitates the universals of nature—changed the very meaning of mimesis. Aristotle's universalism provides the basis for Matthew Arnold's "best that has been thought and known" (and indeed for much of humanist thinking), for one of the distinguishing characteristics of "the best" is its broad range of applicability.

Reflection theory in its Platonic origins implies that culture is less than real or less fundamental than what it reflects, and this implication carries over into the discipline of sociology. So do the more positive Aristotelian twists of this theory—that culture is somehow more profound than the social world and that culture can represent human universals. The two dominant sociological theories of the twentieth century—functionalism and Marxism—both employ the reflection model, and both perpetuate some of its Platonic implications. Both also exhibit the "close-fit assumption" between culture and society that we earlier described as characteristic of social science theories of culture in general. Now, we see where this idea comes from: If one entity "reflects" another, it must match that other entity very closely. Let us examine the cultural implications of these two sociological theories, seeking both the strengths and the deficiencies of their versions of the reflection model.

Figure 2.2 Plato's Reflection Theory Set on the Cultural Diamond

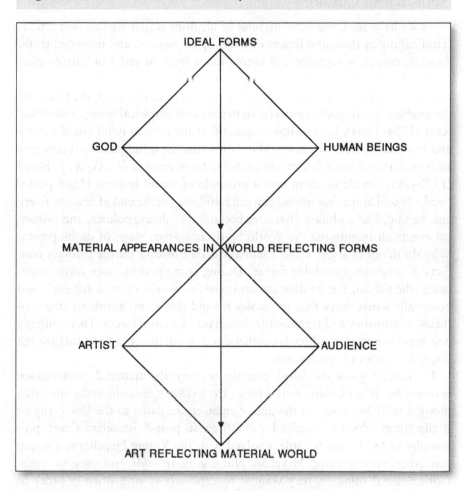

Culture and Meaning in Marxian Sociology

Like all social theorists, Karl Marx and his collaborator Friedrich Engels responded to the intellectual and social currents of their own day, the mid-nineteenth century. In their early writings about culture—and Marx produced his cultural analysis mostly in the early part of his career, before he turned his attention more exclusively to economics—Marx and Engels engaged in the philosophical debate between idealism and materialism. We already met idealism in the Platonic version. Now, we take a look at the debate as it appeared some 2,000 years after Plato, when Marx was a young man.

"From Earth to Heaven": The Materialist Approach to Culture

As we have seen, the basic premise of idealism is that we can best understand culture as the embodiment of ideas, spirit, beauty, and universal truth. As such, culture is separate and autonomous from material or earthly existence. The late-eighteenth- and early-nineteenth-century thinkers known as the German Idealists shared the neo-Platonic sense of the spirit, the idea, and the intellectual category as antecedent to sensuous empirical reality. Immanuel Kant (1724–1804), for example, argued that the human mind could receive and respond to the external world only because the mind possessed concepts such as time and space before experiencing them empirically. G. W. F. Hegel (1770–1831) made idealism into a principle of world history. Hegel postulated a World Spirit that moved toward fulfillment at the end of history. Every age, he said, had a unitary character because its culture, politics, and historical events all manifested the World Spirit at a given stage of development. Why do things change? Hegel maintained that history moves through conflicts between irreconcilable forces. During some periods, one force dominates (the thesis), but its domination breeds new crises (the antithesis), and eventually a new force that reconciles the old thesis and antithesis (the synthesis) overthrows and replaces the dominant ideas and forces. This synthesis becomes the new thesis, breeds conflicts, and so on; history moves on through stages in a series of revolutions.

If idealism gives the ideal precedence over the material, materialism reverses the relationship. Karl Marx (1818–1883) encountered materialist thought in 1836, when, at the age of eighteen, he came to the University of Berlin (from which he received a doctorate in post-Aristotelian Greek philosophy in 1841) and became involved with the Young Hegelians, a group concerned with turning Hegelian philosophy to more progressive ends. Critical social thinkers, they wanted to expose laws of history in order to reform society; thus, they were "idealists" in the everyday sense of the term, as well as in the philosophical sense.

After finishing his degree and realizing that a university career would be impossible for him in Prussia, Marx left Berlin for Cologne, where he edited a radical journal. In this capacity, he received a book from a materialist philosopher named Ludwig Feuerbach that dramatically changed his thinking and caused him to break with the Young Hegelians. Reversing Hegel, Feuerbach argued that material conditions produced the spirit of the age. His prime example: religion. Human beings create gods, Feuerbach contended, but then they take their own creation as real, worship it, and become dependent on it. Religion, although created by people, becomes separated from them, coming to serve as an idealized compensation for real human misery. (Marx would echo this sentiment in his later notorious comment: "Religion . . . is the opium of the people.")

The materialist view for cultural sociology implies that religion, values, art, ideas, laws, and culture in general are the products of material reality and that we should analyze them as such. As Marx put it, materialists assume the direction of causality as from earth to heaven, not from heaven to earth. Cultural research, consequently, should move in the same direction.

Historical Materialism

Profoundly influenced by Feuerbach's materialism, Marx soon became impatient with what he considered its ignoring of history, and he finally came to the conclusion that Feuerbach was as much of an ivory-tower philosopher as the idealists themselves. It is not enough simply to point out the material basis of illusions, Marx contended in *The German Ideology* (1970). That's like saying "Gravity is just an illusion" to a man falling from a tall building or, in Marx's scornful words, like "fighting phrases with phrases."

Feuerbach didn't see, in Marx's view, the social and historical roots of the material world. This recognition led to what is known as Marx's historical materialism. A cherry tree, for example, looks solid, a material "given." Yet Marx pointed out that the cherry tree had been brought to Europe from Asia through trade. It wasn't just "there" but had a specific and lengthy history as a product of human labor. Under the terms of historical materialism, any analysis always started from *homo faber* (man the maker), humans working to sustain themselves through production and reproduction.

Not only material things such as trees but also consciousness itself is a social product, Marx argued, a truth that applies to all we think of as culture. Marx claimed that culture, government, religion, politics, and laws are all "superstructure" resting on a base of the material forces of production and their economic foundations. Changes in the base, it follows, bring about changes in superstructure. Marx succinctly put forth this argument in his preface to *A Contribution to the Critique of Political Economy* (1977:389):

> In the social production of their life, men enter into definite relations that are indispensable and independent of their will, relations of production which correspond to a definite stage of development of their material productive forces. The sum total of these relations of production constitutes the economic structure of society, the real foundation, on which rises a legal and political superstructure and to which correspond definite forms of social consciousness. The mode of

production of material life conditions the social, political and intellectual life process in general. It is not the consciousness of men that determines their being, but, on the contrary, their social being that determines their consciousness.

Marx argued that we must make a distinction between material economic conditions of production and ideological forms. In other words, he said, don't judge a period of transformation (or any other period) by its own consciousness, by what people living in the period think and believe, but instead explain the period's consciousness by the contradictions in its material life. The critical analyst should investigate the social origins of the values or "spirit" of the era.

In this investigation, class interests and antagonisms are the key. As Marx memorably put it, a society's ruling ideas equal the ideas of its ruling class. These ideas and values and cultural practices protect their interests and legitimate their position. The ruling class always seeks to justify its preeminent position by making its ideas seem universal. But does Marx's theory mean that culture—ideas, values, arts, laws, religion, and popular culture—is determined inexorably by a society's material life and the related class antagonisms? It sounds that way, but some contend that Marx did not envision a simple determinism. Raymond Williams ([1973] 1980), a Marxian cultural analyst, suggested that Marx's "determination" doesn't mean "totally predict" but "setting limits, exerting pressures." Economic conditions influence, but do not strictly determine, cultural practices.

Marxian theory made the sociological analysis of culture possible by hypothesizing the nature of the linkages between society and culture, the causal direction, and the principles of the relationship between the two. Like all reflection theories, it simplifies the connections indicated by the cultural diamond, but it offers a substantial theoretical justification for this simplification. Marx's historical materialism gave rise to a rich tradition of cultural research that continues to influence how sociologists think about culture. Let's examine this research with an eye for the useful in understanding culture today.

Research Directions From the Marxian Tradition

Marxist research always entails a social critique and implicitly or explicitly advocates change. Because cultural objects either enhance or obstruct the understanding of social relations, potentially cultural objects fit among the "weapons of criticism" Marx called for and thus can facilitate the historical movement toward socialist revolution. Indeed, this provided the key aesthetic criterion for politically committed Marxists.

An especially influential group of thinkers, the associates of the Frankfurt school, applied Marxian cultural analysis. Their background lay in the post–World War I dilemma facing German Marxists: Should they follow Moscow, support the Weimar Republic, or reexamine Marxist theory? The Institute of Social Research in Frankfurt was set up to follow the last of these options. Here assembled Marxist scholars, most from Jewish families, who sought to reconcile their Marxism with the contemporary world. After the Nazis came to power, most of these Frankfurt school associates escaped from Germany, and many moved to Columbia University in the mid-1930s. Max Horkheimer headed this scholarly community, which also included Herbert Marcuse, Theodor Adorno, and Leo Löwenthal.

Members of the Frankfurt school advanced a new critical theory, which organized empirical cultural analysis around a goal of social reformation. In this spirit, they did a great deal of research on authority and mass culture, seeing both as related to the growing helplessness of people in modern society. They criticized mass cultural products as having become mere commodities that discouraged social protest by making consumers reconciled to their existence. In mounting this critique, the Frankfurt school used the term *culture industry* to stress the antidemocratic nature of popular culture.

In an interesting example of Marxian cultural analysis, Leo Löwenthal ([1944] 1968) compared biographies of notable Americans found in popular magazines published early in the twentieth century with biographies that appeared in the same magazines during the 1940s and found dramatic changes. The early biographies usually described inventors, discoverers, or business entrepreneurs, whereas those of the later period more likely described movie stars, sports figures, and other entertainers. Löwenthal concluded that this change reflected a shift from an economy based on production to one that emphasized consumption and leisure. A related shift had occurred in the amount of detail the biographies contained. Whereas the earlier ones characterized their subjects as extraordinary, later biographies talked about the ordinary lives of their subjects, including information about the brand of cigarettes the movie star smoked or the type of car the baseball player drove. This, too, reflected the shift from production to consumption values that took place during the century, as small-scale business gave way to giant corporations. Löwenthal concluded that the working-class and middle-class readers no longer believed in the Horatio Alger myth that the early biographies offered. (J. Gamson [1994] offers a contemporary version of how America conceptualizes its celebrities.)

Music provides another example of the radical critique of popular culture. Theodor Adorno attacked radio music, produced and distributed by the culture industry, with the charge that popular music on the radio, including jazz, is mere repetition that leads its audience to delight in recognition of the familiar, not the challenge of the new. Psychologically, this results in a childlike regression rather than an intellectual awakening. This line of reasoning typified the Frankfurt school concerns. They ultimately feared that people would become too stupefied by the mass media to protest, or even notice, when their freedoms disappeared.

Meanwhile, in the mid-twentieth century, another theory—functionalism—was proving enormously influential in the sociology of culture and elsewhere. It retained the mirror model of culture while offering a comprehensive account of human social relations. If Marxism views human social life as a bitter struggle to the death, functionalism views it as a systemic tendency toward harmony. We now need to look at functionalism, so different from Marxist theory yet sharing the reflection model, to see its impact on cultural studies.

Culture and Meaning in Functionalist Sociology

Aristotle's suggestion that culture tells about the kind of thing that happens to human beings may be restated in terms specific to a given society. Thus, the culture of the Egyptians tells us about the kinds of things that happen in Egypt, thereby indicating the way Egyptians view their social and natural worlds. In this modified Aristotelian form, reflection theory becomes, for two reasons, a very attractive model for the sociological understanding of culture. First, the idea that "culture reflects society (or social structure)" provides a model of the connection between culture and society and suggests the primary direction of influence. Second, this model allows for the use of culture as social evidence.

Both attributes are part and parcel of the functionalist image of a close fit between culture and social structure, at least in a society that functions properly. The essence of functionalism is that human societies, to maintain themselves, have concrete needs, and social institutions arise to meet these needs. For example, every society needs to rear and socialize its young, so every society has some regular, institutionalized patterned relationships, called families, that perform this function. A healthy society exists in a state of balance or equilibrium in which institutions adapt to one another and operate in a system of mutual interdependence to meet the needs of the society. Failures of fit, which all societies experience to some extent, are described as dysfunctional. It follows from this thinking that every social level—the culture, the polity, the economy, and the social order—provides input to and receives output from every other level. Every level adapts to, or reflects, every other level. Thus, culture reflects society just as society reflects culture.

Problems with this simple functionalist version of reflection theory become obvious when we think of specific examples, such as the degree to which popular television shows "reflect" social reality. What about human beings, we might ask, the creators and audiences, and the other points of the cultural diamond? The classic functionalist reflection model assumes that these human beings are passive and without interests of their own. In addition, the model does not have a place for the independent influence of the organizations of cultural production, the record companies, church hierarchies, symphonies, art galleries, and so forth.

Even the mirror metaphor is less straightforward than it first appears. From the audience's point of view, for example, is a cultural work a mirror of itself or a window into other people? Here, we recall Peter Berger's (1969) point that the same person does not necessarily perform the acts of externalization and internalization. And what about the passage of time? The transience of the mirror image seems to conflict with the real permanence many cultural works have shown, a permanence the humanities have suggested as especially significant.

Moreover, the "social evidence" point—the idea that we can read a society directly through its cultural works—often misleads. We all know, for example, that *Father Knows Best* and other family sitcoms of the 1950s offer a highly skewed portrait of actual American family life during that decade. Cultural objects often idealize certain aspects of social experience, or they emphasize less favorable aspects as a form of social criticism. Or, as Plato recognized, they feature the sensational; few people would suggest that the sexual and criminal shenanigans on the average reality show "reflect" the way contemporary people really live.

So the pure mirror model, in which social structure and culture adapt to one another and serve each other's functional needs, seems a bit hard to swallow. More complex functionalist reflection models do exist, however, and they satisfy some of the objections raised here. To take one effective study, art historian Michael Baxandall (1972) suggests a way for the basic reflection model to represent all of the points and links of the cultural diamond. In his study of fifteenth-century Italian paintings, Baxandall shows how the paintings reflect

1. *commercial transactions.* The contract between a painter and his client—the contract would be the horizontal line on our diamond—stipulated the amount of expensive pigments, the extent of gilding, and the proportion of the work that the master, as opposed to his students, painted.

2. *changing values.* During the century, the emphasis in the paintings—and what the client was willing to pay for—shifted from pigments to pictorial

skill. This reflected changing consumption styles among wealth—specifically a new concern with taste instead of a simple display of wealth—but still reflected class position.

3. *the "period eye."* This is to the cognitive capacity and style of an era. For example, Baxandall notes the large number of containers, cylinders, and piles of grain or other goods in the paintings. He suggests that these appealed to the knowledge and skills of wealthy merchants, who had to develop great facility at gauging volumes because no standard weights and measures existed at this time. Such merchants were often the painters' clients. Note that Baxandall gives us a highly sociological definition of *taste,* the conformity between the discriminations of painters and viewers. "If a painting gives us opportunity for exercising a valued skill and rewards our virtuosity with a sense of worthwhile insights about that painting's organization, we tend to enjoy it: it is to our taste" (34).

In this reflection argument, culture is not a direct reflection of the social world but rather is mediated through the minds of human beings. Renaissance Italian paintings reflect the social experience that produced a certain way of seeing things, a period eye composed of a "stock of patterns, categories and methods of inference; training in a range of representational conventions; and experience drawn from the environment, in what are plausible ways of visualizing what we have incomplete information about" (Baxandall 1972:32). And not only the general social experience of fifteenth-century Italians is reflected but also that of the specific class of men—and they were virtually all men—who produced and bought the paintings. At the same time, the analysis is recognizably functionalist (although as an art historian, Baxandall probably would not use the term). From the position of social structure, the rising merchant class requires a way to demonstrate its wealth and indicate its participation in aristocratic patterns of behavior such as art patronage. From the position of culture, painters require buyers who understand and approve of what they see. The merchants and the paintings, respectively representing social structure and culture here, functionally adapted to one another.

Although a complex reflection model proves more satisfactory than the simple culture-reflects-society view, questions remain. How do cultural works maintain effectiveness over space and time? Twentieth-century people don't have a fifteenth-century period eye yet still respond to the art of the Italian Renaissance. Somehow, we must create new meanings independent from the original period eye, and the reflection model does not help us understand where these come from. Another question asks, "Why are some 'realities' reflected and not others?" Culture is clearly selective in the way that mirrors are not. Reservations about the mirror metaphor, especially in its functionalist version, have led some people to suggest that culture is more a reflection "on" than a reflection "of." Through culture, in other words, human beings may reflect on their individual and social experience.

Let us pause here to review our path. At the opening of this chapter, we saw how culture provides the meanings that human beings find essential. It therefore followed that a sociological understanding of culture would attempt to connect cultural meanings with the social world. A standard approach, rooted in Platonic and Aristotelian cultural theory, is to envision culture as reflecting the social world. Both functionalist and Marxist theories of culture employ the reflection model. Now we look at a quite different analysis of cultural meaning whose effect reverses the direction of reflection: the cultural theory of Max Weber.

Culture and Meaning in Weberian Sociology

Both the functionalist and the Marxian version of reflection theory recognize that culture and social structure exert mutual influence on one another, but both tend to emphasize a causal arrow that goes in one direction. Society (or social structure, the economic base, or class relations) causes (or determines, shapes, or influences) culture. In terms of the cultural diamond, the arrow generally points downward. Yet, if human beings require meaning to organize their lives, culture, as a bearer of meanings, must make something happen in the social world. The arrow must point upward as well.

The social scientist most known for emphasizing this other direction of causality is Max Weber (1864–1920), the German sociologist mentioned in Chapter 1. Like his contemporary Émile Durkheim and like Marx a bit earlier, Weber tried to understand the modern world, especially industrial, capitalist society. Weber did not think that culture simply *caused* social structure. He knew that the influence worked both ways, and in his writing on religion and economic life, he took pains to emphasize that he was looking at "only one side" of the causal relationship and not claiming that religion caused capitalism. The extent to which religion participated in the formation and expansion of the spirit of capitalism interested Weber. He sought correlations between religious beliefs on the one hand and practical behavior and ethics on the other to see how a religious movement might have influenced material culture. In his masterpiece *The Protestant Ethic and the Spirit of Capitalism* ([1904–1905] 1985), Weber made a powerful case for the influence of cultural meanings on economic life itself and thus on the social world.

The Anxious Protestants and the World They Built

Weber introduced *The Protestant Ethic and the Spirit of Capitalism* by noting how the West is unique in many respects: in its specialized science and arts, its highly trained officials, its rational law, and most especially its capitalist economic system involving "the pursuit of profit, and forever *renewed* profit, by means of continuous, rational, capitalistic enterprise" (17). Human greed is nothing new; people have always desired acquisition, and every society has housed its capitalists. Unique to the West, according to Weber, is the capitalist organization of human labor, the separation of business from the household, and the dominance of rational bookkeeping. The central problem, then, is not the origin of capitalism itself but rather the ascendancy of bourgeois capitalism with its rational organization of free labor. Putting the problem another way, Weber claimed interest in origins of the bourgeoisie—those sober middle-class capitalists—and their peculiarities. He wanted to explore the side of the causal chain involving how an economic spirit, or the ethos (distinguishing character) of an economic system, reflected a set of religious ideas.

The analysis starts with an observation: Everywhere in Europe, Protestants flocked to commerce, business, and skilled labor far more than Catholics; they were, in other words, overrepresented in capitalist economic activities. Weber considered the spirit of capitalism as involving an ethic or duty, particularly one's duty in a calling, as exemplified by such aphorisms of Benjamin Franklin as "Time is money." In Franklin's writings, Weber finds a mixture of profit seeking and rational calculation. For example, consider the following:

> After industry and frugality, nothing contributes more to the raising of a young man in the world than punctuality and justice in all his dealings; therefore never keep borrowed money an hour beyond the time you promised, lest a disappointment shut up your friend's purse for ever. (49)

This type of thinking seems unique to Western capitalism.

This spirit of capitalism stood in sharp contrast to the traditional attitude, whereby people work only to live according to custom. Those under capitalism work incessantly for profits, going well beyond their needs and driven by a "time is money" type of self-imposed motivation. The ideal type of capitalist was not a hedonist who enjoyed wealth but an ascetic: "He gets nothing out of his wealth for himself, except the irrational sense of having done his job well" (71). If the spirit of capitalism can't be explained by the desire for luxury, neither can it be explained by material conditions. Weber compared fifteenth-century Florence, where capitalism was advanced but lacked the distinctive later "spirit," to the eighteenth-century Pennsylvania of Franklin, which had more of the spirit than it did capitalism itself. What was the "background of ideas" that made activity directed toward profit into a morally charged vocation?

The answer lies in two Protestant religious ideas: the calling and predestination. Martin Luther's conception of the calling—the particular vocation to which God has "called" every man and woman—gave a moral justification to worldly activity. This interpretation contrasted with Catholicism, wherein such activity was morally neutral at best. Luther stressed that Providence assigned each person a place in God's scheme and a specific job to do. Pursuit of one's vocation, or one's calling, is a way of serving God.

The idea of a calling might encourage pious Protestants to work hard, but it would not make them endlessly pursue profits without stopping to enjoy their gains. This pattern of action came from another strand in Protestant theology, that involving predestination. As theorized by John Calvin, predestination describes the belief that, at the beginning of time, God destined every individual for heaven or hell; people could do nothing to change their destinies. According to Calvin, God is unknowable and his decrees incomprehensible; he has decided everything, and one must trust in his justice without question.

Such a harsh doctrine, Weber reasoned, would produce a feeling of unprecedented inner loneliness for those who believed in it.

> In what was for the man of the age of the Reformation the most important thing in life, his eternal salvation, he was forced to follow his path alone to meet a destiny which had been decreed for him from eternity. (104)

No person, no sacraments, no church, and not even God could help. How was such a religion bearable? Weber said that the Calvinists responded to the psychological pressure by becoming obsessed with seeking hints regarding whether they were destined for salvation. Their clergy made two suggestions: (1) It was one's duty to consider oneself saved (if a person worried openly about going to hell, he or she probably would!), and (2) one might gain self-confidence in one's heavenly destination through worldly activity. Protestants could bolster their conviction of salvation through good works, self-control, and purposeful activity. In contrast to monastic withdrawal, such lives epitomized what Weber called "innerworldly asceticism," in which Calvinists enacted their religious beliefs in the workshops, markets, and households where they lived their lives.

Weber saw the Puritan as a man concerned with monitoring his own state of grace, engaged in endless moral bookkeeping and the methodical

Christianization of his entire life. He labored hard in his calling but did not spend or enjoy his profits. If successful, he just worked harder; he could never rest, for complacency might signify damnation. Such a pattern of behavior had two results: (1) It built up the capital of those who practiced it (all of those unspent profits were available for investment), and (2) it developed an attitude toward hard work as a "good thing" for its own sake, a foreign idea to the traditional assumption that work was just a means to an end. The spirit of capitalism lasted long after the particular religious beliefs themselves (e.g., a strict belief in predestination) had atrophied. Indeed, Weber saw the spirit of capitalism operating in his own day, and in many respects it persists in ours as well.

The Cultural Switchman

In *The Protestant Ethic and the Spirit of Capitalism,* Weber showed how a set of religious ideas influenced the way people worked, spent their money, and ordered their economic lives. The result of a particular religion-based form of economic behavior helped give rise to the Western form of capitalism that has dominated the world economy for three centuries. Thus, this "side of the causal chain" maps onto our cultural diamond as the way that culture causes, influences, or is reflected in the social world.

Weber himself did not want to deny that people pursued their material interests—to this extent he endorsed Marx's *homo faber* as a starting point— but he contended that their ideas, their cultures, shaped just how they pursued these interests. In a famous metaphor, he once compared the role of culture to that of a railroad switchman:

> Not ideas, but material and ideal interests, directly govern men's conduct. Yet very frequently the "world images" that have been created by "ideas" have, like switchmen, determined the tracks along which action has been pushed by the dynamic of interest. (1946:280)

Thus, the Calvinists had material interests (earning a living) and ideal interests (salvation). A set of religious world images involving a calling and predestination set the tracks along which they pursued these interests by making these pursuits meaningful. And along those tracks, Western capitalists and workers still run their economic lives.

Like functionalism and Marxism, the Weberian model that social action reflects cultural meanings has directed much sociological research, especially attempts to explain broad social change. For example, when Jack Goldstone (1991) sought to explain the wave of revolutions that convulsed Europe and Asia in the seventeenth and eighteenth centuries, he showed that sudden population increases triggered a set of factors—government incapacity, elite conflict, and popular discontent—that led to state breakdown and rebellion. But then a new puzzle emerged: Why did these structural factors lead to revolution in the West (England, France) but not in the East (the Ottoman Empire, China)? Goldstone found the answer in Weber's cultural switchman model. The Western religious tradition was linear and eschatological; when a change occurred, such as the coming of the Messiah, it was once and for all. Revolutionary action made sense in this meaning system, for history has a direction, total transformations are possible, and things can get better. Eastern religions, on the other hand, view history as cyclical, not linear. This way of thinking did not "switch" political and economic grievances toward revolutionary action but encouraged a return to previous forms of authority.

The "switchman" operates at the individual level as well. Lisa Keister's research on contemporary Americans focuses on the Weberian link between religion and economic behavior. She finds that conservative Protestants tend to accumulate less wealth than other groups (holding constant such things as education and income) because they adhere to a model of stewardship (money is not your own but the Lord's) that demands that they give their money away freely, while Roman Catholics accumulate more wealth because they have strong family orientations that demand they save and make only low-risk investments (Keister 2007, 2008).

The reflection model—whether we emphasize the causal direction from culture to social world or the reverse—proves most persuasive when used to reveal previously hidden correspondences between society and culture. In other words, although the mirror metaphor can mislead if it is taken too literally and excludes other points of the cultural diamond, it can nevertheless reveal significant parallels between cultural objects and their social world.

Meaning Systems or a Tool Kit?

How far should we go with this idea of cultural/social correspondences? The classical views summed up in the reflection model emphasize a close relationship between culture and human activity, but in recent years this assumption has come under sharp attack. Many sociologists now argue that the culture/social world connections are loose, that all cultures are more fragmented than coherent, and that the Weberian image of culture providing a systematic set of ideas and values by which people orient their behavior is fundamentally misleading.

Two general critiques of the Weberian culture-and-meaning position have been made. First, it is too subjective. Robert Wuthnow (1987) argues that Weber's approach to culture, and that of people in this tradition like Geertz, requires sociologists to get inside people's heads. Wuthnow maintains that we should think of culture as observable behavior rather than a subjective system of meaning generation. Sociologists should not try to be psychoanalysts.

Second, although such a view of culture seems to envision hard and fast rules for behavior, observation shows that people behave in contradictory ways, that they say one thing and do another, and that their cultures do not steer them as Weber suggested. Sewell (1992) posits that the image of cultural rules is too formal and rigid. Instead, he prefers to think in terms of cultural schemas, informal presuppositions that lie behind more formal rules. These schemas can operate at various levels, from trivial points of etiquette to deep values or unconscious binary systems, and can transfer to new situations.

Ann Swidler (1986, 2001) maintains that cultures are more like tool kits than switchmen, in that they contain rationales underlying various lines of action that can be drawn upon in different contexts, but these rationales are not internally coherent. She demonstrates her thesis by showing how middle-class Americans have two distinct ideologies of love. They can articulate the romantic "till death do us part" ideal of a mutual love that weathers all adversity; they also express a second, much more qualified and contingent, "so long as my partner meets my needs" ideology. These ideologies are not just different but contradictory, yet Swidler shows that people readily use both of them. People have multiple cultural repertoires, and they use them more as bases for "echolocation" than as some restrictive road map. The contradictions don't paralyze people, however, as a more systematic meaning underlying action theory would predict, and they don't because people draw on different ideological resources under different situations.

By the end of the twentieth century, many cultural sociologists had come to accept this more fragmented model of culture. The idea of strong culture—coherent meaning systems steering action—had largely given way to a view of looser and contingent relationships between culture and action. The events of September 11, 2001, led many people to reconsider the role cultural meaning systems play in directing behavior. The world scrambled to understand an Islamist worldview that could justify acts of religious terrorism. Under the circumstances, it once again seemed plausible to think of coherent cultural systems, generators of meaning for entire societies.

Meaning, Modernity, and the Clash of Cultures

Conflict between Muslims and the Judeo-Christian West have stained the opening pages of the twenty-first century with blood. The September 11, 2001, attacks on the World Trade Center and the Pentagon; the bombings in

Bali, Saudi Arabia, Madrid, and London; the wars in Afghanistan and Iraq; attacks on Christian churches in Pakistan and Lebanon; the endless bloodshed that Israelis and Palestinians have visited upon each other—all of these horrific events seem to offer evidence of a "coherent" culture rooted in the Islamic world. To some, they even seem to support a "clash of civilizations" thesis.

Originally set forth in a *Foreign Affairs* article that political scientist Samuel Huntington wrote in 1995 and then further expanded in a book published the next year, this thesis argues that since the end of the Cold War, the fault lines in the contemporary world have become more cultural than economic or political. A number of civilizations rooted in different religious cultures interpret the world very differently. These different interpretations inevitably produce fundamental conflicts over meanings. Particularly problematic is the gap between the beliefs, goals, and values of the Islamic arc stretching from Indonesia to Morocco on the one hand and the West— Europe and North America—on the other.

Huntington's thesis of a war between civilizations based on different cultural foundations is hotly debated, and many sociologists think the thesis oversimplifies and obfuscates. Although radical Islamists may indeed see the world in these terms (Wright 2006), Palestinian liberationists have only weak links to Islam, Iraq under Saddam Hussein was militantly secular, and most Muslims abhor terrorism. So to translate Huntington's ideas into a binary image of culture wars would be a mistake, as would assuming that Islamic cultures are any more coherent than other cultures; ideological writings belie the fragmented cultural "tools" that most people use. At the same time, however, we cannot just dismiss the impact of deep-seated differences in the worldviews. "Culture matters," as the title of a book edited by Lawrence Harrison and Huntington (2001) points out, and the challenge is to see how it matters.

Sociologists have had a hard time doing so because, following the lead of its founding fathers, the discipline has supposed that the bases for cultural clashes—religion, ethnicity, and different worldviews—were disappearing. This basic disciplinary assumption appears wrong. Twenty-first century assertions of religious and ethnic particularism are robust. They reveal a more general phenomenon: the failure of modernity to realize its goal of enlightened humanism. Ever since the eighteenth-century Enlightenment, Western social thought in general has regarded the modern era as strikingly different from any that preceded it. Modernity was seen as the stage in social evolution characterized by reason and the rational application of human ingenuity to nature; by popular participation in determining government leaders and policies; by secularization, freedom from superstition and myths; by technological advances, generally involving industrialization; by urbanization; by universal education; and by possible, if not inevitable, victory over disease and want.

The discipline of sociology, furthermore, has been first and foremost the science of modernity. Sociology's founding fathers—Marx, Durkheim, and Weber—all envisioned a modern society in which particular or ascribed characteristics, things we received at birth, such as skin color, family name, religion, or region of origin, would matter less and less. They envisioned a society of specialized knowledge, where positions were filled by individual merit, where human freedom was in tension with impersonal bureaucracies, and where everything was clear and efficient, though possibly soulless as well.

For good or ill, society, even in advanced industrial/postindustrial societies, has not experienced the expected transformations. Affinities of race and ethnicity persist. Religion has not faded away, and the idea of religious war to the death has proved irresistible to many. Traditions, whether genuinely old or invented, have remained compelling. And modernity itself has prompted strong cultural reactions in two directions: postmodernism and fundamentalism.

Postmodernism is the term many people now apply to the culture of contemporary society, just as modernism—abstract art, atonal music, psychoanalysis, stream-of-consciousness fiction, starkly functional architecture, and the anomie produced by rapid social change—was the culture of modern society. Many people believe that society has entered this new stage beyond modernity, a postindustrial stage of social development dominated by media images, in which people connect with other places and other times through proliferating channels of information. If the modern person was characterized by hope and anxiety, the postmodern person is characterized by a cool absence of illusion. Modern minds were skeptical; postmodern minds are cynical.

We will return to the subject of postmodernism in Chapter 7. For now, let's consider only one aspect of postmodern (or late modern) culture, the declining belief in foundational narratives. Earlier eras seemed always to have defining stories (narratives) that produced meaning and constituted the lens through which people interpreted their experience. In the European Middle Ages, for example, the story was Christian history: the Creation, Adam's fall, Christ's life, the period awaiting Christ's return (in which the "present" was invariably located), the Second Coming, and the Last Judgment. The modern period produced equivalent secular narratives that featured the drama of social progress (whereby humanity evolved, through competition, toward ever more complex and higher forms) or the drama of Marxism (whereby class conflicts moved through a series of economic stages from feudalism to capitalism and, ultimately, Communism).

Theorists of postmodernity argue that many people no longer believe in such master stories. Instead exists a growing sense that life is without meaning and that culture is only a play of images without reference to some underlying reality. Postmodern cultural objects exhibit freedom and exuberance; because signifiers need not connect with any specific meanings, a postmodern building can have Gothic spires, Renaissance arches, modern windows, and a Spanish colonial courtyard, and only a fool mired in some meta-narrative would try to interpret such a building. At the same time, the celebration of meaninglessness—making a virtue out of anomie—can result in an empty nihilism. Such developments have produced an exceedingly strong countermovement, one that appears worldwide: the impulse toward religious fundamentalism.

Fundamentalisms appear in many forms: Hindus tearing down the mosques in India; Israeli Jewish settlers basing claims to West Bank land on scriptural authority; Shiite Muslims establishing a puritanical theocracy in Iran; and American Christians demanding prayer in, and sex education out of, schools. All such movements share the vehement rejection of certain aspects of modernity (Emerson and Hartman 2006). Social changes appear to impinge on their most sacred values. Some fundamentalists retreat from "the world," attempting to live according to their own lights, like the Amish in rural America. Others attack.

Although sociology as a discipline generally assumes increasing secularization and postmodernists celebrate it, fundamentalists assert the older claims of religion and traditional social patterns, which they regard as justified by religion. Their single-mindedness and passionate commitment attract many to their cause, for they offer a fixed set of meanings and interpretations, often based on a religious text, that provides stability in a chaotic world. In other words, they offer a culture with clear meanings. The statements of Osama bin Laden and other al Qaeda leaders reveal this very clearly. Ironically, in adhering to a fundamentalist meaning system to ward off chaos, religious radicals end up unleashing that very chaos.

SUMMARY

In this chapter, we considered the relationship between culture and meaning. We saw how human beings require meaningful orientation for their lives and how culture provides such orientation. We looked at the origin and history of reflection theory. We looked at several modern sociological theories of how culture, as a bearer of meaning, connects with the social world. Some of these theories, such as Marx's, perpetuate a classical reflection model whereby culture reflects social structure like a mirror. Others, notably that of Weber, emphasize how social structures respond to cultural meanings. These Weberian theories of culture providing meaning have drawn criticism for being too directive, for giving culture coherence and power that it may not always have. But conflicts between Islamists and the West have given such strong culture theories a renewed plausibility.

If we return to the cultural diamond for a moment, we notice that all of these culture-as-meaning theories share one thing, as Figure 2.3 indicates: They concentrate on the vertical axis of the diamond. The left point of cultural creation, the right point of cultural reception, and the five links beyond the vertical axis are virtually ignored.

Figure 2.3   Reflection and the Cultural Diamond

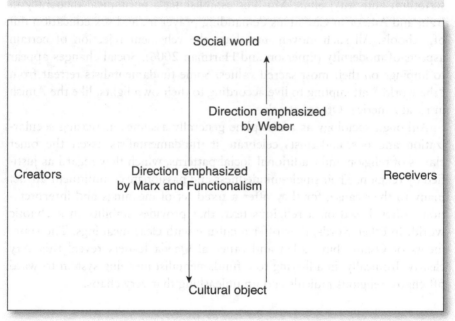

For all their power and plausibility, the theories that concentrate on relating cultural meaning to the social world downplay the role of human agency, of active human beings who produce the ideas, the theologies, the art, the media, and the popular culture that are the vessels of meaning. Similarly, these theories downplay the thoughts and actions of those who receive the cultural messages, who interpret, accept, or reject some of the suggested meanings. In this de-emphasis, they may be considered incomplete. Accordingly, in the following two chapters, we concentrate on the facets of the cultural diamond that have thus far been neglected: the social basis for cultural creation, production, and reception.

QUESTIONS FOR STUDY AND DISCUSSION

1. It has been said that culture works by providing stories—in other words, that people draw upon a cultural repertoire of stories to understand who they are and how they should live their lives. Discuss the pros and cons of this view. How does it relate to the reflection model? What could such stories enable people to do, and how could such stories constrain or mislead people?

2. Must all cultural objects be meaningful? Why or why not? Think of examples of cultural objects that seem saturated with meaning and others that seem meaningless. How could both be part of the same culture?

RECOMMENDED FOR FURTHER READING

Farrer, James. 2002. *Opening Up: Youth Sex Culture and Market Reform in Shanghai.* Chicago: University of Chicago Press. Farrer gives an ethnography of dance clubs, courtship, and the fast life in urban China. He shows how rapid revisions of the sexual culture, responding to both Western and traditional Chinese models, provide meaning and orientation for young Chinese as their world undergoes dramatic social change.

Swidler, Ann. 2001. *Talk of Love: How Culture Matters.* Chicago: University of Chicago Press. Rejecting the coherent view of culture as switchman, Swidler gives a brilliant analysis of how culture works in people's everyday lives.

Weber, Max. [1904–1905] 1985. *The Protestant Ethic and the Spirit of Capitalism.* Translated by Talcott Parsons; introduced by Anthony Giddens. London, England, and Boston, MA: Unwin Paperbacks. Weber's classic is indispensable to the debate over culture and meaning.

Wuthnow, Robert. 2003. *All in Sync: How Music and Art Are Revitalizing American Religion.* Berkeley: University of California Press. Wuthnow takes a close look at how contemporary American religion uses the arts, from hip-hop to modern dance to Renaissance paintings, to convey spiritual meanings.

3

Culture as
a Social Creation

W e have seen that culture possesses meaning. Cultural objects are meaningful to human beings living in a social world; conversely, the social world, otherwise random and chaotic, is meaningful because of the cultural lens through which people view it. But pressing questions remain: Who makes specific cultural objects? How are they endowed with meaning? What types of creators and creative operations does the left point of our cultural diamond represent?

As a cultural creator, consider Bessie Smith. Regarded in her own time as the "Empress of the Blues" and since as a singularly important figure in American music, Smith established the "classic blues" style in the 1920s. *Classic* may seem an odd term for blues singing (odder still, the term is never applied to male singers), but this specific musical form, tinged with jazz, combines African American country blues rooted in the Mississippi Delta with a vaudeville style of showmanship. With her extraordinary vocal gifts, flamboyant lifestyle, and great popularity, Bessie Smith seems to fit the standard image of exceptional individuals who create cultural objects by shaping and bending symbolic expressive forms to their will. This creative-artist-as-genius view holds that Bessie Smith took a form of Negro folk singing, polished it, and delivered it with a smooth sophistication to audiences a long way from the Delta. Accounts of Smith's precocious talent (she made her musical debut in Chattanooga at the age of nine), domineering personality (she refused to let any other blues singers appear on the bill with her), and mature death (she died in an auto accident in Mississippi at 39; one story tells that she bled to death because the hospital would not treat Negroes) support this story of individual cultural creation.

The singer who distills the experience of her people into the blues, the reformer who leads a social movement based on a new vision of social justice, the artist who works feverishly in a lonely studio, the prophet with burning eyes who brings a message from God, the animator who dreams up a character called Mickey Mouse, the poet who transforms the beauty of nature into a simple haiku, the praise singer who comes up with an innovative song to celebrate the chief—all of these figures we recognize as cultural creators. In moments of inspiration, these individuals create something altogether new, something moving, entertaining, brilliant, and often either profoundly disturbing or delightful. Such gifted people—the van Goghs and Bessie Smiths, the Disneys and Jeremiahs—change the cultural world in which human beings live.

So the answer to the question "Where does culture come from?" at first seems to be "from the efforts of individual geniuses." But this individualistic answer seems to work best for individual cultural objects such as a blues style or a haiku. What about culture in the broader sense of a "historically transmitted pattern of meaning"? It is harder to think of culture at this level as "coming from" anywhere. It seems always to have been there.

Sociology suggests an alternative to both the unsatisfying "it has always been that way" view at one extreme and the un-sociological "individual genius" view at the other. This alternative posits culture and cultural works as collective, not individual, creations. We can best understand specific cultural objects—the haiku, Jeremiah's prophesy, or Bessie Smith's singing—by seeing them not as unique to their creators but as the fruits of collective production, fundamentally social in their genesis. In this chapter we explore the background and implications of the sociological approach to cultural creation. In the following pages, we try to indicate how a fuller picture of Bessie Smith's singing emerges when viewed as a collective product, the result of Smith's concrete location in a particular social world, a context with competing cultural traditions and individual opportunities, organizations, and markets.

This view of culture as a social product originates in the work of Émile Durkheim on religion. We begin the chapter, therefore, by reviewing Durkheim's analysis and considering what happens when we follow his suggestion to view culture as collective representation. We then examine four contemporary sociological approaches to the collective production of culture: symbolic interactionism, the study of subcultures, research on whether cultural changes precede or follow social changes, and the social basis for creative innovations. As we proceed, we return often to the case of Bessie Smith to see how a sociological understanding of cultural creation can enrich our understanding of her music.

Durkheim and the Social Production of Culture

Émile Durkheim (1858–1917) was a French sociologist working in the late nineteenth and early twentieth centuries. He follows Marx and Weber as the third "founding father" of the discipline of sociology. Like these other two, he tried to understand how modern societies worked.

To these founders of sociology, as to modernist poets and artists such as William Butler Yeats, the modern world seemed fractured, divided, and increasingly unglued (Yeats 1956:184):

> Things fall apart, the centre cannot hold;
> Mere anarchy is loosed upon the world . . .

Social chaos—"mere anarchy"—seemed a real possibility. Over and over, the question "What can hold society together?" troubled thinkers of the early twentieth century. Durkheim investigated everything from suicide to religion to systems of education to science to sociological methods with this central question in mind. In his theory of collective representation, he thought he had found the answer.

The Problem of Modern Social Life

In modern life, Durkheim observed, people can be sorted in many ways: They have different occupations, different fields of knowledge and expertise, different beliefs, and different life experiences. Durkheim compared this to an earlier, less differentiated social state, which he called mechanical solidarity, wherein people join together because of their similar lives. In simpler times, he reasoned, each member of a society did the same type of work (e.g., farming), followed the same religion, raised and educated their children, and thought and believed and hoped and feared in pretty much the same way. Each member of the society could say confidently, "My people do this" or "My people believe this." The shared beliefs and understandings of a people constituted their collective consciousness, and this collective consciousness governed their thoughts, attitudes, and practices.

Change came when societies grew in size and density and people began to specialize. The most obvious form of specialization is the different types of work people do, but institutional specialization occurred as well. In the past, for example, teaching the young what they needed to know, performing religious rituals, and making the transitions of birth and death took place within the family, and the society as a whole exerted strong pressures against deviation. Modern institutions—schools, mosques, and hospitals—separate these life processes from the family, as well as from one another. Durkheim asked, just as we still ask, Under such conditions of specialization and differentiation, how can such societies hold together?

Durkheim considered a number of possible answers to this question. At times, he stressed the need for people to exchange with one another, a state he called organic solidarity; in effect, the farmer exchanges his produce with the teacher who, in return, educates his children, just as the organs of the body exchange with one another. At other times he proposed professional associations as a future source of cohesion. Although he never settled on a single solution to his problem, Durkheim believed that every society must have some kind of collective representation, some tie that binds that demonstrates to the society's members their undoubted connection to one another.

Social Bonds: The Role of Religion

Durkheim's search for collective representation and how it worked led him to take a close look at religion, which he viewed as the most fundamental bond among people of earlier times. His magnificent study of the social production of religion, *The Elementary Forms of the Religious Life* ([1915] 1965), emerged as his most influential work in cultural studies. Durkheim wrote this work toward the end of his career, when his thinking had changed from an early emphasis on structural influences on social behavior to a greater concern with culture and meaning. In *The Elementary Forms of the Religious Life,* Durkheim looked at what he regarded as the most primitive forms of religion—the totemism of Australian Aborigines and certain Native American groups. Why study primitive religion if his interest leaned toward human society today? Durkheim began with a functionalist postulate: A human institution such as religion cannot rest upon error or superstition; instead, it responds to a profound human need. Consequently, he looked at primitive religions to see the "constituent elements" fundamental to all religions.

Durkheim's analysis of religion centers on four key ideas: (1) collective representation, (2) the distinction between the sacred and the profane, (3) the origins of the sacred, and (4) the social consequences of religion.

First, Durkheim argued, religion provides the basis for all categories of thinking, and religion and categories of thinking alike are "collective repre- *1* sentations which express collective realities" (22). How does he make this argument? Human beings, he pointed out, cannot conceive of time and space independent of socially agreed-upon divisions, even though we know they are arbitrary and not natural. The seven-day week, for example, is a social convention of Western societies; one we recognize as artificial (in Nigeria, the Igbo have a four-day week), yet thinking of time without resorting to this convention proves impossible. Durkheim pointed out all categories of thought, all essential ideas, as social. Human beings are "double"—we possess an individual biological component and a shared social component, our participation in a collective consciousness—and our categories of thought, including our sense of the religious, come from that second social component. Hence, religion and culture are collective representations.

But how does the society, the collective, make its presence felt within us? Durkheim answered this question in the next two steps of his argument. He started by asking, What do all religions have in common? The answer is not that they all believe in some supernatural or divine being; Buddhism doesn't, for example. There is a simpler answer: All religious beliefs divide the world *2* into sacred and profane. Now, nothing special determines the nature of the sacred; virtually anything can fit this category. As said in Chapter 1, bread, the homeliest of foods, becomes sacred in the Christian communion. Similarly, Native American and Australian groups sanctify such animals as snakes, insects, and carrion eaters that other cultures despise. Its absolute separation from the profane and its inapproachability with impunity characterizes the sacred—the biblical story of Uzzah, who touched the ark of God and died on the spot, reminds us of this—and the core of religion lies in this separation.

> A religion is a unified system of beliefs and practices relative to sacred things, that is to say, things set apart and forbidden—beliefs and practices which unite into one single moral community called a Church, all those who adhere to them. (Durkheim, [1915] 1965:62)

Durkheim traced our sense of the sacred by looking at totems, central to "elementary forms" of religion. He pointed out that many simple societies are organized around clans, kinship groups distinguished by names like "the kangaroo clan" or "the people of the white eagle." Each such name represents the clan's totem, which serves as the emblem of the clan; this image or representation of the clan appears on its property and the bodies of its members, especially when the clan gathers together. More than just a name or an emblem, however, the totem is sacred, and all sorts of ritual prohibitions surround it—a taboo against eating it, for example. These tribal peoples base their entire cosmologies, their classifications of human beings and nature, on the totem, thus imposing a sacred/profane structure on the entire universe.

Up to this point, Durkheim has argued that the sacred/profane distinction organizes and classifies all social and natural beings and that this distinction emerges in its most elementary form in the totemic religions of tribal people. But where do such people get the idea that the totemic emblem is sacred? Clearly, not from the object itself, for the totem often personifies a rather lowly animal. Durkheim answers this question from the heart of his cultural analysis, suggesting that the totem symbolizes two things: the totemic principal (or, we would say, God) and the clan. "So if it is once the symbol of the god and of the society, is that not because the god and the society are only one?" (236). The god of the clan, in other words, is the clan itself.

How does Durkheim justify this conclusion? Society, he suggested, arouses a sensation of divinity in human beings through (1) its power or control over us, shown in its ability to cause or inhibit our actions without regard for individual utility, and (2) its positive force, the "strengthening and vivifying action of society." When a member of society lives in moral harmony with his comrades,

> he has more confidence, courage, and boldness in action, just like the believer who thinks that he feels the regard of his god turned graciously toward him. [Society] thus produces, as it were, a perpetual sustenance of our moral nature. (242)

People think this moral support must result from some external cause, some force always represented with religious symbols, and they respond to the force with respect and awe. Two sorts of reality seem to emerge—that associated with the force (sacred) and that associated with the everyday (profane).

Using the example of Australian clans, Durkheim shows how people awaken to a sense of religious force. The Aborigines, like most hunter-gatherers, experience their lives as having two phases: times of scattered wandering in groups and times of gathering for a ceremony called the corroboree. The first phase, normal everyday life, contains things "uniform, languishing, and dull." But during the corroboree, people come together to sing, dance around the fire, enjoy a normally forbidden sexual freedom, and celebrate until they drop from exhaustion. In such a gathering, life is emotional, people are animated by powerful forces and passions, and each sentiment is echoed back by another until the energy and exuberance grow like an avalanche. Durkheim referred to this stage as one of "collective efferves-cence." When taken up by such collective effervescence, people feel unlike themselves or, almost literally, "carried away."

Because their lives have such very different phases—the routine everyday and the effervescent corroboree—the Aborigines believe they participate in two separate worlds: the profane, flat and dull, and the sacred, charged with energy and excitement. Thus arises the religious idea of the sacred and the profane and the absolute separation between them. Why does the force felt during sacred time get associated with the totem? Durkheim reasoned that because the totem provides the clan name, totemic emblems abound during the gathering of the clan. Because of its visibility during these times, the totem comes to represent both the scene and the strong emotions felt. It becomes a collective representation.

Therefore, Durkheim concluded, the rational folks who equate religion with superstition are wrong. The religious force is real enough, but the source of the force is not what the believer thinks: "The believer is not deceived when he believes in the existence of a moral power upon which he depends and from which he receives all that is best in himself: this power exists, it is society" (257). The religious force comes not from a totem or a god but from the experience of the social. Religion, therefore, encompasses the system of ideas by which people represent their society. And because religion provides the source of the classifications through which we apprehend the world, all of human culture becomes a representation of the social.

Culture as Collective Representation

Durkheim's analysis of religion points to all cultural objects as collective representations. They represent not just a particular society but social experience itself. We recognize the functionalist thread here: Groups and societies need collective representations of themselves to inspire sentiments of unity and mutual support, and culture fulfills this need.

We have seen before, in reflection theories, the idea that culture represents society. Rather than assuming a straight reflection, however, Durkheim's analysis shows a more complex picture of how cultural objects, such as religious beliefs, can represent our experience of the social in all its force. Culture, including religion, is a collective representation in two senses. First, the cultural objects we began with—a painting, a social movement, a prophecy, an idea, or a blues song—are not simply created by an individual touched by genius or inspired by God. Instead, people bound to other people—people who work, celebrate, suffer, and love, like the clan members in Australia—produce them. Second, in their cultural products, people represent their experiences of work, joy, pain, and love. Durkheim's cultural theory gives us the social mechanism whereby cultural creators produce, in Wallace Stevens's words, "a tune beyond us, yet ourselves."

The implication for sociological research would be that if one tried to understand a certain group of people, one would look for the expressive forms through which they represent themselves to themselves (and to others, although this function would have secondary importance). A business organization, a youth gang, a nation, a family, or any identifiable social group will develop collective representations through which it demonstrates its collective solidarity to itself and others. The sociologist can come at this collective representation process from the other direction, from the analysis of a particular cultural object, as well. In the planning for possible disasters, one researcher has shown, for example, optimistic scenarios (cultural object) that avoid worst-case thinking demonstrate a particularly American cognitive orientation (collective representation), and a dangerous one (Cerulo 2006).

What would it mean, then, to call Bessie Smith's blues collective representations? It would imply that even songs about individual pain represent group experience, in this case that of African Americans in the South during the early twentieth century. For example, many of Smith's songs tell of losing a man. On one level, we could regard this theme as the expression of the universal problem of lost love; at another, personal level, this theme could express a very specific problem of how one woman lost one man at one particular time. On an intermediate level, however, a social representation occurs as well, and this specific representation speaks to the difficulties of sustained relationships among impoverished blacks in the rural South. "Frosty Morning Blues," for example, begins, "Did you ever wake up on a frosty morning and discover your good man gone?" Sharecroppers living in unheated shacks—and most Southern blacks endured this condition during the time Bessie Smith was singing—would have loathed to leave their beds on cold mornings; their shared experience of this common misery lends a collective weight to the individual's particular misery of being abandoned. This collective understanding of the pleasures of warm beds and the pain of cold floors "on a frosty morning" can be said to "strengthen and vivify," in Durkheim's language, even the bawdy development of the frosty-morning metaphor: "Oh my damper is down and my fire ain't burning and a chill's all around my bed." Both the humor and the pathos of the song, and of Bessie Smith's blues more generally, represent the social world in which they originated.

The Collective Production of Culture

Applying Durkheim's insights constitutes what we call the collective production approach to cultural meanings. This approach tries to take away the mystery about the creation of art, ideas, beliefs, religion, and culture in general by revealing the many social activities, such as interaction, cooperation, organization, and contestation, involved in the formation of what we designate as cultural objects. If culture is a collective representation, as Durkheim argued, the collective production approach investigates the nuts and bolts of just how the collectivity represents itself.

Collective production theory has two sides. One involves the interactions among people and how these interactions themselves generate culture. This version of collective production theory stems from the branch of social psychology known as symbolic interactionism. In the remainder of this chapter we look at such interactions and how they work on both the small group level and the broader societal level. The second type of collective production looks less at interactions and more at the organization of cultural producers and consumers, including such things as culture industries, distribution mechanisms, and the markets for cultural products. Chapter 4 examines these studies, generated by what is usually called the production-of-culture school and rooted in organizational and economic sociology.

Symbolic Interactionism

Most branches of social theory assume certain things as given. For example, although we might try to explain how the norms of a society constrain its members to act in one way and not another, the norm itself—say, the norm of apologizing if you bump into someone—is taken as a given. Or, we might examine certain roles, such as the role of a teacher or a mother, to see how they are enacted, but we largely take the roles themselves for granted. Symbolic interactionism concerns how people actively construct and learn their norms and roles. The basic insight of the interactionists holds that the human self is not a preexisting Platonic form but is shaped through social interaction. An early theorist of this school was Charles Horton Cooley, who coined the term "looking-glass self" ([1902] 1964). According to Cooley, an interaction comprises three phases: (1) The self imagines another's response to his or her behavior or appearance, (2) the self imagines the other person's judgment, and (3) the self has an emotional reaction, such as of pride or shame, to that judgment. For example, a little girl runs and bumps into a boy in her playgroup. The girl observes the boy's expression of pain and anger, and she imagines that he thinks her clumsy or thoughtless. She understands his probable judgment of her action (he may say, "Hey, watch out," or give her a scornful look), and she responds emotionally (she feels embarrassed or ashamed at having hurt him or provoked his anger). Such interactions establish the norm of apologizing when accidentally bumping into someone else, for the apology constitutes a second interaction sequence to restore the social harmony that the first disrupted.

All social learning does not take place through two-person interactions, of course. George Herbert Mead (1934) pointed out that the developing child first learns to take the role of another person. This constitutes the "play" stage; the child plays at being a teacher or plays with an imaginary friend. Later comes the more complicated "game" stage, wherein the child learns to take on and take into account a variety of other roles. Mead used the analogy of the baseball game: The runner must know what the shortstop is likely to do, what the fielder will try to do, and so forth. Children move from play to games as they develop more complex responses to those with whom they do or might interact. Ultimately, the child learns to take into account the response of the *generalized other*, Mead's term for the society— he calls it "the organized community or social group which gives to the individual his unity of self" (1934:154)—with which the individual always implicitly interacts. This generalized other is the source of morality, and children are socialized into understanding what it expects.

> It is in the form of the generalized other that the social process influences the behavior of the individuals involved in it and carrying it on, i.e., that the community exercises control over the conduct of its individual members; for it is this form that the social process or community enters as a determining factor into the individual's thinking. (155)

Where does culture come in? From the symbolic interactionist point of view, the human individual—the self—is wide open to influence. As we saw in our earlier discussion of meaning, biology or our innate nature gives little direction to our lives, so we must develop our own guidelines, and we do so in the course of our interactions with one another. Symbolic interactionism suggests that human interactions create culture, just as Durkheim's corroboree created totemic religion. Once created, cultural objects are perpetuated and transmitted through their repeated expression and the socialization of new group members—for example, the young. Symbolic interactionists are interested in the micro-settings through which this process happens.

Consider a classic paper by Howard Becker (1953) on how people learn to smoke marijuana. Many people think of getting high on marijuana as simply a biological response. On the contrary, Becker argued, a complex process of social learning must take place. The novice smoker interacts with more experienced users, often with members of a marijuana subculture (at the time of the study, the early 1950s, marijuana smoking was primarily confined to jazz musicians and similar bohemian subcultures). From these experienced smokers, novices learn how to smoke (e.g., to hold the smoke in their lungs), what to feel (the experienced smokers identify and label such feelings as floating or time distortion), and what to enjoy. If the interaction process breaks down—for example, if a new user tried to smoke a joint while alone—the novice would unlikely develop the habit of or the taste for marijuana. But with all of the interaction processes completed, the novice "becomes" a marijuana user, with smoking part of his or her identity.

Similarly, one "becomes" a blues singer through interactions, not just through inborn talent. Bessie Smith's immediate musical heritage was not call-and-response work songs in the cotton fields—the blues' birthplace—but the vaudeville stage and tent show circuit played by black performers in the early twentieth century. On the vaudeville circuit, female singers developed a smooth, sophisticated style of singing, a far cry from the earthy blues style of the fields. Indeed, it might be said that Smith innovated not to sophisticate a folk idiom but instead to rough up this slick, cabaret singing. And even that wasn't strictly her own innovation. An immediate predecessor of Smith's, Ma (Gertrude) Rainey, traveled with touring companies throughout the South introducing down-home elements into the vaudeville style. Rainey discovered Smith and took her into her company, the Rabbit Foot Minstrels, where the young girl's singing and showmanship developed. After leaving Rainey's troupe, Smith worked the Southern circuit with tent shows, pursuing her career in the world of segregated music. Bessie Smith's identity as a blues singer, in other words, grew out of her interactions with other musicians.

Identity is a key concept for the symbolic interactionist approach. One's own identity or sense of self—"I am a blues singer" or "I am a brother-in-law"—develops through interaction with others and requires confirmation from others. Once again, we enter the realm of meanings here; the self tries to project a certain set of meanings onto those with whom it interacts and in return tries to interpret the meanings constructed by partners in the interaction. Erving Goffman (1959) analyzed this process by using the metaphors of theatrical performances: When it interacts, the self is an actor performing a role before an audience. If the performance succeeds, the self confirms a certain identity both to her partners in interaction and to herself.

A striking example comes from research on the homeless. In their study of homeless street people in a Texas city, David Snow and Leon Anderson (1993) found that the down and out constantly try to do what Snow and

Anderson call "identity work": They manage their interactions in such a way as to foster a specific set of impressions. Some construct their identities in terms of distancing; they stress that they are "not like the other guys who hang out down at the Sally" (215) and therefore don't need the services of the Salvation Army or other relief agencies. Others embrace the homeless role—"I'm a bum, and I know who my friends are" (221)—declaring themselves proud of their freedom and clever at surviving in the harsh world they inhabit. Still others construct elaborate fantasies about their past histories or future prospects. One homeless man told the researchers at great length how the next day, "I'm going to catch a plane to Pittsburgh and tomorrow night I'll take a hot bath, have a dinner of linguine and red wine in my own restaurant, and have a woman hanging on my arm" (226). In all of these activities, the homeless conduct impression management in their interactions to control the meanings they present to others.

Again we see the cultural position as distinct from the biological one. A biologically based argument that Snow and Anderson cite (Maslow 1962) suggests that human beings have a hierarchy of needs; they require certain things to survive—food, clothing, and shelter—and only once these needs have been met do people have the luxury of worrying about meanings, identities, or symbolic representations. On the contrary, respond Snow and Anderson, the homeless, who may not know where their next meal is coming from or where they will sleep that night, are nevertheless adept manipulators of words and symbols, compelled to construct and project specific identities. Like all people, they use culture—in this case, the resources of language and storytelling—to enact their social performances and make their world meaningful to themselves and others. (For a similar example of performing identity to achieve specific goals, see Cheris Sun-ching Chan's 2009 study of how life insurance agents operate in front of a skeptical clientele.)

Although the homeless must make up their own culture and identities with few resources and limited precedents, most interactions that transmit culture and form identity call on a known and shared history of the community. The generalized other is usually concrete, with specific characteristics, in more stable social worlds, so the cultural objects that serve as collective representations do not have to be made up on the spot. Among the Yoruba in Nigeria, children learn to greet their parents by kneeling in front of them before speaking. This kneeling is a form of etiquette, and the practice constitutes a meaningful cultural object. Through socialization into this practice, the child learns something about Yoruba relationships (the child must respect the adult) and behavior (the child must show respect in a particular way). The child also learns her collective identity. She is a Yoruba because she thinks and acts this way, and she thinks and acts this way because she is a Yoruba.

Subcultures

Speaking of Yoruba culture or identity evokes the image of an undifferentiated generalized other, a community to which all Yoruba belong. People, however, belong not simply to a single group or community but to a variety of them. Mead (1934) identified two types: abstract social groups, such as debtors, that function as social groups only indirectly and "concrete social classes or subgroups, such as political parties, clubs, [and] corporations, which are all actually functioning social units, in terms of which of their individual members are directly related to one another" (157). If these relations to one another prove strong enough to counteract some of the influences of the societal generalized other, the group becomes a subculture.

We might well refer to the worlds of marijuana smokers, homeless men, or traveling vaudeville performers as *subcultures*. As the name suggests, a subculture exists within a larger cultural system and has contact with the external culture. Within the subculture's domain, however, operates a powerful set of symbols, meanings, and behavioral norms—often the opposite of those in the larger culture—that bind the subculture's members. Thus, we might speak of the hip-hop subculture, the gay subculture, or the cyberpunk subculture. A subculture doesn't just refer to consumption tastes—we don't speak of the subculture of Volvo owners or pizza lovers—but to a way of life. Teenagers especially flock to, and produce, subcultures, for they have the means to express themselves through consumption, they desire to differentiate themselves from other age groups and even other teenagers, and they are not yet anchored by the institutions of adult life (Hebdige 1979).

Sociology's interest in subcultures began in the early twentieth century with the Chicago School of urban studies. Research focused on unassimilated subcultures—immigrant groups and criminal gangs—and the questions posed involved when and how such subcultures would assimilate into mainstream American life (Thomas and Znaniecki 1918–1920; Thrasher 1927). While the youth subculture research carries on this tradition in the sense that youth groups tend to be short-lived (youth grow up, and subsequent cohorts of teens want to distinguish themselves from their elder siblings), contemporary scholarship often focuses on more permanent subcultures such as those associated with professions. In the aptly titled *Wild Cowboys,* Robert Jackall (1997) uncovers the subculture and "habits of mind" of the law enforcement officers—New York homicide detectives and the district attorney's prosecutors—as well as the criminals who interact with them in the tight world of New York's big-time drug trade. The detectives seek to transform chaos into order as they pursue cases—small-time drug dealers killed by other dealers—that no one else cares about. In the detectives' subculture, this is an intellectual challenge as much as a moral one. Detectives' near obsession with solving cases that everyone regards as "public-interest homicides"—that is, slayings in which everyone is glad the victim is dead—mystifies people outside this subculture.

Subcultures, with their elaborate symbols and meanings, develop by people interacting with one another and therefore have been of great interest to sociologists oriented toward symbolic interactionism. Gary Alan Fine (1987), for example, studied how members of Little League baseball teams produce their own temporary subcultures. Drawing on extensive participant observation, interviews, and questionnaires with ten Little League teams in three cities, Fine explored how social interaction in the Little League context socializes boys into adult male roles and gives rise to what Fine calls the "idioculture or self-culture" of the group. In this socialization process, adults (coaches, parents) emphasize effort. They exhort the team to try harder by maintaining that a boy or a team must "want to win" and that a player must always "give it his best shot." The unspoken assumption is that success or failure depends on internal motivation—on character, in other words—and not on physical talent, compatibility among team members' skills, or luck. The boys themselves emphasize "proper behavior," which they regard as the expression of appropriate emotions and emotional control: Big boys don't cry.

Little League teams develop an elaborate linguistic and symbolic code known only to the team members. One team, for example, designated a foul ball hit over the backstop as a "Polish home run." An outsider hearing jokes such as "Don't hit a Polish home run" might guess, based on his or her knowledge of American ethnic jokes about Poles, that the team referred to some inept play but would have no idea of the specific act being referred to. Little League teams generate hundreds of such private, shared meanings.

What are the roots of this idioculture? Fine's causal argument is sketched in Figure 3.1. The interacting preadolescent group—the team—responds to general cultural values, such as the importance of winning. The boys also participate in a preadolescent cultural system familiar to youths from coast to coast; what ten-year-old hasn't sung "A Hundred Bottles of Beer on the Wall"? Some of the cultural objects in this system come from the media, and some come from such institutions as summer camps where boys from different communities come together and trade information. The boys pick up both direct and indirect messages from adults, and they feel the influence of biological pressures, including an acute discomfort around girls. The most notable characteristic of this peer culture is a desperate longing to fit in with the other boys, coupled with a scorn for outsiders.

Figure 3.1 Cultural Production in a Little League Baseball Team

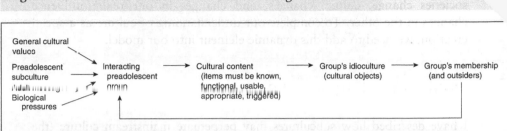

In such a context, events transform into culture. Not just any event or object can undergo transformation into a cultural object, however. For a symbol or expression to enter the idioculture, it must draw on known information (e.g., ethnic slurs about Poles); it must be functional (nicknames help identify players, some of whom might have the same first name); it must be usable (coaches forbid certain four-letter words, well known in preadolescent subculture, so they do not enter most teams' idiocultures); it must be appropriate (the nickname "Maniac" stopped being appropriate when a player improved); and it must be triggered repeatedly (the expression "Polish home run" would have been forgotten had not so many foul balls gone over the backstop). Subcultures also interact with and perpetuate one another. On a college campus racial "wannabes" (whites who embrace hip-hop), Goths, and Christians mutually define one another through their mutual antagonism (Wilkins 2008).

Subcultures make meaning, producing cultural objects significant to insiders and mystifying to outsiders. They often emphasize opposition, as in youth subcultures built around music and style (Hall et al. 1980; Hebdige 1979). In this sense they exhibit the more general behavior of constructing symbolic boundaries, ways people distinguish between "people like me" and "those others." Michèle Lamont (2000) shows how French and American working-class men make elaborate discriminations between regular guys like themselves and people who operate very differently, even though their class positions sometimes are much the same. Sometimes, the creation of such boundaries is less about meaning than about avoiding the meaningful. Nina Eliasoph (1998) studied how small groups like environmentalists and country dancers work to avoid meaningful talk, especially about politics, to keep their groups cohesive.

Up to this point, we have considered the specific social world in which interactions take place, such as a subculture, as a relatively stable collectivity

ple smoothly socialize. This is an incomplete view. In reality,
ge, culture changes, and changes in one realm influence
other. To complete our understanding of culture as a social
creation, we need to add this dynamic element into our model.

Cultural Innovation and Social Change

I have described how subcultures may perpetuate mainstream culture (the
Little League teams) or defy it (the marijuana smokers), but sometimes they
set out to change it. Although a relatively rare event—most subcultures just
want to be left alone—many social movements start out as subcultures. To use
Weber's terms, they move from the separation of otherworldly asceticism to
the reforming or even revolutionary engagement of innerworldly asceticism.

China offers a good example of how a separatist subculture became a
movement for revolutionary social change. What became known as the
Boxer Uprising of 1900 began as the Spirit Boxers, a subculture of peasant
youth during the late Qing dynasty who were devoted to martial arts and a
ritual involving the divine possession of a believer by one of the popular
gods (Esherick 1987). In 1898, the terrible poverty and dislocation brought
about by the flooding of the Yellow River combined with increasing anti-
Westernism in response to escalating imperialist and missionary activities to
transform the Boxers into a militant nationalist movement, the Boxers
United in Righteousness. Their slogan was "Revive the Qing, destroy the
foreign." Over the next two years, the number of Boxers grew, as did their
attacks on Chinese Christians and the foreigners themselves, finally culmi-
nating in a siege of the foreign enclave in Beijing that fell by a foreign expe-
ditionary force amid great bloodshed.

Although secret societies or spirit possession cults were not unusual in
the late Qing, specific social pressures—increasing foreign demands and
routine poverty exacerbated by natural disaster—turned what had been an
"otherworldly" subculture into a movement bent on radical social transformation. The very meaning of the Boxers' cultural objects changed.
Martial arts, for example, initially represented individual discipline and
self-control to the Spirit Boxers. To the Boxers United in Righteousness, it
meant aggressive Chinese nationalism. How would we describe this in
terms of the cultural diamond? Did a change in the social world (increasing
foreign pressures) produce a change in the cultural object (martial arts)?
Or did the development of a cultural object (the increasing popularity of
martial arts among youth) produce a change in the way the young Chinese
viewed the social world?

Cultural response to social change need not take the dramatic form of a secret society or revolutionary movement, however. We can see cultural adaptations to changing circumstances in how communities respond to demographic pressures. Maria Kefalas (2003) studied how a white working-class neighborhood in Chicago, feeling threatened by poor African American neighborhoods on its fringes, developed a strong culture of place to protect the residents' ideas of the good life. In everything from how they clean their kitchens (obsessively, even behind the refrigerator) to how they honor their veterans (seriously) to how they landscape their small lawns (precisely), residents of Beltway construct their neighborhood as the "last garden," cultivated to ward off the urban jungle that lies beyond the clearing.

Which came first, the ideal of the garden or the perception of racial and class threat? We need to take a closer look now at the relationship between cultural innovations and societal changes.

Cultural Lags and Leads

Reflection theories of either the Marxist or the functionalist stamp, as discussed previously, could not answer these questions very well. If culture passively reflects the social world, which the reflection model usually implies, change must come from that world first. In this view, innovations in music, art, theology, ideas, popular culture, literature, and expressive behavior must all be responses to social changes. Now, although clearly something is right about the idea that social shifts produce cultural changes, such a deterministic position suggests that the social world always changes first, with culture lagging behind.

The "cultural lag" hypothesis was put forward by a sociologist named William Ogburn ([1922] 1936), who maintained that sociologists should distinguish between "material culture" and "adaptive culture." Material culture is just what it sounds like: "home, factories, machines, raw materials, manufactured products, food stuffs and other material objects." When this material culture changes, the nonmaterial culture, which includes practices, folkways, and social institutions, must change in response. Adaptive culture comprises the portion of nonmaterial culture that adjusts to material conditions. It always takes awhile for the adaptations to catch up with material changes, and this gap is the "cultural lag." Ogburn used the example of the American forests. At one time, social practices (large-scale timbering, clearing forests for agriculture) matched the material conditions (vast forests). The destruction of the forests constituted a dramatic change in American material culture, but many years passed before serious efforts at conservation and reforestation were made at the level of adaptive culture—hence the cultural lag.

Ogburn believed that changes in the material culture usually precede changes in the adaptive culture. In some sense, this is true by definition (adaptation means adapting *to* something). Such a belief fits reflection theory in both its functionalist and Marxian forms. At the same time, we can easily come up with examples wherein nonmaterial culture leads, not lags behind, material conditions. Max Weber's account of how the spirit of capitalism burned hot in backwoods eighteenth-century Pennsylvania provides one such example. For another, consider the worldwide changes in cigarette smoking. Neither a material change (there was no scarcity of tobacco) nor a material discovery (the dangers of smoking to health had been known for years) prompted the abrupt decline of smoking among the American and (later) the European middle classes. The change in attitude came when the large generation born after World War II became concerned (some might say obsessed) with health and fitness. For baby boomers, the body—exercised, slimmed, and well cared for—represented an ideal of youth and strength. They demonstrated high status not with martinis, fur coats, and silver cigarette cases but with expensive mineral water, jogging, and disdain for smokers. As a cultural object for this group, the cigarette came to mean a foolish disregard for health.

The idea that culture always lags behind material change also goes against our experience with dramatic cultural change. As the humanities have long emphasized, now and then a genius, a prophet, or an innovator bursts onto the scene and shakes up existing cultural conventions. At a collective level, some new cultural movements—abstract expressionism, punk music, New Age spirituality, the African American female novelists of the 1970s, prime-time serials, or the rage for physical fitness—emerge and prosper without any direct push from the social. So we need to understand this cultural innovation, where culture seems to lead, not lag behind, social change, or where cultural change seems to bear no direct relation to changes happening in the society at large.

Cultural Innovations

A random event—a boy hits a ball over the backstop—gets processed by group interaction. The symbolic representation of the event functions in its usefulness for building group solidarity, identifying norms, and separating the insiders from the outsiders. Cultural creation has occurred, and a cultural innovation—the "Polish home run"—gets established. More generally, the collective production approach to culture suggests, although innovations may occur randomly and unpredictably, some patterns as evident: (1) Certain periods prove more likely to generate innovations than others, (2) even the innovations follow some conventions, and (3) certain innovations prove more likely than others to become established.

Let's look at these points in order. A number of cultural analysts argue that cultural creativity does not take place at a steady rate but shows dramatic peaks and valleys. During periods of relatively little change, conventions remain stable, the community in question generally shares ideas, and the status quo remains unchallenged; individual selves and the generalized others live in harmony, Mead might say. At other times, cultural creativity explodes. Thinkers come up with new ideas and systems of ideas that circulate among men and women concerned with public affairs. Artists defy the conventions of their genres. Long-standing relations, such as those between the sexes, get overturned. Behaviors change in everything from dress to living arrangements to occupational goals. In much of the world, the 1960s represented such a period of intense cultural ferment.

What causes such a burst of cultural innovation? "Unsettled times," says sociologist Ann Swidler (1986). A "disturbance in the moral order," says Robert Wuthnow (1987). A loosening up of the dominant ideology, says Marxian critic Raymond Williams ([1973] 1980). The common point they make seems that under certain conditions—massive demographic shift, war, or sudden economic change—the old rules, cultural and social, no longer apply. A moral vacuum occurs, and in such a situation people cast around for new guidelines, new meanings with which to orient their lives. Failure to find such meanings brings the experience of anomie, the disorientation that Durkheim attributed to rapid social change. Cultural innovation—the production of new meanings—emerges as a response to incipient anomie. It reorients people and gives them their bearings in the new social circumstances.

Think again of the middle and late 1960s. The United States experienced a controversial war; unusual but unevenly distributed economic prosperity; legislation bringing the agenda of African Americans, other minorities, and (later) women into mainstream politics; and a demographic bulge (the baby boom) going through its teenage years. This combination laid the ground for extraordinary cultural change. Ideologies, fads, artistic movements, behavioral changes—from cohabitation to long hair to the drug culture to Pop Art to the Black Panthers to Women's Liberation to acid rock—all represented cultural responses to the unsettled times of the 1960s. The slower pace of cultural change from the mid-1970s to the end of the century was a consolidation period that resisted dramatic changes (Steensland 2007).

The innovations of the 1960s were not just an American phenomenon. The withdrawal of colonialism from Nigeria, as elsewhere in Africa, stimulated a burst of artistic and intellectual activity. In contrast, the failure of such economic programs as the Great Leap Forward and Mao's increasing uneasiness over the future of the Chinese Communist regime lay the groundwork for the Cultural Revolution, clearly an innovation in the extent and ferocity of its repression. In Europe, youth culture, spurred by the baby boom, consumerism, and left-wing politics, shook the traditional establishment.

Does this mean that cultural lag theorists were right—that culture changes in response to the social world? Although the arguments of Wuthnow and Swidler may seem to suggest this, the issue of what leads what depends largely on when you start the analysis. We could say that the ongoing Chinese Communist revolution (social world, material culture) led to the Cultural Revolution (cultural objects, adaptive culture). However, we could just as legitimately say, rather, that earlier changes in the Chinese culture (modernization, the impact of the West) led to changes in the Chinese social world (the Communist Revolution).

Although certain periods seem to exhibit more cultural change than others, the second premise of the collective production approach to innovation is that cultural innovations may not be as dramatically different as they first seem. Cultural creators typically respond to conventions rather than ignore them. Howard Becker (1982), for example, distinguished four types of artists: the integrated professionals, the mavericks, the naive artists, and the folk artists. Three of the four types are conventional. Folk artists follow the conventions of their craft. Integrated professionals perpetuate the conventions of their own particular art world (Becker uses the term *art world* to encompass all of the people whose various activities—from making paintbrushes, for example, to writing art criticism—go into the production of a certain kind of art). Mavericks ostentatiously defy the art world's conventions, but the key point is that only those who know the conventions in the first place can recognize their very unconventionality. They act conventionally unconventional, like teenagers who express their nonconformity with adult values by conforming to a rigid teenage dress code designed to appall their elders. Only naive artists not attached to a collective production world may be said to innovate without regard for convention, but their very lack of connections makes the work of such artists virtually unknown. Thus, their innovations have neither audience nor influence.

This brings us to the third premise on innovation: Cultural creators may produce something new, but not all such innovations will become established. We saw this in Fine's (1987) Little League study; a new symbol or nickname will wither unless conditions allow it to become known, used, functional, apt, and repeatedly triggered. On a larger scale, Robert Wuthnow (1985) suggested that ideological innovations of the modern era will unlikely last unless the state is hospitable to them. Looking at the

Reformation in Europe, he pointed out that monarchs always favored some version of Luther's reforms, for the Reformation downgraded ecclesiastical authority and thus removed Rome and the church hierarchy as a major rival to royal authority. Whether or not the Reformation took hold in a particular country, therefore, resulted from the king or queen's power in comparison to the landed aristocracy, which favored Rome. Countries with a relatively strong monarchy, such as England, embraced the Reformation, whereas countries with a monarchy dependent on the landed aristocracy, such as France, did not.

Similarly, though innovative, Bessie Smith's singing so succeeded for other reasons. It caught on, or became established, only because of a specific set of conditions, including her lucky timing: In 1920, a singer named Mamie Smith (no relation) made the first blues record, *Crazy Blues*, and opened up a vast new market for the record industry. Within a few years, Okeh, Paramount, and Columbia's "race record" series sought singers for the African American market. Bessie Smith signed up with Columbia, and her recordings for the company provided the basis for her immense popularity. She continued to tour the vaudeville circuit in the South, but the Columbia recordings had created an audience in the North as well. She played in large Northern cities under the auspices of the Theater Owners Booking Association. (TOBA was considered the best management and booking agent for Negro performers, but its demands gave it the nickname among the stars of "Tough on Black Asses.") Indeed, much of Smith's reputation for innovation stems from her introducing a Southern musical form to a Northern audience.

Bessie Smith's story, unquestionably one of individual talent, is also one of record companies and vaudeville circuits, artistic mentors and new audiences, and expanding markets and skilled promotion. Her blues provided both a collective representation of African American life in the segregated South and a collective product of an entertainment industry. Although her genius was her own, her creation was social.

SUMMARY

In this chapter, we traced some sociological theories of the creation of culture. We saw how sociologists followed Durkheim in regarding culture as collective product or representation rather than as exclusively the work of individual creators. Cultural objects, by this reasoning, express aspects of the social world and are produced by the collective activities of members of this world. We saw how interactions among people create new cultural objects—practices, beliefs, symbols, and expressions—and how such cultural objects bestow meanings on the human experience. We saw how cultural innovation, creating new meaning, occurs at the microlevel of subcultures and the macrolevel of ideological shifts. We saw that creativity, along with its recognition and its establishment, depends on social conventions and social institutions.

So far, we have concentrated on creators of culture on the one hand and the social world on the other. We have paid only minimal attention to two things: the audience or recipients of culture (the right point on our culture diamond) and the organizations of production and distribution that tie all of the points together. Yet we have seen in the example of Bessie Smith the vitality of organizations and audiences to any understanding of cultural creations as collective representation. The next chapter discusses these two—the right point of our cultural diamond and the organization as links among creators, receivers, and cultural objects.

QUESTIONS FOR STUDY AND DISCUSSION

1. Think of some ways in which culture works as "collective representation" in contemporary life. Where might we find vestiges of what Durkheim called "organic solidarity"? What are some contemporary sacred symbols? Do we still need such symbols outside of religious life?

2. Identify a subculture within a larger cultural formation. For example, you might think of a youth gang, a religious cult, a tight ethnic group, or a student fraternity; perhaps you can use a group with which you have had personal experience as your example. Discuss how your subculture erects and maintains its symbolic boundaries.

3. If cultural objects are social creations, where do inspired individuals come in? Does a sociological theory of culture ignore the creative genius of people like Leonardo da Vinci, Toni Morrison, Isadora Duncan, or Yo-Yo Ma?

RECOMMENDED FOR FURTHER READING

Becker, Howard S. 1982. *Art Worlds.* Berkeley: University of California Press. Becker gives readers a lively account of how a wide variety of human activities and interactions produce art and how whether or not a cultural object gets the label of "art" is itself a product of interactions and negotiations.

Durkheim, Émile. [1915] 1965. *The Elementary Forms of the Religious Life.* Translated by Joseph Ward Swain. New York: Free Press. No summary can capture the rich detail of Durkheim's study or the precision of his analysis.

Lamont, Michèle. 2009. *How Professors Think: Inside the Curious World of Academic Judgment*. Cambridge, MA: Harvard University Press. Lamont looks at a strange subculture indeed—that of university professors—and explores how these opinionated and argumentative characters come to agree on what constitutes "good work."

Smith, Philip. 2005. *Why War? The Cultural Logic of Iraq, the Gulf War, and Suez*. Chicago: University of Chicago Press. Smith offers a neo-Durkheimian analysis of how nations have binary codes (sacred/profane) and how these influence the interpretation of events in times of crisis, thereby producing decisions and reproducing underlying culture.

4

The Production, Distribution, and Reception of Culture

Many Americans and Canadians proudly display Eskimo soapstone carvings in their living rooms.[1] Rounded, polished, and smooth to the touch, these miniature sculptures of polar bears, seals, and fur-wrapped children adorn any number of urban middle-class homes thousands of miles from the Arctic. The carvings seem profoundly natural, the innocent, simple renditions of what the Eskimos see around them. By now, of course, readers of this book have learned to be wary of anything referred to as "natural." The sociological approach to culture maintains that practices or objects that seem natural, even inevitable, are not. Like Marx's cherry tree, they have a history embedded in social relations—as do the soapstone carvings.

According to anthropologist Nelson Grayburn (1967), military men stationed in the far north during World War II and other visitors noticed the Eskimo penchant for carving or whittling. The Eskimos looked on this activity as making toys, not art, doing something to amuse the children and pass the time during the dark months of an Arctic winter. An entrepreneurial Canadian artist named James Houston saw something else in these little carvings—namely, the appeal they would have for non-Eskimo viewers and buyers in the cities to the south. With the encouragement of the Canadian Department of Northern Affairs (now called Indian and Northern Affairs Canada), which was responsible for the Eskimos' welfare, Houston set up a system of production for the market he had so astutely identified.

At first there were problems. Because the Eskimos worked with extremely hard materials such as ivory and bone, carving took a long time. Ivory, moreover, was increasingly rare. These things hardly mattered when the carvers were producing for their own amusement, but the organizers from down south and their marketing outlets in lower Canada and the United States were spiritual heirs of Benjamin Franklin— "Time is money"—and the leisurely rhythms and small quantities of craft production did not fit their requirements. They convinced the Eskimos to work in soapstone, both readily available and easy to carve, so they could turn out the finished carvings more quickly.

The content as well as the materials of these carvings required some regulation. When Eskimo inmates in a tuberculosis hospital decided to make some money with their carving, they turned out sculptures of American cars and kangaroos, causing another course correction. The entrepreneurs destroyed these carvings and impressed on the carvers that the customers in Toronto and New York seeking "real" Eskimo art wanted seals and bears, not kangaroos. No doubt bemused by what the white people in warm climates found interesting, the Eskimos dutifully turned out the roly-poly animals as required. Encouraged to fashion figures from their traditional religious mythology, carvers in another Eskimo community happily obliged even though they had been devout Anglicans for generations.

Just as the entrepreneur had envisioned, the carvings caught on and found their market. The same system of production and distribution remains today. The Eskimos got a new source of income, the gallery owners in Canadian and American cities got their percentage, the entrepreneurs made money, and coffee tables from Winnipeg to Atlanta display fat little seals that their owners assume to be traditional folk art. Local crafts deemed "authentic" can often find global markets (Wherry 2008).

This story demonstrates our previous suggestion: Cultural objects are not simply the "natural" products of some social context but are produced, distributed, marketed, received, and interpreted by a variety of people and organizations. This kind of self-conscious production, marketing, and distribution system applies to ideas as much as tangible cultural objects. During the years leading up to the Iranian revolution, the Ayatollah Khomeini taped speeches propounding his brand of fundamentalist Islam during his exile in Paris. His followers smuggled the tapes into Iran, and the faithful secretly listened to them on cassette players. International broadcasters similarly package ideas and frame news events and then distribute them throughout the world.

In this chapter, we explore the production and distribution of culture, from ideologies to mass consumer culture. We have already glimpsed some of these processes—recall Bessie Smith with her "race records," touring companies, and newly created Northern audiences—and now we take a closer look at the organizations and processes whereby cultural objects move beyond their creators to those who ultimately experience, consume, and interpret them. We start with the production-of-culture school of cultural analysis. The chapter then proceeds to a discussion of audiences and cultural reception in which we consider the implications of the fact that the receivers of a cultural object come to it not as blank slates but as people conditioned by their cultural and social experiences. Finally, we look at two opposing interpretations of the production-reception link: the pessimistic view of the "mass culture" theorists and the more optimistic view held by scholars of "popular culture."

The Production of Culture

Many sociologists believe it is insufficient simply to point out, following Durkheim or Marx, that culture is a collective product. We need to understand just how culture—and the cultural objects that compose a culture—is produced; moreover, we need to learn what impact the means and processes of production have on cultural objects themselves. This type of analysis came out of industrial and organizational sociology during the early 1970s, when sociologists trained in industrial sociology, systems analysis, and economic analyses of business firms began applying their models to cultural production.

This production-of-culture approach, in the words of Richard Peterson (one of its founders and foremost practitioners), looks at the "complex apparatus which is interposed between cultural creators and consumers" (1978:295; see also Peterson and Anand 2004). This apparatus includes facilities for production and distribution; marketing techniques such as advertising, co-opting mass media, or targeting; and the creation of situations that bring potential cultural consumers in contact with cultural objects. Placing racks of paperbacks in a supermarket, signing a new singer with a record company, legwork done before and after an evangelical revival, organizing a blockbuster museum exhibit, and generating buzz for a new fashion designer—all of these activities are grist for the production-of-culture mill.

The Culture Industry System

We can begin thinking about cultural production by working from a framework developed for mass-produced cultural objects. Paul Hirsch (1972) developed a useful model that he calls the "culture industry system"—in other words, the organizations that turn out mass culture products, such as records, popular books, and low-budget films. Hirsch pointed out that such cultural objects share a number of features: demand uncertainty, a relatively cheap technology, and an oversupply of would-be cultural creators. In the light of these factors, the culture industry system works to regulate and package innovation and thus to transform creativity into predictable, marketable packages. Figure 4.1 shows how Hirsch's system works.

Starting at the left, we see the creators (the artists, the geniuses, the talent) transformed into the technical subsystem that provides "input" for the rest of the system. This input must cross the boundary at Filter #1. Recall that there is an oversupply in the technical subsystem; it contains many more would-be singers, filmmakers, and novelists than the overall system requires. At the input boundary, the creative artists employ "boundary spanners," such as agents, to bring their work to the attention of the producing organization, or they may act as their own agents, for example by uploading their music video on YouTube. Producing organizations employ their own boundary spanners: talent scouts who check out new bands, editors who read through piles of manuscripts, and directors who look for promising screenplays.

The managerial subsystem consists of the organizations that actually produce the product: publishing houses, film studios, and record companies. Sometimes these are large firms, but sometimes they are not. For example, in the publishing business virtually everything can be subcontracted out, so a "publishing house" might consist of a single individual with a telephone. Sometimes it is not even that. In Nigeria, authors can arrange to have their books typeset and run off by the local newspaper printer; the name of a fictitious "publisher" then appears on the book even though no such organizational entity exists. In another twist to the managerial subsystem, although Hirsch thought of culture-producing organizations as turning out a large number of similar products, in some cases an organization exists only

Figure 4.1   The Culture Industry System

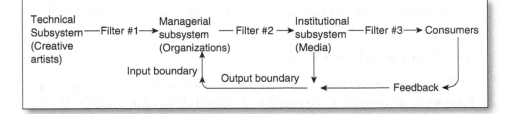

to produce a single cultural object. Called project-based organization, this is characteristic, for example, of independent filmmaking wherein contracts tie the director, producer, and actors together only for the duration of the project (Faulkner and Anderson 1987).

Strategies that the managerial subsystem employs to manage innovation include maintaining contact personnel at both boundaries, overproduction of products coupled with the recognition that most will fail, and unremitting attempts to influence or co-opt media gatekeepers. At the output boundary, the producing organization employs boundary spanners to reach the mass media—the crucial target of promotional activities—with news about the "product" (Filter #2). Media gatekeepers (the institutional subsystem) include such people as disc jockeys, talk show hosts, book and film reviewers, and that portion of the press that covers culture and its creators. For large firms, publicity and sales departments cultivate relations with the media, who serve as surrogate consumers. There is plenty of room for corruption here, as in the occasional payola scandals wherein record companies bribe disc jockeys to promote their latest records.

The ultimate consumers—the public—typically hear of new products through the media (Filter #3). If *Entertainment Weekly* gives a film an A, the magazine's readers will be more inclined to see the film. Although the producing organizations are highly dependent on such media exposure and work hard to get it, they also work hard to avoid needing it, either by producing a fairly homogeneous product or by convincing consumers as much. An example of the first strategy emerges in the various lines of romance novels. Readers know precisely what a Harlequin romance will be like; they know the basic plot formulas, the degree of sexual explicitness, and the length. That being the case, Harlequin does not need to advertise or promote each individual new novel. Instead, it promotes the lines—Harlequin Romance, Harlequin American Romance, Harlequin Silhouette Romantic Suspense—and emphasizes the homogeneity of the lines by giving each new title a number. The second strategy is to indicate more product homogeneity than actually exists. Promoting the "new Quentin Tarantino film" or the "latest album by Wilco" is a way of trying to bypass the media (who may say, after all, that this latest album by Wilco is not as good as the band's earlier ones) by convincing consumers that if they liked earlier work by a certain singer or director, they will surely like the new product.

Two types of feedback take place in the culture industry system. The first comes from the media and consists of airtime, reviews, and general media attention. The second comes from consumers and is measured by sales of tickets, CDs, or books; by jukebox plays; and by sales of related products (a hit movie like *Spider-Man 3* is surrounded by an enormous cloud of products, from books to lunch boxes to stuffed animals to, finally, the movie video itself). Producing organizations interpret both types of feedback to assess the popularity of an artist, the effectiveness of their promotional activities, and implications for similar future productions.

Notice that we can superimpose Hirsch's model on the horizontal axis of the cultural diamond. Doing so emphasizes what should already be clear: The actual cultural object, the product of the managerial subsystem, is of minor importance in the total system. This is especially true for the mass culture products Hirsch had in mind, which are overproduced; the producing organization has no great stake in any one product so long as a certain percentage of its products are hits.

Hirsch developed his culture industry model specifically for tangible mass culture products, but with minimal modification, it could be applied to high culture, ideas, or any other cultural object. If, for example, we take a certain theological stance (let's say a feminist reading of the Bible) as our cultural object, we can think of a religious denomination in analogous terms to a culture industry system, turning out theological messages as its products or, in other words, as cultural objects. The technical subsystem consists of seminary graduates looking for positions. The managerial subsystem is the churches of the denomination (for simplicity, we can assume a congregational polity like the Baptists, in which individual churches "call" their own pastors). Newly ordained graduates ask boundary spanners such as mentors from the seminary to help them locate a position; meanwhile, churches send out their own boundary spanners in the form of pastoral search committees to canvass the "talent." A would-be pastor's feminism may be an asset or a liability for any given church. Once the pastor attains a ministry—has been taken on by a culture-producing organization in the managerial subsystem—his message, via sermons, rituals, and setting a pastoral example, would go out to the consumers, the members of the congregation. An institutional subsystem such as the local press may feature the new pastor and his innovations; in rare cases, churches employ a more elaborate use of radio or television to broadcast sermons and services. The most important medium, however, is word of mouth. Feedback from the congregation comes directly to the pastor and the lay leaders of the church. More dramatic feedback, analogous to ticket sales, comes from membership changes. If the pastor is popular, or if his innovative combination of biblical literalism and feminism goes over well, word spreads in the community and the congregation grows. On the other hand, if he is at odds with his congregation, or if the fit between his theology and their piety is a poor one, church members may vote with their feet, causing membership to decline and prompting the church to go back to the technical subsystem in search of new talent.

The model of the culture industry system can be applied to cases from nonindustrial societies as well. In many West African societies, for example, young men want to join the secret societies that perform masquerades (in this system, the cultural object) on ritual occasions. Only a specific secret society is allowed to put on a specific masquerade. There is an oversupply of would-be masquerade dancers in the technical subsystem, and these young men may encourage kin and patrons to spread the word about their performing abilities. The secret society itself is equivalent to the managerial subsystem, and its members would scout for talent. (The roles of the boundary spanners are especially interesting in this case because no one actually knows or can admit knowing who the members of a secret society are; nor can the members reveal themselves.) The institutional subsystem operates via word of mouth; if a secret society is especially good at masquerading, people from neighboring villages may show up at the proper time to try to catch the performance. Negative feedback is also popular; village youth may mock a poor masquerade, and the secret society may have to rework its performance accordingly.

By these examples, we can see that analytic models such as Hirsch's help us understand how culture-producing organizations work. Such organizations attempt to produce a regular flow of products and reduce uncertainty. However, despite the controlling efforts of the managerial subsystem, a great deal of unpredictability comes from the market—those ticket buyers, congregants, audiences, consumers, and potential converts who ultimately determine the success of a cultural object. We need, therefore, to examine the nature of markets more closely.

Cultural Markets

Richard Peterson (1978) studied the production of cultural change in country music, and his research offers a good example of how market changes can reverberate throughout a culture industry system. Peterson described the production of country music. The culture industry system for this music (to use Hirsch's terms) was fairly small, generally rural and white, and had a high degree of integration among its subsystems. Record companies or their subunits were themselves devoted to country music. Singers traveled the performance circuit—including Nashville venues, state and county fairs, and country music festivals—and often sang live on country radio stations. Country stations, advertising such products as seed, fertilizer, and chewing tobacco, appealed to a rural audience. In this system, the artists and country disc jockeys often knew each other, and the deejays who played country music exclusively knew the music and its performers very well. There was, finally, a close fit in the lifestyles of performers and their audience.

Change came in the form of a hip-swinging white kid named Elvis Presley, who created a sensation in the mid-1950s by mixing the traditional country sound with black rhythm and blues. Feeling threatened by the explosive demand for rock and roll, and fearing that their own brand of music might get swamped, country singers banded together to form the Country Music Association, dedicated to the preservation and promotion of their musical style. The CMA was extremely, and paradoxically, successful in its efforts. Peterson showed the dramatic increase in the number of country music stations that occurred during the 1960s and early 1970s. This increase brought with it some unexpected consequences. The new stations, now competing for a broader market, needed to extend their audience appeal beyond the traditional country music fans. So, they began taking some of the hard edges off the country sound, playing songs that sounded less twangy and more like rock. These stations (the institutional subsystem) called themselves "modern country radio," and they began to resemble the "top 40" stations. Disc jockeys (gatekeepers at Filter #2) who served the new stations no longer knew very much about country music; they preferred, and played, the songs that sounded most like rock.

Some recording artists gained immense popularity due to the expansion of the country music sound, but many of the old troupers found themselves cut out of the "modern country" market as rock and easy-listening styles prevailed. Old singing styles such as cowboy music were squeezed out entirely. The record industry responded to the changing market in its choice of talent (Filter #1). More singers felt compelled to adopt a crossover strategy, singing country-rock blends. Traditionalists formed a new organization, the Association of Country Entertainers, to fight the dilution of the country sound but with limited success. Record companies favored crossover sounds; modern country radio, eager to capture an ever wider audience and show advertisers they could reach affluent urban consumers (no more ads for chewing tobacco), emphasized familiar songs and recent hits. Country music became less and less distinguishable from other popular music.

In this case, a large new market worked to diminish the artistic distinctiveness of a cultural object, but the opposite can happen as well: Increased market size can result in cultural differentiation. Consider a case from a very different time and place, nineteenth-century Paris. Harrison and Cynthia White (1965) showed how the French dealer-critic system rose in the mid-nineteenth century to challenge the dominance of the Royal Academy and serve the growing bourgeoisie. The conservative academy, with its annual juried salons, favored huge paintings of classical, patriotic, and religious subjects and rarely exhibited paintings of landscapes or humble subjects. But the growing market of middle-class householders did not want monumental depictions of "the death of Caesar" or "Jesus scourging the moneylenders" on their living room walls. They wanted what was pretty, familiar, and a pleasure to the eye. At about the same time, technical changes in the manufacture of pigments made it possible for artists to leave the studios and paint in the open air. The new market organized by independent dealers coincided with the new technology, as well as with the needs of an increasing number of painters to have a steady income, something that the academy salons could provide only to a tiny minority. The cultural objects that resulted from this new combination of dealers, critics, buyers, and painters were fresh, vivid renditions of natural scenes and middle-class life, with all of the brush strokes showing and nary a martyr or classical hero in view. In this manner, Impressionism, originally the work of a few salon rejects, was established as one of the most important and popular innovations in the post-Renaissance visual arts.

A similar innovation-through-exclusion process took place with American novels during the nineteenth century (Griswold 1981). At this time, American copyright laws protected Americans but not foreigners, which meant that publishers had to pay royalties to native authors but not to English ones. As always, there was an oversupply of manuscripts, and as always, publishers wanted to maximize profit, so American publishers favored English novels. This preference led to a curious result. American writers who wrote about the same subjects that English writers wrote about—love and marriage, money and achievement, the joys and sorrows of middle-class social life—were blocked at Filter #1 because the publisher could get that kind of novel from English authors without paying royalties. (The English authors made no profits on works published in the United States, either, and they complained bitterly about the American "piracy.") Accordingly, those American novels that did get published tended to deal with unusual, non-middle-class subjects, often telling about men or boys who fled society and had adventures in the wilderness. Many of the classics of our literature—*Moby Dick, Huckleberry Finn, The Deerslayer*—follow this model. Critics ever since have speculated on the peculiarities in the American character or psychology that produced so many "men outside society" novels and so few "love, money, and manners" novels. A production-of-culture analysis, however, suggests that such novels resulted from quirks in the American copyright law, not in the American character. When the United States finally adopted international copyright in 1891, most of the thematic differences between American and English novels simply disappeared.

No matter how stable a system may be, cultural markets respond to social change. As we saw in Chapter 3, it is probably pointless to debate what leads or lags behind what. There seem to be certain "unsettled" periods when both the social world, including its economic and political arrangements, and the expressive objects that we call culture change more rapidly than usual. Such fertile times produce new ideologies and genres, and under such circumstances, cultural markets and cultural forms change together.

An example of dramatic social and cultural change producing a new cultural market and new cultural forms to satisfy this market comes from early-twentieth-century China. During the late nineteenth century, China experienced severe political crises, including the Boxer Uprising discussed in Chapter 3, caused by the Qing dynasty's increasingly apparent incapacity to defend China against foreign incursions. Urban Chinese, especially those living in treaty ports with foreign enclaves and rapid industrialization such as Shanghai, had a growing appetite for news of all kinds, and the number of newspapers and presses grew dramatically (Lee and Nathan 1985). With more and more Chinese becoming literate and demanding both news and new ways of thinking, some writers took upon themselves the obligation to instruct their fellow citizens about the changing world. Others, inspired by the growing urban market, simply wanted to entertain readers and make some money. And for many, the impulses toward entertainment and instruction were intertwined.

Beginning about 1910, "butterfly fiction," which depicted true love and ill-fated lovers, was immensely popular, especially in Shanghai (Link 1981). These stories and novels were written by educated men whose employment prospects had been destroyed by the end of the civil service exam system in 1905. Drawn to Shanghai, they saw their chance with the booming readership, especially that huge urban middle class who wanted to read but didn't want anything too challenging. The butterfly love stories were non-Western and affirmed some traditional Chinese values, but at the same time, they glorified true love and marital choice. This happened at a time when, for many urban Chinese, family-arranged marriages began giving way to a freer choice of mates. Thus, butterfly fiction may be seen, after Durkheim, as a collective representation, reflecting and addressing new ways of thinking about love and marriage. But it was also a response to a distinctive urban context of literary production shaped by the migration of educated men (technical subsystem), a vigorous press (managerial subsystem), interacting circles of socially aware intellectuals (institutional subsystem), and an ever-increasing market of literate Chinese.

Modernization and urbanization—along with war, pestilence, and economic upheaval—are the most earthshaking occasions of cultural creativity, but social reconfigurations on a smaller scale can also be culturally productive.

Anthropologist Ulf Hannerz envisions culture as made up of "a network of perspectives, with a continuous production of overt cultural forms" (1993:68). This network model brings together the perspectives rooted in a particular subculture with particular experiences on the one hand and a cultural production apparatus with a very different social position and agenda on the other.

David Grazian showed how such a network has operated in the case of the Chicago blues (2003). In the postwar period, the perspective of African Americans on the Chicago South Side shaped their urban, re-imagined southern blues tradition. Blues music remained largely within the black enclave until the 1960s, when a gentrifying area on the North Side gave rise to a bohemian but affluent subculture in the Old Town area. Entertainment venues in and around Old Town and Lincoln Park offered blues musicians more money than ever imaginable before. By the 1970s, urban boosters were steering tourists to the Old Town/Lincoln Park area where they could enjoy "authentic" Chicago blues without running the risks of actually going to the South Side ghetto neighborhoods. Thus, the "Chicago Blues" grew from a subcultural perspective being disseminated to a (now global) market characterized by a radically different racial and economic profile.

The Production of Ideas

Much production-of-culture thinking draws on the culture industry model where the cultural products in question roll off the assembly line ready for mass consumption. We can envision the various subsystems involved in producing TV shows or romance novels. But our definition of cultural objects is much broader, embracing concepts and ideas. Does it make sense to think of these as "produced"? The basic image of cultural objects requiring creators and recipients and having some relationship to the social world that produces or receives them is the same whether we are talking about revolutionary ideologies or new video games. Specifically, creators produce an excess supply of all cultural objects, from art to theology, fashion to poetry, and ideas to Web sites. These cultural objects similarly compete for public attention, whether the attention comes in the form of belief (e.g., an ideology or theology), institutional development (e.g., publication, staging, filming), canonization (awards, institutional approval), hits (Web sites), or sales (mass culture).

Even patriotism can be seen as a cultural object produced through collective action. When cultural objects align with a particular national ideology, they are afforded special attention or privileges. France offers a centuries-long example: Johnson (2008) argues that the French Revolution spared the Paris Opera House because of its belief that its very lavishness appropriately

represented French culture. Mukerji (1997, 2009) argues that a century earlier gardens and canals were cultural objects that represented the French
monarchy, while in the contemporary world DeSoucey (2010) shows how
foie gras has come to express French patriotic sentiments, a case of what she
aptly calls "gastronationalism."

But ideas have to compete for attention just like every other cultural
object. William and Denise Bielby (1994) used the quote "All hits are flukes"
to title their analysis of how television network programmers develop "interpretive packages" promoting concepts for development as primetime series.
Writer-producers generate an oversupply of ideas for possible series that
could get developed by the networks, put into their primetime schedules, and
then picked up by local affiliates. As they pitch these programs to top network executives, advertisers, and affiliates, network programmers—the
middle link in the system—frame these concepts in terms of the reputation
of the people involved, the genre, and imitation (the new show is compared
to a successful predecessor). Reputations are the most important form of
currency here in terms of predicting which shows will get picked up.
Interestingly, however, no relationship seems to exist between how the program is pitched and what its eventual ratings (market success) will be; all hits
are indeed flukes. The early stages of this process involve no product, only
an idea in the form of a brief synopsis that the networks show to advertisers
and affiliates; "the pilots exist only as scripts, and the programmers themselves have yet to see the product they are describing" (Bielby and Bielby
1994). So, before the actual filming, the series concept must have made it
through an institutional gauntlet.

Even such disembodied television concepts as "interpretive packages" are
anchored by their institutional context, of course. What about ideas that have
no such anchorage? Once an idea has been put into words or symbols (a
manifesto, a peace symbol), it is a cultural object. So, which of these ideological cultural objects fall by the wayside, and which have social influence?

As alluded to earlier, several sociologists have suggested that some times
and places are richer in their ideological production than others. Robert
Wuthnow (1987) focuses on times of breakdown in the moral order: When
the old ways of doing things, the old understanding of social relationships,
no longer seem to work, people cast around for new ideas. Such times are
fertile for ideological production.

Ideological oversupply takes place, especially in turbulent times, so the
various ideas have to compete for resources, just as the potential primetime
series have to compete for advertisers. Wuthnow describes the competition for
resources as "selection," using an explicitly Darwinian metaphor to suggest
why some ideological movements survive whereas most do not. Successful

selection gains stability through institutionalization in which the state or some other powerful institutional actor embeds the ideology into its practices. Not all resource-rich ideas win this ultimate prize of institutionalization. Amy Binder (2001) compared two ideological contenders—Afrocentrism and creationism—in terms of their institutionalization in school curricula; the former has been distinctly more successful than the latter.

But what part does the consumer play in this range of examples? In this discussion of the culture industry system, we have given short shrift to this vital element. So far we have concentrated on the connections among cultural creators, objects, and receivers—the lines (diamond-wise) among the three points captured by the "culture industry system" or the "market"— but we have not focused on the right point of the cultural diamond, the consumers, receivers, or audiences for cultural objects. It's time to do so. In the spirit of Hirsch's model, we might call cultural receivers the "interpretation-producing subsystem." In the next section we look at how receivers interpret cultural objects in order to produce their own meanings.

Reception

Despite all of the strategies employed by core firms in culture industry systems, a great deal of uncertainty remains. Record companies cannot predictably produce hit records anymore than publishers can reliably turn out bestsellers. Pastoral recruitment committees often find that their taste in ministers turns out to be at odds with the preferences of their congregations. Brilliant ideas fall on deaf ears. The ultimate success of a cultural object depends on its listeners, viewers, audiences, or consumers—in other words, on the cultural recipients who make their own meanings from it. For although the meaning of a cultural object may be initially suggested by the intentions or period eye of its creators, the receivers of culture have the last word.

We need to consider how and with what degree of freedom receivers make cultural objects meaningful. A basic postulate of the sociological approach to reception is that what Eviatar Zerubavel calls a "social mind" processes incoming signals (1997). Zerubavel argues that we should not conceive of the mind as either just a brain (the province of neuroscience) or just an individual mind shaped by individual experience (the province of psychoanalysis). In between these two endpoints of the most universal and the most particular comes the social mind, a group perspective formed by interpersonal communication and the province of a cognitive sociology that would "highlight our cognitive diversity as members of different thought communities" (11; see also DiMaggio 1997).

Our social minds—as members of particular groups and categories—shape what we pay attention to, what we get emotional about, and what meanings we draw from environmental signals. For example, European and American Jews may detect anti-Semitism in artworks like Wagnerian operas that might seem benign to others. Indeed, a history of oppression or victimization shapes a group's mind toward paying attention to subtle references to their oppression; groups not sharing this social mind often regard the victimized groups as being unduly "touchy." We can think of many ways in which different types of people—for example, men and women, gays and straights, Muslims and Christians, teenagers and parents—seem to view the same thing very differently, and these differences are to a considerable extent predictable products of the social mind.

The point is that to think of the reception of cultural objects, we need to understand that this reception, the meaning drawn from the cultural objects, is not firmly and undeniably embedded in the object itself or subject entirely to individual quirks. People's social attributes, their positions in a social structure, condition what they like, what they value, and even what they recognize in the first place.

Audiences and Taste Cultures

Survey research supports what common observation shows: Different types of people watch, buy, enjoy, use, read, and believe different cultural objects. Devotees of dogfights tend to be working class and male; devotees of opera tend to be upper class and white. Mainstream Protestants tend to be more affluent and educated than Pentecostals. People who drink vintage champagne tend to have higher household incomes than people who drink Night Train. A vast amount of research—both market studies and leisure time surveys—confirms the reality of cultural stratification.

The link between cultural taste and socioeconomic position is not always straightforward, however. Many cultural objects—detective novels and popular television programs, for example—cut across class, regional, ethnic, and gender boundaries. Moreover, social strata differ in the breadth of their cultural participation. To put it simply, upper-middle-class and middle-class people do more of everything than working-class people. Thus, whereas a working-class man may be knowledgeable about sports, popular music, and television, his middle-class counterpart is likely to be knowledgeable about fine arts, classical music, serious fiction, *and* sports, popular music, and television, to the extent that Peterson called these people "cultural omnivores" (1992; see also DiMaggio 1987). This broader cultural repertoire allows the middle-class person to operate in a variety of social settings, switching his or her presentation of cultural knowledge to suit the occasion. In sharp contrast, one of the deprivations of ghetto dwellers is that although they may understand and adroitly negotiate the complex system of signification in which they live, their cultural skills are not transferable to the world outside the ghetto (Wilson 1987).

Putting forward a powerful theory of the consequences of taste, French sociologist Pierre Bourdieu (1984) argues that culture may be thought of as capital. Like economic capital, cultural capital can be accumulated and invested; moreover, it can be converted into economic capital. Take a simple example: Two workers, on the basis of job performance, are equally qualified for a promotion. Their boss, an enthusiast for Japanese culture, has scrolls and wedding kimonos on the walls of her office, reads modern Japanese fiction, and enjoys going out for sushi. Worker A is able to talk with her about a favorite Mishima novel or the merits of a new sushi bar. Worker B lacks the cultural capital—the background of knowledge and taste—to pick up on and respond to his boss's interest (or, even worse, he is heard to mutter something about being revolted by the thought of eating raw fish). All else being equal, which worker is more likely to develop a friendly relationship with the boss and get promoted?

Bourdieu mapped out the relationship between economic capital and cultural capital. Sometimes they correspond, as in the case of wealthy people able to purchase and patronize the fine arts, but at other times economic and cultural capital are at odds. Students, for example, are often high on cultural capital but low on economic; poorly educated but financially successful entrepreneurs or blue-collar workers may be high on economic capital and low on cultural. The latter usually try to raise the cultural capital of their children by seeing that they get a good education, preferably at prestigious schools. (The research based on and extending cultural capital theory is immense; see for example Lizardo [2006] on the role played by social networks, Chan and Goldthorpe [2007] on whether it is status more than class that is linked to cultural capital, and Baumann [2007] on the fluidity of cultural capital in Hollywood.)

Although economic capital may be bolstered, increased, or undercut by forms of noneconomic capital, the types of readily negotiable noneconomic capital may vary from place to place. After studying middle-class Frenchmen and Americans living in two major cities (Paris and New York) and two provincial towns (Clermont-Ferrand and Indianapolis), Michèle Lamont (1992) found that the kind of cultural capital Bourdieu stressed—knowledge of the arts, refinement of taste—was more important in Paris than in any of the other locations. In provincial towns, what might be termed *moral capital*—a reputation for honesty, decency, and reliability—is more important in deciding who is admirable. In addition, Americans generally respect money, sheer economic capital, more than the French do.

Although exquisite taste and appreciation of artistic genres may be particularly Parisian, research indicates that possessing or not possessing cultural capital can explain a variety of social stratification outcomes. For example, let us say that getting a college degree and a well-educated spouse are both "prizes" valued by a given society. Let us further imagine that people having the same amount of wealth but different amounts of cultural capital (measured by such indicators as attendance at arts and musical events or reading serious literature) compete for these prizes. DiMaggio and Mohr (1985) showed that individuals with high amounts of cultural capital are more likely to win both the degree and the educated mate than their less culturally sophisticated counterparts.

Because people believe that cultural capital matters, groups naturally tend to inflate the value of what they already possess and try to prevent other groups from getting any. Historian Lawrence Levine (1988) documented how upper-class white Americans, feeling threatened by new immigrant groups, segregated their cultural institutions as "high culture," supported and honored by everyone but not too available to the masses, who might misbehave. Museums and other high-cultural bastions of this period often were not open on weekends and evenings, for example, ensuring that those who had to work for a living couldn't make much use of them. (Again, recall those lions guarding the doorways of art museums and libraries.) Similarly, Nicola Beisel (1990) showed how the same elites used anti-vice laws to make certain forms of popular entertainment, such as burlesque, illegitimate.

It seems clear that (1) the reception of various types of cultural objects is often stratified by social class and (2) that people may consciously or unconsciously use culture to support their social advantages or overcome their disadvantages. Note that the second point is not dependent on the first. As Peterson pointed out, people with higher educations have more cultural experiences from all levels—high, low, mass, elite, common, rare, you name it—to work with. They have a broader cultural repertoire, and this breadth may be more socially useful than having a refined knowledge of philosophy or the fine arts.

Bonnie Erickson (1996) showed that in the workplace, displaying knowledge of elite cultural forms is rare, probably because it is not an effective strategy for gaining compliance. What is effective is cultural variety, being able to navigate in different cultural seas. This cultural variety seems to come from having broad social networks, where one network might tune a person in to the latest *American Idol* winner, another to the latest Pulitzer Prize winner.

Next, we consider how an understanding of different types of recipients can illuminate the understanding of cultural objects as meaningful, shared symbols embodied in forms.

Horizons of Expectations

A German literary critic named Hans Robert Jauss provided a key for sociologists trying to understand cultural reception. Helping formulate the theory of literary reception aesthetics in the 1970s, Jauss (1982) pointed out that when a reader picks up a book, she does not come to it as an empty vessel waiting for its contents to fill her. Instead, she locates it against a "horizon of expectations" shaped by her previous literary, cultural, and social experience. A reader interprets the text—finds meaning in it—on the basis of how it fits or challenges her expectations. In constructing the text's meaning, she finds her horizon of expectations changing as well.

Jauss's reception aesthetics makes it possible to link the cultural and the social in the process of meaning construction. For example, in a study of how readers (book reviewers and literary critics) from three places interpreted the novels of a writer from Barbados named George Lamming, I found that different audiences interpreted the same books in very different ways (Griswold 1987). West Indian readers said Lamming's autobiographical novel *In the Castle of My Skin* was about the ambiguities of identity; the British readers said it was about how a youth, any youth, comes to maturity; American readers said it was about race. Given their differing horizons of expectations, and given the complexity and ambiguity of the novel, three related but distinct sets of meanings emerged among the three categories of recipients.

The concept of a horizon of expectations extends well beyond literature and offers a way to understand how any cultural object may be interpreted by people with specific types of social and cultural knowledge and experience. More than this, it suggests how any event may be transformed into a cultural object by being made meaningful. Of particular interest to sociologists is the additional virtue that this model offers rich comparative possibilities. Consider what would at first seem not a cultural object at all but a tragic event: the death of a child. In the United States, people generally regard such an event as a horrible accident, an intrusion of chaos into the predictability of our lives. The very meaninglessness of such a death can be made meaningful—rendered a cultural object—by setting it against our horizon of expectations about babies: Babies are individually valuable and cherished and rarely die. Thus, the death of an infant is a horrifying anomaly. In a Brazilian slum, on the other hand, a child's death has a different meaning altogether. Anthropologist Nancy Scheper-Hughes (1992) showed how parents in the squalid settlements outside a city in northeastern Brazil set infant mortality against a horizon shaped by extreme poverty, violence, and powerlessness. Given this horizon, these mothers (and sometimes fathers, though the men are often absent) respond to a child's death with little emotion. These Brazilian parents regard their babies as potential human beings, not actual ones. For people with such a horizon, an infant's death doesn't mean "One of our children has died" but "A creature that was never fated to live has departed. He was an angel, not a human, and has returned to heaven."

Looking at the different interpretations that people construct from the same cultural objects may reveal deeply held social assumptions. If we think of a television show as "shared meaning embodied in form," for example, we find that different groups of people share different horizons and therefore construct different shared meanings from the same cultural object. Tamar Liebes and Elihu Katz (1990) studied the way groups of viewers in Israel interpreted the primetime soap opera *Dallas*. Moroccan Jews who had immigrated to Israel saw *Dallas* as being about the bonds of kinship and how difficult family life could be. Russian emigrants interpreted the series as a none-too-subtle critique of capitalism. And native-born Israelis, just like a control group in Los Angeles, did not regard the program as reflecting any social reality at all; for them it was simply slick television entertainment.

Explicitly or not, many considerations of how producers of meanings attempt to engage a receiving group's horizon of expectations use the framing model. If cultural creators can frame their product or message so it resonates with a frame that the audience already possesses, they are more likely to persuade that audience to "buy" (an idea, a product, or a taste). Political propaganda operates this way quite overtly. Barry Schwartz (1996) has shown how FDR's administration, working to mobilize support for American involvement in World War II, keyed its pro-war message about the present to the Lincoln frame from the past. Counting on the collective memory that honored Abraham Lincoln's resolve in the face of war, the administration legitimated American military action by fitting it to the public's horizon of expectations that included the sacred place that Lincoln held.

In contrast, sometimes the creators of cultural objects have no idea how they will be received. Technical innovation offers some amusing cases of this. Wiebe Bijker (1995), a historian of technology, points out that the meaning of a newly invented artifact does not reside in the artifact itself; technologies acquire their meanings in social interactions. Thus the question of whether something "works" is something to be explained: It works for what and for whom? He takes the towering "ordinary" bicycle (with a huge front wheel and small back wheel) of the late nineteenth-century as an example. Did the "ordinary" work? It certainly did not work for women, older men, or anyone concerned about safety or ease of use. On the other hand, it worked fine for the macho young men riding around the parks trying to impress the girls with their daring. When the technological innovation of safer bikes with wheels of equal diameters came along, the young men did not accept them because of their safety or comfort but only when they were shown to be faster.

By now the question arises: If every group has its own distinctive horizon of expectations, can such groups of people construct any meanings they please? Can cultural objects be interpreted in any way whatsoever, or do the form and content of cultural objects constrain the meanings found in them? Both the academic world and the general public have vigorously debated this question, which essentially concerns how much freedom cultural receivers have as meaning makers. Let us examine this ongoing controversy.

Freedom of Interpretation: Two Views

At the point where human beings experience cultural objects, they react, construct interpretations, and make meanings. We have seen that different groups can construct somewhat different meanings out of the same cultural objects. But how much freedom do people have to make these meanings?

Theoretically, there could be two opposing answers: (1) People can make any meanings whatsoever (receivers are strong/cultural objects are weak), and (2) people must submit to whatever meanings are inherently contained in the cultural object (cultural objects are strong/receivers are weak). At one extreme is unlimited freedom: People can do anything they want with the cultural objects they receive. French structuralist Claude Lévi-Strauss (1966) once referred to the human mind as like a bricoleur or tinkerer, the sort of handyman who could fix or make things out of whatever bits and scraps of material happened to be around. Following this bricoleur logic, the recipient of a cultural object can make meanings virtually independent of the cultural object itself. We've all heard jokes to this effect: A sixteen-year-old boy asks another what a particular book is about, and he replies, "It's about sex." Asked what the movie he saw last night was about, he then replies, "Oh, it was about sex, too." And so on. Presumably, this young man would find a bowl of cereal, a passage from *The Merchant of Venice,* or a trip to the Laundromat to be "about sex."

This view, however—that recipients can make cultural objects mean anything, that virtually any bit of culture can be "about sex" or anything else— denies autonomy to cultural objects themselves. It implies that there are no distinctions, no better or worse, richer or poorer, inspirational or depressing, or elevating or pornographic cultural representations, only different kinds of people experiencing the cultural object and assigning different meanings to it. Meaning becomes entirely a function of the receiver's mind. Such a position is anathema to a traditional humanities-based approach to culture (though it is held by some contemporary literary critics). Social scientists are uncomfortable with it as well, for it denies culture's role as a collective representation. If anything goes, or if any person's interpretation is as good as the next, culture's capacity to serve as a means whereby people "communicate, perpetuate, and develop their knowledge about and attitude toward life" (Geertz 1973:89) is undermined.

The other extreme position holds that cultural meanings are tightly controlled and that receivers have virtually no freedom of interpretation. According to this view, people ignorant about the conventions of a particular cultural object may not understand it, outsiders to a subculture may not "get it," and scholars and specialists may labor to ferret out the hidden meaning of a text or symbol, but there is *a* meaning. Such a conviction, which for many people seems no more than common sense, has been called the "proper meaning superstition." Even though a cultural creator may aim for a particular interpretation or response to a work, our own experience suggests that people vary enormously in their responses to a cultural object.

When we push these positions to their logical extremes in this way, neither seems justified. Two schools of thought in the social sciences, however, essentially represent these extremes in a somewhat more presentable form. The first, mass culture theory, leans toward the strong culture/weak receivers side, suggesting that cultural objects can essentially overwhelm their helpless recipients. The second, popular culture theory, sees people not as helpless in the face of the cultural onslaught but as active makers and manipulators of meaning. These two schools offer very different conceptions of how human freedom and cultural power relate. Assumptions from each pop up in the public discourse over, for example, the influence of news media on presidential elections or the effects of lewd lyrics in popular songs. We need, therefore, to examine their assumptions and sort out their implications.

Seduction by Mass Culture

In my earlier discussion of the production of culture, the expression "culture industry" referred to the organizations that produced cultural objects for a market. It was a neutral term, implying neither good nor bad. In the view of mass culture theorists, however, there is little good about the culture industry.

Those who adopt the mass culture perspective see the culture industry as the technology for producing mass entertainment on a hitherto undreamed-of scale. Such entertainment aims at a low common denominator of taste, emphasizing the lurid over the moral or intellectual, to capture as wide a market as possible. Mass cultural products render their recipients numb and apathetic. This apathy, in turn, leaves these passive recipients ripe for political tyranny, while their sheer numbers force cultural producers to come up with ever more violent, sensational, and shocking materials to get a response from their jaded audience.

We have seen this view before as far back as Plato and more recently from the Frankfurt school. During the 1950s, when television was transforming cultural participation in the United States and Europe, criticism of mass culture came from both the political Left and the political Right. The Left saw the capacity for political criticism buried under the mindless drivel of mass entertainments; the Right saw the capacity for cultural critique, for refinement of taste, buried. Both Right and Left agreed that independent thought was imperiled, both worried about media-induced brainwashing, and both drew dark historical parallels with Roman emperors who diverted the plebeians with "bread and circuses" while the empire crumbled.

Of particular concern was the impact that mass culture might have on children, assumed to be impressionable and vulnerable to its messages. A typical specimen of this school was *Seduction of the Innocent* (1954), a book written by clinical psychologist Frederic Wertham, with excerpts appearing in *Ladies' Home Journal*. Discussing comic books, especially those depicting crime, he castigated comics for contributing to illiteracy, delinquency, and sexual perversion, as well as for glorifying violence as a means of solving problems. He was especially outraged by the interplay of the comics' messages about violence and sexuality with their advertisements:

Comic-book stories teach violence, the advertisements provide the weapons. The stories instill a wish to be a superman, the advertisements promise to supply the means for becoming one. Comic-book heroines have super-figures; the comic-book advertisements promise to develop them. . . . The stories feature scantily clad girls; the advertisements outfit peeping Toms. (217)

In such an indictment, we recognize the effects cited by the Frankfurt school (numbing and incitement to mindless violence), as well as the degradation, brutalization, and sexual explicitness deplored by conservative thinkers. Although the violence and sexual explicitness of contemporary mass culture make Wertham's worries about comic books seem downright quaint, the concern with mass culture's possible negative effects remains.

From the early 1970s until the present, for example, many sociologists have examined how mass cultural products perpetuated racial and gender stereotypes. A good example of this type of research focuses on children's books.

Mass culture's relation to violence is another evergreen topic, as in the legal actions involving rap singers, whose music seems to many people to promote violence toward the police and women. Popular music and especially television receive constant scrutiny for their impact on their audiences, particularly on children, although such scrutiny has had little inhibiting effect on the culture industry. Counterarguments cite freedom of expression, market demands, and the fact that mass culture only "reflects" the culture at large. In the view of mass culture critics, however, no horizon of expectations is robust enough to withstand the constant onslaught of violence and perversion. All audiences, they believe, are innocent, and all can be seduced.

The opposite view, however, holds that people are too knowing, too canny to follow cultural objects down the garden path. This view speaks not of mass but popular culture.

Resistance Through Popular Culture

In some ways, the term *popular culture* is a redundancy. Culture is public, and all culture must be popular to some extent; unpopular culture, like a TV pilot that fails to attract an audience, just goes away. But the term has come to mean the culture of the people, and here *people* means the common people, the non-elite majority—hence, the commonly heard contrast between high culture (or serious culture or good culture or Culture) and popular culture.

Popular culture clearly includes mass cultural products such as television shows, popular magazines, and off-the-rack fashions. It also includes, and emphasizes, the wisdom, common sense, values, and way of life of "the people," especially the nonpowerful and nonwealthy—those groups who, according to Bourdieu, lack both economic and cultural capital. In this respect, it draws on the old anthropological "way of life" definitions of culture. As indicated in the Snow and Anderson (1993) study of the homeless, all people need meaning in their lives; meaningfulness is not just a luxury indulged in by the well-to-do but a human necessity. Popular culture, so the theory goes, is the system of meanings available to ordinary people.

Among sociologists, the reevaluation of popular culture began in the 1960s, when previously dominated and ignored groups—minorities, gays, women, and the poor—demanded respect as never before. Now many social scientists, as well as scholars in the humanities, felt uncomfortable with the old attitudes toward soap operas for women as trivial, black English as sub-standard, or the practices of the poor as irrational and dysfunctional. Scholars examining previously despised works, genres, and systems of meaning found them to contain complexities and beauties; at the same time, deconstructing previously esteemed works, genres, and systems of meaning, they found widespread representations of class hegemony, patriarchy, racism, and illegitimate canonization.

The reevaluation of popular culture occurred in two ways, and both of these approaches involve an image of the audience that is far from passive. First, scholars examined popular culture itself in search of hidden meanings that had been accessible to its recipients but missed by academics and other disdainful elites. For example, in separate studies Tania Modleski ([1982] 1984) and Janice Radway (1984) took a new look at an almost universally scorned form of popular literature, women's romance novels. Radway, who used focus groups to talk with readers about their interpretations of the romances, discovered they had distinct criteria for assessing the quality of what was usually dismissed as homogeneous formulaic novels. Moreover, the novels themselves were seen to contain a theme of the male who moves from arrogance to nurturing. This nurturing male was especially attractive to women readers, typically nurturers themselves who longed to be cared for in kind. Modleski found Harlequin romances to contain a revenge theme— the heroine almost dies or otherwise abandons the hero, causing him pain until she returns—and suggested that this subject represented women's collective fantasy of getting back at their oppressors. In both studies, and in this type of analysis as a whole, the popular audience is seen as decoding meanings that are especially satisfying in light of its social experience.

In the second form of reevaluating popular culture, the recipient is seen not only as decoding meanings to which elite recipients have been oblivious but also as actively constructing subversive meanings. Mass cultural objects may indeed be patriarchal or represent the "ideas of the ruling class," as the theory goes, but people do not have to accept these meanings imposed, as it were, from outside. They make their own meanings.

John Fiske (1989) used the analogy of mass culture being like a supermarket. People may pick up mass-produced items from the cultural supermarket, but when they cook (make meanings), they mix these supermarket goods with whatever they have in the pantry at home, thereby individualizing and transforming the final product—sometimes with surprising results. For example, Fiske studied audience reactions to *The Newlywed Game,* a television game show wherein couples scored points when each could accurately predict the other's responses to questions, which usually had risqué overtones. Although couples that exhibited high levels of agreement were the winners in the program's formal terms, it was the losers—those who disagreed with each other—who won roars of approval from the audience. Fiske saw this reaction as a case of people creating counter-hegemonic cultural objects and subversive meanings. The rules of the game supported marital harmony under generally patriarchal authority, but the audience cheered for the rebels.

Both the popular culture theorists like Fiske and the mass culture theorists like Wertham are essentially concerned with reception, and both share the value of human freedom, but they interpret the relationship between cultural object and receiver very differently. Figure 4.2 presents a schematic of their differences on the cultural diamond. In the mass culture model, cultural objects impose their (simple, sensational) meanings on their audiences, but in the popular culture model, the audience makes new meanings.

As the global spread of mass communications technology increases, it remains to be seen which view of the cultural object/recipient relationship proves more accurate. Because cultural objects are interpreted not in isolation but by interacting human beings, it seems likely that distinct interpretations, or reinterpretations, will continue to emerge from groups having distinct experiences. The real danger, not envisioned by either mass culture or popular culture theory, may be that people will stop interpreting cultural objects at all.

Figure 4.2   Mass Culture and Popular Culture Theories on the Cultural Diamond

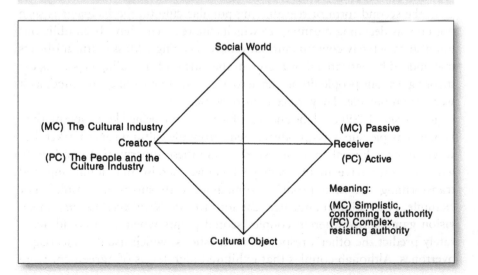

Like the native-born Israelis and Los Angelenos in the study of *Dallas,* people bombarded with cultural objects may simply reject the idea that these objects are socially meaningful. We take up the prospect of abandoned meaning in Chapter 8. For now, suffice it to say that such an intellectual disengagement of the receivers of culture from the cultural objects themselves may be a far more frightening idea than anything that the mass culture theorists envisioned.

SUMMARY

In this chapter, we explored the points and links of the culture diamond. Having already examined cultural objects and social meanings and the collective creation of those objects, we considered here the production-of-culture linkages among creators, objects, and recipients. We considered the role of recipients themselves, who bear socially shaped horizons of expectations and are engaged, actively or passively, with the culture they experience. Either through their numbed passivity or their grassroots power, these recipients, in turn, affect their social world.

Our analytic model is complete. But models themselves are no good unless they can tell us something about the world in which we live. In the next two chapters, we apply our analytic devices to social problems and business and organizational transactions. In these two chapters, we observe with a sociologically informed eye the operation of cultural meanings in the real world and the influence they exert.

NOTE

1. Native North Americans of the Canadian Arctic, who used to be called Eskimos, now prefer to call themselves and be called Inuit. I follow Grayburn (1967), who used the term *Eskimo* in his research; the soapstone sculptures are commonly referred to as *Eskimo art.*

QUESTIONS FOR STUDY AND DISCUSSION

1. Apply some of the theories from cultural sociology to explain the origin, production, and reception of new forms of music (e.g., hip-hop, the resurgence of folk music in the 1960s and 1970s, or your favorite) or new genres of television (reality shows, soap operas, or your favorite). Who are the creators, who are the receivers, and what is their relationship to the social world? What institutions mediate the connection?

2. Imagine an artwork that is violently offensive to some particular religious group. The members of this group demand that it be censored (e.g., removed from the museum, library, or textbook). Drawing on your knowledge of cultural sociology, hold a debate on this censorship versus the question of artistic freedom.

RECOMMENDED FOR FURTHER READING

Grazian, David. 2008. *On the Make: The Hustle of Urban Nightlife*. Chicago: University of Chicago Press. Place and even time can be cultural objects, produced and consumed by people with their various agendas and horizons. Grazian shows how in urban Philadelphia "the night" is produced as a fantasy world of clubs, restaurants, and sexual freedom, which is consumed by college-age youth who then go on to produce their own fantastic nightlife identities.

Harrington, C. Lee, and Denise D. Bielby. 2000. *Popular Culture: Production and Consumption*. Oxford, UK: Blackwell Publishers. Harrington and Bielby have collected analyses of the nuts-and-bolts production of both standard and bizarre examples of popular culture.

Lamont, Michèle. 1992. *Money, Morals, and Manners: The Culture of the French and the American Upper-Middle Class*. Chicago: University of Chicago Press. Lamont compares how the French and the Americans assign status to others on the basis of their cultural refinement, their integrity, and their wealth.

Levitt, Peggy. 2007. *God Needs No Passport: Immigrants and the Changing American Religious Landscape*. New York and London: New Press. Levitt shows how transnational migrants with strong cultural ties to two places reproduce and adapt their religious faiths. Some become cosmopolitans, some choose one context over the other, and some become "religious global citizens," for whom the bonds of faith outweigh those of the nation.

Peterson, Richard A. 1997. *Creating Country Music: Fabricating Authenticity*. Chicago and London: University of Chicago Press. Peterson, one of the founders of the production-of-culture approach, demonstrates its power in this analysis of the early years of country music.

5

Identities, Problems, and Movements

S ome things clearly need fixing. Any society produces pathological, dysfunctional, cruel, shameful, and maybe even evil conditions. Political or
moral leadership entails getting people to recognize the problem and then to
set about solving it.

This view of social problems sees them as objective: The situation in question is real, can be identified, and can be objectively measured, and just
about everyone will agree that the situation is indeed "a problem" once they
know about it. Sexually transmitted diseases are an example. We can clearly
identify an STD as any disease spread primarily though sexual contact; thus,
syphilis is an STD, whereas cancer is not. We can objectively measure their
occurrence: X percent of the population is currently infected with syphilis as
opposed to Y percent in 1950. And surely everyone would agree that STDs
are a social problem; in fact, they used to be called "social diseases." No
decent society can do less than put resources toward reducing the incidence
of STDs and working toward cures for them.

Although this objective view of a social problem is attractively straightforward, its assumptions are vulnerable. What is an STD? Certain types of
cancers are more common to people who have had syphilis, even though
they crop up years after the syphilis has been cured; are such cancers STDs?
Diseases like preeclampsia are associated with pregnancy; because pregnancy is "sexually transmitted," should preeclampsia be considered an STD?
Depression may result from a sexual relationship gone sour; is depression an

STD as well? Posing questions like these clearly shows that there is no "bright line" separating STDs from other forms of illness; the line results from a social decision.

As for objective measurement of rates of occurrence, this is much harder than it seems. STDs are stigmatized and disproportionately associated with poor people or people on the margins of society like heroin addicts who spread AIDS with needles. Such people are notoriously difficult to count—similar to the problem the U.S. Census has with counting the homeless—or to bring into the medical system for testing. So, any statement about the rates of an STD in a population, and especially a statement about a trend over time, is an educated guess.

Even with a less than precise definition and measurements, surely there can be no doubt that STDs are social problems, can there? Yes, in fact, many people question this. Traditionalists argue that sex outside of marriage is "the problem," and if that problem were solved, STDs would largely disappear. Defenders of privacy rights regard required testing for STDs to be an invasion of privacy, so in many states pregnant women cannot be compelled to be tested for HIV, despite the risk to their babies. This position defines the "problem" as the government prying into people's private concerns. In the notorious Tuskegee experiments, the U.S. Public Health Service allowed some poor black men to leave their syphilis untreated for years, defining their disease not as a problem but as an opportunity for medical research (Jones 1992).

So, social problems are not always clear and straightforward, as the objective approach seems to assume. Instead, they are constructions (Loseke 1999). The essence of the constructionist approach is that only when a situation has meaning for a specific group of people and that meaning is a negative one can the situation get defined as a social problem.

In other words, a social problem is a cultural object, produced by specific agents; Loseke calls them "claims-makers." It is interpreted by a specific group of recipients, whom Loseke regards as the "audience" for the claims being made. "Simply stated, a social problem is created when audiences evaluate claims as believable" (37). If recipients accept the producers' definition, it becomes "a problem," and if they become mobilized to take action, it becomes a social movement.

To understand the implications of this constructionist approach, we begin with the claims-makers (creators) and audience (recipients). Calls for action are generally aimed at some collectivity. This might be an organization, as when advocates address a church to raise money for that cause, or it might be a group of people that share a sense of being a "we," as when Y-ME

National Breast Cancer Organization targets its pink-ribbon appeals to women. In other words, the construction of a social problem depends on the prior construction of a collective identity.

Constructing a Collective Identity

Identity can also be seen either as objective or as a construction. Recent thinking emphasizes the constructionist view, which thinks of identities as not so much given and fixed but malleable, fluid, and subject to interpretation. People can easily change their group memberships, the causes they support, or the people they hang out with. With greater effort, they can change their religious and institutional ties, their physical appearance, or their occupations; with even greater effort, they can change their citizenship or their sexual characteristics. An Algerian Muslim man could become a French Catholic woman; such an identity change would be radical but not unheard of. Moreover, what it means to be a man or a woman, a Muslim or a Catholic, is subject to interpretation.

Alberto Melucci (1989) has emphasized how collective identity is not fixed but a process. Consciously or not, you have to work at being a woman or a Catholic or an Algerian; otherwise these are just labels, categories that have little to do with your behavior. In his words,

> *Collective identity is an interactive and shared definition produced by several interacting individuals who are concerned with the orientations of their action as well as the field of opportunities and constraints in which their action takes place. . . .* Collective identity formation is a delicate process and requires continual investments. As it comes to resemble more institutionalized forms of social action, collective identity may crystallize into organizational forms. . . . In less institutionalized forms of action its character more closely resembles a process which must be continually activated in order for action to be possible. (34–35; italics in original)

We see in this definition the link to social problems and social movements. When a collective identity is activated, it produces a shared way of thinking (a social mind) that perceives certain situations as troubling and in need of attention. This cognitive activation can lead to action.

To better understand collective identity as a construction rather than an objective "given," let us consider race and ethnicity, which seem to shape identity very powerfully. Sociologists once thought that increasing modernization would erode ascribed differences like those of race and ethnicity, religion and kinship group, nationality, and even gender. This convergence model—modern individuals and societies would become more and more alike—was compatible with a view of eventual racial and ethnic assimilation, known in the United States as the melting pot, wherein ethnic and racial differences would disappear into a homogenized American identity. And while the world at large was not envisioned as a huge melting pot, modernization theory supported the idea of Marshall McLuhan's "global village," in which media technology would link all humanity, with ethnic, racial, and national differences growing less and less important.

The 1960s changed the picture dramatically, both in the United States and abroad. At home, the civil rights movement brought African Americans' lack of assimilation to the forefront of American consciousness. Soon after, other ethnic groups—Native Americans, Poles, Italians, Hispanics, and Irish—began asserting ethnic pride. They emulated the Black Pride rhetoric, and they were reflected in and assisted by the culture industries that produced and promoted festivals—Cinco de Mayo has become more of an American holiday than a Mexican one—and mass cultural goods for ethnic niche markets (Jacobson 2006). Racial and ethnic divides shifted but did not disappear (Lee and Bean 2007). The old melting pot ideal no longer seemed either accurate or desirable. This change had parallels worldwide: Nationalist leaders of newly independent countries and the generation of political leaders that followed them rejected the convergence model and asserted their own distinctiveness. Third World nations declared their independence from either U.S. or Soviet domination, regardless of whether they were actually able to get along without support from one of the two big powers. In the 1970s, the human rights movement focused attention on the treatment of minority groups within nations. All of these new movements emphasized and even celebrated persistent ethnic differentiation.

Expressive culture played a major role in both American and foreign expressions of ethnic pride. If African leaders of the 1940s and 1950s wore suits from Savile Row and Paris as they negotiated with representatives of the colonial powers, the next generation of African leaders wore agbadas and dashikis. Often, however, they wore military uniforms, as political and economic changes proved more intractable than cultural changes. And cultural distinctiveness, often centered on differences in language and religion, tore apart many new nations as the old dreams of assimilation and convergence seemed more and more distant.

Cultural assertiveness of a specific collective identity, however—based on ethnicity, race, religion, language, or some combination of these—is likely to persist for a number of reasons. First, its expression through cultural objects is psychologically satisfying yet often relatively low cost. An

African American youth can wear a cap with a Malcolm X symbol or follow specific hip-hop groups more easily than he can effect change in his school, his neighborhood, or his job opportunities. Even when cultural allegiance is extremely costly, as in the enmity between Serbs and Croats in the Balkans, an individual may find it easier to apply simple rules of affiliation—she's a Serb, so she's my enemy—than to negotiate new interaction patterns. Second, such assertiveness engages the ethnic or racial group's intellectual leaders, who then have a stake in its perpetuation. If urban schools with a large Puerto Rican component in the student body start offering courses in Puerto Rican poetry, someone has to teach them, and these teachers then have a stake in their continuation. Third, political leaders seeking votes find it easy and convenient to appeal to ethnic sentiments, as shown by the political luminaries who turn out for the St. Patrick's Day parades. This is why the issue of a gay Irish group marching in New York City's parade has been so vexed: On one hand, the parade is privately sponsored so theoretically the sponsors can exclude whomever they want, but on the other hand, New York's politicians are reluctant to alienate the gay community. The interaction between cultural and political agendas escalates the conflict, and because it is "colorful," the media treat the dispute to lavish coverage.

The cultural expression of ethnicity is less straightforward than might first appear, precisely because collective identity is a process and not a given, a construction and not an objective fact. Ethnic and racial groups have their subdivisions, often invisible to outsiders, and the question of whose culture gets promoted and taken as the culture of the entire group may be hotly contested. In the United States, many Spanish speakers resent being lumped with one another as "Hispanic," pointing out that Dominicans and Argentineans have little in common. West Indians and African Americans eye one another warily; Koreans fear the economic inroads being made by Thais, while Thais look over their shoulders at Vietnamese. These divisions get played out in local negotiations over multiculturalism. It is all very well to represent different cultures in the curriculum, but how many cultures? Do differences between northern and southern Italians get expressed in the Columbus Day celebration—traditionally associated with Italian ethnicity—and how do the claims of Native Americans get represented in a celebration of the "discoverer" of their lands?

Ethnicity itself is a cultural object, with different creators and different recipients, all constructing different meanings. When I'm in Europe, I'm clearly an "American"; when in America, I'm variously a "WASP," an "Anglo," a "Yankee," a "white," and a "Midwesterner." To a radical Islamist, I might be a "Crusader." And in Nigeria, I am—along with anyone else having white skin—a "European." My person is a cultural object with ethnic characteristics that different creators use to communicate with different audiences (cf. Morning 2009).

Nigeria exemplifies some of the difficulties of ethnic representation. Within this country of some 88 million people are at least 250 distinct languages associated with different ethnic groups (some put the count as high as 400). The three majority languages—Hausa, Yoruba, and Igbo—are spoken by roughly two thirds of the population. Although no one is happy with English as the lingua franca, none of the three majority linguistic groups wants to give way to another, whereas the many minority groups fear domination by the "big three" and therefore strongly support the use of English for commercial and governmental transactions. Thus, the evening news broadcast by the Nigerian Television Authority (NTA) is read in English; at the close of the program, the announcer says goodnight in Hausa, Yoruba, and Igbo—much to the disgust of the minority Nigerians, who strongly protest this bit of symbolism. What seems a low-cost gesture to NTA is an arrogant expression of would-be cultural domination to the Efik, Ibibio, Tiv, and dozens of other minority ethnic groups.

Racial and ethnic affiliations seem natural, matters of blood and bone. But once again, sociologists point out, both are cultural constructs. This is a key argument of the burgeoning field of whiteness studies (e.g., Wray 2006). A person who is one-eighth black is "white" in Jamaica but "black" in Louisiana. Trinidadians and Belizeans, who come from countries a thousand miles apart and regard themselves as having little in common, become ethnically lumped as "West Indians" when they immigrate to Britain, just as British racists apply the derogatory term *Pakis* to Hindu Indians, Muslim Pakistanis, and any other South Asians who happen to be around. A "Paki" is not a person but a cultural object.

Even though people may be lumped together by outsiders or by historical circumstances, they may also take advantage of this imposed ethnicity. Stephen Cornell (1988) studied how Native Americans came to recognize a shared identity and common political agenda. For Native Americans living on reservations during most of the twentieth century, tribal and subtribal affiliations were the significant markers of identification both to themselves and to others with whom they came into contact. But in the 1950s and 1960s, increasing numbers came to such cities as Los Angeles and Chicago, seeking the economic opportunities that their desolate reservations lacked. Here, they clustered in the same down-and-out neighborhoods, dealt with the same bureaucracies, hung out at the same bars, and sometimes were subject to the same prejudices as "dirty Indians" or "red niggers." Now the cultural identity that mattered was not Oglala or Cree but "Indian." This recognition of shared identity led urban Indians to assert common cultural and political claims. One of the most visible and influential fruits of this new supratribalism was the aggressive organization known as AIM (American Indian Movement), which pressed Indian issues in the 1970s. The collective identity of Native America expanded further in the late twentieth century; the number of Americans who identified themselves as "Indians" tripled between 1960 and 1990 (Nagel 1995).

Cultural expressions of ethnicity, like the African American holiday of Kwanzaa, designed by a California professor in the late 1960s, are often cases of the "invention of tradition," not of venerable ritual. Ethnicity and race are artificial constructs, collective identities that are the results of historical contingencies. At the same time, they exert enormous motivational influence, instilling fierce loyalties and equally fierce hatreds. Heterogeneous states and social groups (e.g., communities, schools, and organizations) are thus obliged to find ways to acknowledge and perhaps celebrate cultural diversity while constructing a common culture, of which the different ethnic or racial groups are subcultures, that successfully claims the primary allegiance of every citizen. No simple task, this is made harder by local habits and prejudices. Many Chinese in Malaysia feel stronger ties to Chinese elsewhere than they do to Muslim Malays, who have severely restricted their opportunities. Some American Jews donate vast amounts of money to Israel, often more than they do to local charities. The claims of ethnicity, resting on what has been termed a "constructed primordialism" (Appadurai 1990), remain strong enough to frustrate the cosmopolitans, resulting both in indisputable pride and in unspeakable bloodshed.

Gender and sexualities have followed a parallel path. In the 1970s feminist theory, popular cultural representations of women's concerns (*Ms. Magazine* [1971]; *Our Bodies, Ourselves* [1973]), legislative changes (Title IX [1972]), linguistic changes (from "he" as a universal pronoun to "he/she" or the somewhat self-conscious use of "she" as the universal), and "women's studies" programs challenged male-centered norms. As with "whiteness," however, soon "masculinities" and heteronormativity were themselves undergoing deconstruction. By the turn of the century the thinking had evolved from male/female or gay/straight binaries to seeing genders and sexualities in systemic terms, the roles and identities contingent rather than fixed, performed rather than biologically mandated. (For representative recent work on the construction of gender, see Silva 2008; Schilt and Westbrook 2009; Anderson 2009; for a empirically well-grounded study of sexual collective identity construction, see Armstrong 2002).

So race, ethnicity, gender, sexuality, and indeed all collective identities are constructions, not givens. At the same time, we must recognize that these particular constructions (and other key bases for collective identity like gender and religion) create powerful "we" groups that influence our thinking and behavior in multiple ways. One of these ways is that people making claims about a social problem will try to reach people through their collective identities, saying, for example, "You, as a Latina or as a black woman or as a Roman Catholic, ought to be concerned about this." In the next section, we examine how this process works.

Constructing a Social Problem

Poverty, crime, teenage pregnancy, high infant mortality rates, racism, urban decay, unemployment, drugs, drunk driving, inadequate health care—and on and on. Most of us can reel off a list of pressing social problems without hesitation. Although such a list has roots in problems that cause human suffering universally—such as violence, hatred, and premature death—the forms that these problems take are specific to each culture and society.

Americans regard teenage pregnancy as a social problem, for example. For the Hausa of Nigeria, where most girls marry at the age of twelve or thirteen, young women who reach their twenties *without* having children are the problem. For the Chinese, whose government addresses its population problem by vigorously enforcing a one-child-per-family policy, any pregnancy is problematic. If the family has no children, the problem is whether or not the baby will be a son (desirable) or a daughter (less desirable). Infant girls often show up abandoned near orphanages, left to the charity of strangers so that the parents can try for another pregnancy (virtually all babies in Chinese orphanages are females or severely handicapped males). If the family already has a child, the pregnancy must be hidden or else the mother may be forced to abort. Even in America, labeling "teenage pregnancy" as the problem may be misleading. Few would regard a pregnant nineteen-year-old with a working husband as worrisome, but many such are included in statistics and stories about the "dramatic rise in teen pregnancy." Kristen Luker (1991) found that concerns about "babies having babies" has more to do with public disapproval of the welfare system, racial prejudices, and concerns about teenage sexual activity than with actual demographic changes.

Media define and focus attention on social problems. Consider *The Jungle,* Upton Sinclair's indictment of the meat-packing industry that helped provoke passage of the Pure Food and Drug Act, or *Uncle Tom's Cabin,* Harriet Beecher Stowe's sensational depiction of the horrors of slavery that transfixed northern U.S. readers. If culture can draw attention to social problems, can it also sometimes create the problem? And if so, what might be the role of culture in the solution of these problems it has helped bring about?

Making Trouble

We have seen that culture imposes meanings on an otherwise chaotic and random universe. Cultural systems turn events and objects into cultural objects with meanings specific to each culture; a business card is meaningful to a Japanese in a way that it is not to an American. In just this way, we can see how certain phenomena in the social world are made meaningful and transformed into cultural objects and, more specifically, into social problems.

Consider what takes place when things that "just happen" become cultural objects. We have all seen the fatalistic bumper stickers that proclaim "Shit happens." The world *is* full of painful occurrences, private tragedies, and large-scale and persistent deprivations; life is neither fair nor kind nor naturally and obviously meaningful. Sometimes, though, the human misery that "happens" is transformed from a mere happening into a meaningful cultural object, and the cultural object gets designated as a social problem. When this transformation takes place, it becomes possible for people to seek solutions, for the existence of a "problem" implies the existence of a "solution." (Thus, we do not regard death as a "problem," for it has no "solution.")

What happens when we see poverty as a social problem in the United States? In this case, it becomes a cultural object read against a horizon of expectations (e.g., America is a rich country), interpreted (e.g., given our abundance, America should not have any significant poverty), assumed to have a creator (e.g., what forces and actions shape this cultural object of American poverty?), and seen as something to be overcome (e.g., with a "War on Poverty," Lyndon Johnson's program of the 1960s). If poverty is not seen as a social problem—the poor are always with us—its more painful consequences can be alleviated, but poverty itself is not seen as something to be solved. Considered as a cultural object, on the other hand, poverty (and any other social problem) can benefit from the same type of cultural diamond analysis as any other cultural object, asking who creates the definition of the problem, who receives and interprets it, what meanings it contains, and in what social world it is meaningful.

From Happening to Event to Social Problem

First, let's consider how "happenings" turn into "cultural objects." The creation of a cultural object is like the creation of an event, which anthropologist Marshall Sahlins (1985) describes as the relationship between a happening and a structure, a relationship created by interpretation. How do happenings become cultural objects identified as social problems? It appears that for a cultural object first to be created and then to be identified as a social problem, it must articulate with an interlocking set of ideas and institutions. Schematically, this process looks like Figure 5.1.

Consider the social problem of drunk driving, a case that sociologist Joseph Gusfield (1981) examined closely. The relevant set of happenings might include auto accidents; traffic fatalities; transportation patterns, including the American reliance on cars and the under-funding of public transportation; car design emphasizing style or affordability over safety; and American individualism, including an attitude that seatbelts limit one's personal freedom. How, asked Gusfield, out of all these, have the American people singled out the "drunk driver" as the single meaningful cultural object and social problem?

The answer lies in American ideas and institutions. Our culture emphasizes individual responsibility, so a fatal accident must be some individual's fault; blaming it on "the system" is not the American way. Our history of temperance movements has left a lingering association of alcohol with immorality (taxes on liquor and cigarettes are called "sin taxes"). The flip-side of our emphasis on personal freedom (with the car and the open road emblematic of this emphasis) is our belief in personal control. Drunkenness is individually "sinful" in two ways: The individual has made a bad decision (to get drunk; to drink and drive), and she has given up her ability to control herself, her body, and her car. Hence, the concept of the "killer drunk" fits a number of strands in our common web of ideas. It fits our institutions as well. Auto manufacturers and liquor distillers support the

Figure 5.1   Transforming Happenings Into Cultural Objects

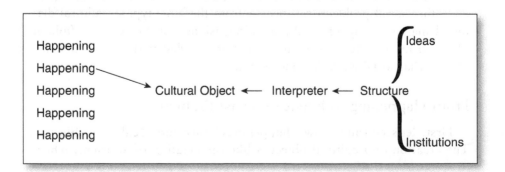

construction of the "problem" as poor individual decision making rather than booze or unsafe (or too many) cars. And our legal system is better equipped to take on individuals who may have committed criminal acts than to go after organizations or systems (though in recent years, class action suits have made inroads).

Even the response to auto fatalities fits the ideological and institutional context. Mothers Against Drunk Driving (MADD) has been highly effective in getting tougher laws on the books and enforced. The very name of this organization sets up a morality play pitting the mother defending her young against the villainous drunk driver who imperils them. It also forecloses debate (who would be *for* drunk driving?) and renders certain solutions (e.g., better public transportation, a high tax on gasoline) unthinkable. MADD accords prestige to women who have actually lost children in accidents involving drunk drivers. A grieving mother is a powerful image in Christian societies, not because Christian mothers love their children more than other mothers but because the image of the *pieta*—Mary holding the dead Christ—is a familiar cultural icon. The maternal grief evoked by MADD focuses attention squarely on individuals—individuals who drink, drive, kill, die, grieve, and act—and not on organizations or systems.

In Nigeria, death on the highway is also an event and a cultural object, but its meaning within the cultural system is quite different. A deadly combination of deteriorated roads, nonexistent traffic law enforcement, crowded conditions, uninhibited drivers, and vehicles that are often overloaded and poorly maintained give rise to enormous carnage on the roads, a fact that all Nigerians acknowledge. The Nobel Prize–winning playwright Wole Soyinka has made danger on the highways a recurring theme in his plays. But Nigerians don't point to the drivers, the pedestrians, or the vehicles as the social problem; for them, the problem is "the road." In Nigerian culture, the road is always a place of danger as well as excitement, a place where witches and destructive spirits lurk to trap the unwary (Bastian 1992). Ben Okri's novel *The Famished Road* (1991) tells of a road that actually devours its victims. As Gusfield (1981) would point out, by defining a public problem in such a way—constructing it as a cultural object with meanings involving spirits and fate—the Nigerians are focusing attention on some types of solutions (placate the spirits; don't travel) and not on others (fix the roads; build sidewalks).

Thus, social problems tend to show a comfortable fit with the ideas and institutions of the society in which they are found. Witches are a social problem in Nigeria because the surrounding culture contains a set of ideas that support a belief in witchcraft, a set of remedies to counter a witch's influence, and a set of institutions, including media—especially the tabloid press, always eager to spread the word about new cases of witchcraft—and markets eager to trade in remedies against bewitching. Suspected witches are killed, and innocent people (often children) are killed to make medicine against witches. As the sociologist W. I. Thomas (1966) pointed out long ago, if people define a situation as real, it is real in its consequences.

The Career of a Social Problem

If social problems are culturally defined, it stands to reason that problems wax and wane in popularity over time. Stephen Hilgartner and Charles Bosk (1988) tried to identify what accounts for the "rise and fall of social problems," beginning with what gets identified as a social problem in the first place. These authors envision a public arena in which competition takes place among the conditions that potentially could be labeled as social problems. This competition occurs in two forms: (1) in the framing or definition of the problem itself (e.g., Is the problem one of drunk drivers or of overreliance on automobiles?) and (2) in capturing the attention of institutions—government, media, and foundations—that have limits on their resources or "carrying capacities." Those conditions that get selected as social problems are phenomena that have specific characteristics: They are or can be made dramatic; they resonate with deep mythic themes in the culture; and they are politically viable, often because they are linked with powerful interest groups. Winners in this competition achieve the status of widely acknowledged social problems. Making similar arguments, Adut (2008) shows that publicity is essential for transforming sexual transgressions into scandals, while Auyero and Swistun (2008) show that toxic environmental contamination requires interpretation if it is not merely to produce uncertainty rather than action.

Consider the AIDS epidemic as an example. In the early 1980s, it became clear to epidemiologists and some members of the homosexual men's community in a few cities that a new, highly contagious, and invariably fatal disease involving the collapse of the immune system was spreading widely. Yet it was several years before public arenas—including federal and local government, the medical establishment, and much of the gay community itself—took alarm and identified AIDS as a major social problem (Shilts 1987). Within the American gay subculture, a strong emphasis on sexual freedom as political expressiveness meant that, for some time, medical warnings about safe sex fell on deaf ears. The disease was highly dramatic, especially in the wasting away of its youthful victims, but few media outlets exploited its dramatic potential at first, for it was believed to be confined to members of a stigmatized group. The same was true outside the United States. For several years, governments in East Africa were reluctant to address AIDS, despite its epidemic proportions in their countries, because they associated the disease with male homosexual behavior, which Africans consider abhorrent. Because of this association, the disease was "culturally impossible" and therefore did not merit recognition as a social problem. In both East Africa and the United States, AIDS did not initially resonate with mythic themes, nor did it link up with powerful political actors; indeed, quite the opposite.

As Hilgartner and Bosk might predict, once AIDS could no longer be ignored, there was competition over the very definition of the "problem": Was it AIDS, sexual promiscuity, or (as some religious conservatives claimed) homosexuality itself? Although the struggle over problem definition was fierce, the gay men's viewpoint was helped by their high level of education, political savvy, and access to the arts and media. By the mid-1980s, gay men and their supporters had dramatized the epidemic in highly effective ways, through the NAMES Project Foundation AIDS Memorial Quilt, plays such as *The Normal Heart* that reached a liberal and affluent constituency, books such as Randy Shilts's *And the Band Played On,* and public rituals, such as releasing hundreds of balloons for each AIDS death, that offered good visuals for the evening news. Celebrities helped, both those who died of AIDS (Rock Hudson, Liberace, Michel Foucault, Perry Ellis, Arthur Ashe) and those who used their prominence to urge support for AIDS research (Elizabeth Taylor). Not only did the gay men's associations engage in lobbying, but the rapid spread of the disease and its identification with non-gay populations also removed the stigma associated with it; if "normal, decent people" could get AIDS from a routine blood transfusion, it became everybody's problem. Under the conservative Reagan administration, the U.S. Surgeon General sent a brochure to every household regarding safe sex, and condoms moved off pharmacies' back shelves into the limelight.

Media attention continues to be intense and crucial, as in a notorious Benetton advertisement showing not the firm's clothes but a family embracing a young man dying of AIDS (the pieta motif again). AIDS-related cultural objects command attention. Tony Kushner's play *Angels in America* won the Pulitzer Prize in 1993, and Michael Cunningham's novel *The Hours* won it in 1999; both have AIDS as a central theme. The widely praised film of *The Hours,* with such box-office stars as Nicole Kidman and Meryl Streep, has magnified the impact of this work. In making such a film, actors like Kidman and Streep become "operatives" in Hilgartner and Bosk's model, helping AIDS compete for public attention.

The career of AIDS offers a clear example of how cultural values and themes shape (or obstruct) the very definition of a social problem. The social problem itself is a cultural object, with those who produce or create it (as a social problem), those who constitute its public or audience, and a set of meanings that interpreters use to relate it to the social world. Not all social problems appear with the relative suddenness of AIDS, however. Some, such as poverty or crime, are always present but rise and fall in terms of public attention. Others are associated with long-term structural changes. But whether the situation is new or old, once its creators (operatives, claims makers) have succeeded in getting it defined as a social problem, the question becomes, Will anyone be moved to try to solve it? Will the social problem generate a social movement? For this to happen, the problem (as cultural object) has to connect with an audience (as recipients) in such a way that some of the recipients are moved to action.

Constructing a Social Movement

Even if a particular audience recognizes something as a social problem, that in and of itself does not mobilize anyone to do anything. Poverty might be acknowledged as a social problem, for example, but if people take a fatalistic view (the poor are always with us; there's nothing that can be done) or a judgmental one (their poverty is their own fault), this recognition will not produce any action. And of course the definition of whether or not there is a problem requiring some action varies across cultures; most Americans and Europeans view female genital mutilation as a social problem whereas many Africans regard it simply as a tradition.

Social movements require motivating people to recognize that a problem exists, to accept the possibility of its being solved, and to regard a certain line of action as being likely to produce this result. "The trick for activists," according to William Gamson (1995:85), "is to bridge public discourse and people's experiential knowledge, integrating them in a coherent frame that supports and sustains collective action."

What is needed to bring off such a trick? Connecting an audience to a problem requires casting the problem in such a way that the audience accepts its relevance. This is usually seen as a problem of framing.

According to sociologist Erving Goffman (1974), a frame is an interpretive scheme that enables people to make sense of what they experience. For example, at the sight of a crippled beggar in Calcutta, a Hindu frame might prompt the observer to interpret the beggar's condition as the result of sins in a past life. A Christian frame might suggest that the beggar's suffering is a God-sent opportunity for charity. And a social activist frame sees the same suffering as bearing witness to economic injustice.

David Snow and colleagues have shown how social movements need to align the frames (interpretive schemata) of potential recruits. Frame alignment is "the linkage of individual and SMO [social movement organization] interpretive orientations, such that some set of individual interests, values and beliefs and SMO activities, goals, and ideology are congruent and complementary" (Snow et al. 1986:464; see also Benford and Snow 2000). An SMO supporting some new environmental protections, for example, might try to acquire the mailing lists of other environmental organizations under the assumption that the SMO's goals and the values of these individuals would be congruent. Other times, an SMO seeks to get individuals to extend their frames or to draw specific conclusions in line with the SMO's goals. For example, an activist promoting registration of all firearms might assert, "As parents (family frame), you have to be concerned about keeping guns out of the wrong hands (gun control frame)." The frames of individuals are to a great extent defined by their sense of collective identities. If someone doesn't consider himself "a parent," the gun control activist's efforts at frame alignment will fail.

Framing leads to action only when recipients accept the proposed fit between problem and solution. When Amy Binder (2001) compared creationist and Afrocentric attempts to change school curricula, she found that the creationists had less success because few people believed that Christian evangelical students faced discrimination, so curricular change was a solution without a problem; on the other hand, there was widespread acceptance of the educational problems of African American youth, so the proposed solution got a hearing. The framing of the problem also suggests the relevant institutional solutions. If sexual harassment is seen as employment discrimination, its solution focuses on employers; if it is seen as a problem of violence, its solution focuses on criminal law (Saguy 2003).

The framer (creative agent, claims maker) needs to bridge the gap between his or her view of the problem and the audience's view. But the framer also needs to stir people up, to move people. This requires making not simply a cognitive appeal but an emotional one. Movement activists will often use stories (Polletta 2006) or art—posters, masks, street theatre, or music—to reach the hearts of potential converts to their cause.

Eyerman and Jamison have written a book called *Music and Social Movements* (1998) with a two-pronged subtitle "Mobilizing Traditions" that nicely captures their argument. Activists draw on traditional musical forms to convey their messages to relevant audiences, to move them emotionally, and thus to mobilize them for action. Civil rights leaders used hymns like "Lift Every Voice" and spirituals like "Let My People Go" to move African Americans to more active forms of protesting their condition. Earlier in the twentieth century, the Wobblies (Industrial Workers of the World) drew on both traditional folk music and popular songs to propagate their message about the working man, and union members ever since have sung "Solidarity Forever" and "Joe Hill." In songs like "Deportees" and (more obliquely) "This Land Is Your Land," Woody Guthrie used traditional folk idiom to carry a savage critique of capitalism. Music, in this analysis, helps fashion what they call a "cognitive identity" whereby people link their sense of being a "we" with a specific form of oppositional action. Music makes this link because it is an effective type of "exemplary action"; it suggests how the audience should feel and what they should do.

> [T]he exemplary action of music and art is lived as well as thought: it is cognitive, but it also draws on more emotive aspects of human consciousness. As cultural expression, exemplary action is self-revealing and thus a symbolic representation of the individual and the collective which are the movement. . . . This exemplary action can also be recorded in film, words, and music, and thus be given more than a fleeting presence. (Eyerman and Jamison 1998:23)

Sandra Barnes (2005) similarly shows how gospel music mobilizes congregants for community action.

"More than a fleeting presence" highlights the critical role played by media. Social problems are always competing for the attention of relevant audiences. Media help problems win and hold this attention. A novel like *The Hours* appears, and the small but influential class of people who read serious fiction is reminded about the personal tragedies involved in AIDS. Then *The Hours* wins the Pulitzer, and newspapers, TV, magazines, and other media trumpet this event; people hear about the book, and its subject, even if most will never actually read it. Then a film is made, and filmgoers who don't think much about AIDS but are fans of Nicole Kidman get reminded of the scourge. Media amplification of this sort helps fix a social problem in the minds of a necessarily fickle public.

For better or for worse, media can shape both the problem and its solution for huge masses of people, constructing a social movement in ways that are anything but the outcomes of democratic deliberation. Arvind Rajagopal (2001) suggests that in India's political and moral vacuum following the decline of the Congress Party's hegemony, Hindu nationalism was one of many social movements that offered competing solutions to India's lack of direction during the 1980s. The Vishva Hindu Parishad, founded in 1964, was a cultural organization devoted to spreading Hindu values, using traditional Hindu symbols and popular culture to encourage Hindu identification and a turn from materialism to a spiritual/scientific ideal. Not a party, it has been closely associated with the Hindu-nationalist Bharatiya Janata Party (BJP). But Hindu nationalism was only one ideological position among many.

Then in 1987 producer Ramanand Sagar began showing the Ramayan serial—based on the epic tales of Lord Ram—on state-controlled Indian television. It was hugely popular, and it seemed to offer a solution.

> While Ram Rajya, the golden age of the rule of Ram, has long been held as a utopia, and has repeatedly been utilized as a mobilizing symbol, the realist convention adopted in Sagar's dramatization and the extended serial format of the presentation gave the symbol a discursive detail and a verisimilitude it can seldom have had before. Moreover the claim of a panacea for modern society in ancient Hindu culture, offered as a nationalist message on a state medium, had clear political implications. (Rajagopal 2001:104)

Rajagopal links the televised epic to the violence in Ayodhya beginning in the early 1990s and to the political success of the BJP.

We can translate his account into the conceptual scheme of this chapter. Creative agents frame the problems of Indian society in such a way that they appeal to an audience whose collective identity is more "Hindu" than "Indian." Activating the Hindu identity constructs the problem as one of falling away from Hindu traditions, allowing them to be defiled by irreligious institutions (the secular state) or competing religions (Islam). The solution is an aggressive religious nationalism, and the media amplification helps mobilize public sentiment around this solution. The results of this social movement, in both electoral outcomes and ongoing religious violence, continue to this day.

SUMMARY

Most people regard social problems as malfunctions in the social system, and as such, the problems demand solutions. A social problem may be complex; apparent problems may be symptomatic of larger, underlying problems; entrenched economic or political interests may stand in the way. But all problems, we believe, have solutions if only enough resources, ingenuity, and moral courage are brought to bear on them.

Thinking of social problems less as givens and more as cultural objects draws attention to the artificial construction of any one problem and the implied meanings conveyed when a problem gets defined in one way and not another. Very different interests are engaged in constructing a particular problem as "homosexuality," "sex outside marriage," or "a highly contagious virus spread by bodily fluids," and very different lines of action—different solutions—are implied. This is not to suggest that social problems, however defined, have no relation to human suffering.

People do sicken and die of AIDS, no matter what cultural object is being constructed as "the problem." Applying a cultural diamond analysis to a social problem does suggest, however, that such problems, like all cultural objects, have specific creators and recipients. They also have careers; like any cultural object, a social problem can rise in popularity, become institutionalized, or fail to win an audience and disappear. Understanding this allows us to construct other formulations of a problem and imagine solutions.

In this chapter, we have seen how social problems involving economic inequality, ethnicity, and modernity itself are cultural constructions rather than natural events or random happenings. One may apply a cultural diamond analysis to virtually any social problem. If we set up the cultural object to be, for example, (1) "illegal drugs entering America and threatening its citizens," we are appealing to an audience of Americans fearful of attacks on their way of life. We are invoking images of contamination from foreign sources. We are implying solutions: declaring a national "war" on drugs, strengthening the national defense against penetration by drugs, and taking military action against the foreign producers. It is not surprising that the creators of this cultural object are the federal government. Cultural creators create problems for which they have solutions, and governments know how to wage war. If the drug problem were defined differently so that the cultural object was (2) "poverty and despair that prompt a narcotic-induced withdrawal from reality," the solution would not be war but relieving poverty and despair, something that governments are less successful at doing. It is not surprising that academics and armchair social critics construct this second cultural object more often than politicians and government administrators do, for professors and critics are not responsible for providing the solutions. There are many other ways to construct the cultural object of drugs as a social problem. We could call the problem "sin," "laws attempting to regulate private behavior," "poor individual decision making," or "wicked drug dealers." Different cultural creators, a different intended audience, and different meanings and solutions exist for each such cultural object.

All cultural objects are not equal, however, for different ones will be able to mobilize different resources. Calling a "war on" anything enables the government to take action, whereas constructing the same thing as "sin" precludes government action. As a practical matter, the best cultural object for embodying a social problem is one that (1) unambiguously isolates happenings and turns them into events relevant to the cultural object, (2) captures the attention of a larger or powerful set of recipients, and (3) suggests solutions that are within the capacity of the relevant institutions. Thus, "segregation" is a well-formed social problem for the government to construct as a cultural object because it meets all three criteria, whereas "racial hatred" is not, for it is diffused among various happenings and its solutions are beyond government capacities. On the other hand, the parents of a family can tackle the problem of racial hatred among its members but can do little about segregation.

A cultural object, as we have seen, is an interpretation, a set of meanings that fit a context of ideas and institutions, that translate random happenings into events, and that suggest attitudes and actions. Social problems are cultural objects in exactly this sense. Tracing the links among the problems, their creators, their receivers, and their social worlds will help illuminate those solutions that might work, those that probably will not, and those that have not yet been imagined because of how the problem has been constructed.

QUESTIONS FOR STUDY AND DISCUSSION

1. Select an ethnic collective identity like Inuit, West Indian, or North African. How would it be described (1) as an objective reality and (2) as a cultural construction? What would be involved in perpetuating such a construction? Suppose members of the group migrated—Inuit in Toronto, West Indians in London, North Africans in Marseilles. What would happen to their collective identity and that of their children? Consider this question from both the objectivist and the constructionist point of view.

2. Bring in the editorial page of your local newspaper and use it to identify a social problem that is currently capturing public attention. Discuss how this social problem came to be identified and how it is being posed. What are some other ways in which this problem could have been constructed? Why does it take the form that it does and not one of the alternatives?

3. Compare the careers of two potential social problems, one successful (e.g., capturing public attention and resources) and one not. Use actual examples. Describe the social problem arena, the claims makers or operatives, the framing that goes on, and the principles of selection that determine the outcomes.

4. Much of the social movement literature talks about specific organizations pursuing specific goals. What if the object of analysis is an unorganized collectivity without any specific goal or direction, perhaps without a sense of collective identity? Think of a social category like "teenage females" or "managers working for large corporations." How, according to the constructionist and framing models, could these groups come together as a social movement?

RECOMMENDED FOR FURTHER READING

Armstrong, Elizabeth. 2002. *Forging Gay Identities: Organizing Sexuality in San Francisco, 1950–1994*. Chicago: University of Chicago Press. Armstrong shows how a collective identity like gays or lesbians is not static but changes according to the social and ideological context. In her study of gay and lesbian organizations over three decades, she shows how the collective identity changed from a narrow focus on homophile issues to a radical political agenda associated with the New Left and then to a consumer lifestyle.

Lichterman, Paul. 2005. *Elusive Togetherness: Church Groups Trying to Bridge America's Divisions*. Princeton, NJ: Princeton University Press. In his study how nine Protestant churches address community problems, Lichterman finds that successful mobilization involves a fit between a congregation's internal culture and its definition of the external problem.

Polletta, Fancesca. 2006. *It Was Like a Fever: Storytelling in Protest and Politics*. Chicago: University of Chicago Press. Polletta shows how storytelling creates internal solidarity while dramatizing the movement's cause to external audiences.

Saguy, Abigail C. 2003. *What Is Sexual Harassment?* Berkeley: University of California Press. Saguy compares how the problem of sexual harassment is constructed in France and the United States and the legal and policy differences that result from the different framings.

6

Organizations in a Multicultural World

People who work for organizations think of themselves as practical types, looking to get the job done, improve the bottom line, or implement the policy. Yet just like those who tackle social problems, organization men and women often find themselves dealing with the expressive and the symbolic—in other words, with culture. Many of the ambiguities of organizational life derive from the role that cultural objects play, both within the organization and impinging on its operations from outside. In this chapter, we explore how culture affects the ways people conduct business transactions, how governments try to implement programs, and how organizations try to produce and market products—like hamburgers, for instance.

McDonald's in Israel wrestles with reconciling fast food business objectives with Israel's religious laws and ethnic sensibilities (McGreal 2006). Israelis adore American popular culture, and nothing is more emblematic of all things American than a Big Mac. Nothing is less kosher, either, and therein lies the problem.

Two faces of Israeli religious culture bear upon the issue. On the one hand, most Israelis are Jews who do not actively practice their religion. Israel has many thriving non-kosher restaurants, and the stratum most likely to patronize McDonald's, the young and with-it, are the least likely to be religiously observant. On the other hand, Orthodox Jews act as a cultural watchdog, ready to pounce on anything that seems too blatantly disrespectful of religious doctrines.

With 120 outlets in Israel, of which 11 are strictly kosher, McDonald's has made numerous accommodations—all controversial—to the cultural context:

- It changed its iconic yellow and red signs to blue and white, the colors of the Israeli flag, for the kosher restaurants.
- It uses only kosher beef, potatoes, and milkshake mix in all of its restaurants.
- It will open no branches in Jewish settlements in the occupied territories.
- It insists that Arabic-speaking employees use only Hebrew when working.

The endless dilemmas facing McDonald's typify the complexities of reconciling global and local cultures. Global culture, strongly influenced by American popular culture and spread by the media and travelers, makes the Big Mac available as a cultural object, as shown in Figure 6.1. In this case, the cultural object is created indirectly by an American corporation and directly by Israeli franchisers aiming for Israeli consumers. The global burger as a cultural object means (Meaning #1) up to date, American, fresh, youthful, and trendy. But locally, the Big Mac and other McDonald's fare are cultural objects, too. As constructed by religious conservatives, they are (Meaning #2) non-kosher, non-Jewish, alien, assimilationist, and an affront to religion and Jewish identity. McDonald's franchisers want to capitalize on the first set of meanings and reach the audience with whom it resonates and to isolate the second set—McDonald's knows an Orthodox Jew is never going to chow down on a Quarter Pounder with Cheese anyway—and keep it from influencing the national market.

Making profits, doing business generally, getting results—these activities are more complicated in a global economy where local and international cultures clash, where incompatible meaning systems must be reconciled, and where the people doing business or working for an organization cannot avoid managing meanings just as much as they manage money, products, and people. This chapter explores three ways in which culture affects the ways organizations accomplish their objectives, or fail to, in a rapidly changing world. We begin by considering organizational cultures, first at the individual level, examining the relationship between culture and motivation, and then at the group level, examining cultures that can emerge within organizations. Second, we look at some research on the ways in which national cultures shape organizational outcomes. And finally, we explore the problems of those organizations and programs that must operate across a multiplicity of cultures.

Figure 6.1   McDonald's in Israel

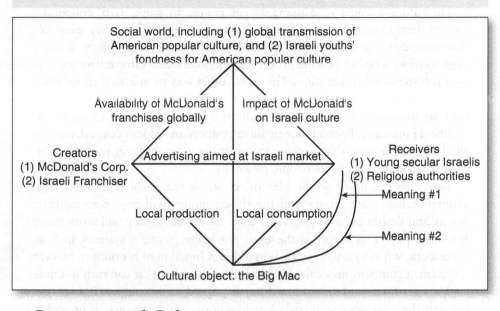

Social world, including (1) global transmission of American popular culture, and (2) Israeli youths' fondness for American popular culture

Availability of McDonald's franchises globally | Impact of McDonald's on Israeli culture

Creators
(1) McDonald's Corp.
(2) Israeli Franchiser

Advertising aimed at Israeli market

Receivers
(1) Young secular Israelis
(2) Religious authorities

Meaning #1

Local production | Local consumption

Meaning #2

Cultural object: the Big Mac

Organizational Cultures

Organizations operate within and across cultures, but they also produce cultures of their own. Managers and workers create and receive cultural objects—shared meanings embodied in forms—that may facilitate or obstruct the organization's operations. We can think of this exchange of meanings as operating at two levels: the individual or small group level and the level of the larger group ("the workers") or even the organization as a whole. Let us first consider the microlevel, where group subcultures arise to create a meaningful working world.

Culture and Motivation

Any organization has goals, and therefore any organization faces the problem of motivating its members to work for these goals. We see this most clearly in organizations that seek to make a profit, but it is true for all types of organizations. For example, Penny Becker (1999) has shown that churches of the same denomination can have wildly different congregational cultures. Motivating the members of a church that thinks of itself as a family is very different from motivating members of a church that thinks of itself as a community activist or as a detached provider of religious services. Leaders and communicators have to work with and through the local culture, regardless of the organizational type.

How does a leader or a manager get people to work hard, cooperate, extend themselves for the good of the whole, or do anything they wouldn't otherwise do? This is a standard problem faced by the management of every organization, whether a corner grocery, a religious sect, a government agency, or a transnational corporation. The most direct way to motivate compliance is through the exercise of force: Most people will respond most of the time if they are threatened with a whip or a gun. But raw power is inefficient, not to mention inhumane. Prison labor or slave systems are seldom cost-effective in the long run; nor are they options for most contemporary organizations. So how do managers motivate people to work?

One theory is based on the idea of economic man, which goes like this: Human beings want money and the things money will buy. Because their wants and desires are always greater than their means, they will work more for more pay. This theory is the basis for wage payment systems such as piecework, whereby a worker's pay is a direct function of his output. In such a system, a company may calculate that the average worker can turn out nine widgets per hour, and the standard pay is pegged to this output. If a worker exceeds the established standard of production—in other words, if he makes ten widgets per hour when the standard is nine—he gets a bonus. If he only turns out six widgets, on the other hand, his earnings may get docked.

As plausible as it sounds, the economic incentive theory often doesn't seem to work. Studies of work units have repeatedly shown that a group will establish a reasonable rate of production, one that its members can achieve without much difficulty, and most individuals in the group will not exceed it (Homans 1950). Those who produce more are derisively called "rate busters," just as overachievers in school are sometimes scorned as "teacher's pets." The social pressure exerted by the group will usually bring the rate busters into line. Similarly, those who fall behind will be helped by other group members even though it is not in the latter's economic interest to do so.

We have seen this phenomenon before: the creation of a subculture, with its own meanings and practices, that buffers its members from external influences. The same thing that happens in Little League teams and among pot smokers also happens in government bureaucracies and business firms. As with those examples, we can reinterpret organizational subcultures in terms of the cultural diamond. What the external culture creates as a cultural object—an incentive system wherein extra effort "means" more pay—is received by subculture members who have a distinctively different horizon of expectations. For them, the piecework system "means" inequalities within the group that make everyone's life more difficult and that, perhaps, encourage management to raise the standard level of expected production. So the group creates its own cultural object, an amount of output that "means" a reasonable level of production and group harmony. However, the managerial audience for such an output level sees it as indicating workers' recalcitrance and inability to perceive their own economic interests.

Saleswomen in department stores of the early twentieth century, for example, set up their own "counter cultures," whereby they ignored the management incentive system in favor of a "stint," an amount of sales they judged to be a fair day's work (Benson 1986). Each worker monitored her sales, and as she approached her day's stint, she would slacken her selling efforts, perhaps by doing some stock work off the selling floor. Those who had already made their stint for the day would steer sales to those who were behind. Eager beavers who ignored the stint and tried to generate too many sales were labeled "grabbers" and risked social isolation from the department's subculture unless they changed their ways.

Similar accounts of the subversion of managerial objectives by small-group worker cultures occur worldwide. When American firms open operations in other countries, for instance, they often have a problem with nepotism or other forms of particular favoritism. To the American executives, individual employees should be judged and treated on their own merits; showing favoritism is a form of corruption. But to the local employees, favoring someone from your home village (in China), your family (in Italy), or your ethnic group (in Nigeria) by promoting that person over others who are equally qualified means expressing appropriate group solidarity. Similarly, what looks like a bribe to Westerners looks like a legitimate monetary show of respect and gratitude, perhaps delivered before the fact, to many people in developing countries.

If neither sheer economic incentives nor the forceful imposition of bureaucratic rules can be counted on to motivate desired behavior in workers, then, what does work? Organizations have tried a variety of approaches, all involving the attempt to create a certain type of organizational culture in which hard work and commitment to the goals of the organization are part of a meaningful complex of activities and attitudes. Some organizations have applied structural solutions to the problem of bureaucratic alienation—for example, by having few hierarchical steps and by locating decision making at relatively low levels (cf. Burns and Stalker 1961). Instead of a tall, thin organizational chart, these firms have a short, fat one; they typically stress informality and accessibility, encourage innovation, and avoid such status markers as executive cafeterias. The closer the average employees are to the centers of decision and control, managerial reasoning runs, the greater influence they have over outcomes, and the less social distance there is between top management and everyone else, the more "everyone else" will identify with and contribute to achieving the goals of the organization.

A second way of ensuring that employees share the goals of the organization is to foster a preferred type of organizational culture directly by selectivity at the recruitment stage and by active socialization. This strategy is perhaps most notable among Japanese organizations. With sufficient selectivity and intense socialization, even high employee turnover may not disturb the organizational culture (Harrison and Carroll 1991). In her study of flight attendants, Arlie Hochschild (1983) analyzed how airlines promote an organizational culture of caring for customers by (1) selecting flight attendants who are naturally sympathetic, extroverted people and (2) training them to have the proper emotional responses, including feeling genuine concern for the passengers' comfort and genuine satisfaction when a passenger is happy. Hochschild calls this "emotion labor," or the selling of feelings for wages, and she regards it as a little-noticed form of gender discrimination (the airlines and the passengers expect more emotion labor from women than from men). The point here, however, is not whether or not the airlines' recruitment and training are exploitative but simply their success in instilling an organizational culture among their employees.

Structural and cultural attempts to motivate organizational commitment often go hand in hand. Typical of this combination is a high-tech engineering company studied by Gideon Kunda (1992). The firm's organizational structure, all parties agree, is decentralized, vague, and constantly changing. This ambiguous structure is compatible with the firm's strong and oft-asserted culture of self-management (lines of authority aren't important), joint decision making (specified positional responsibilities are beside the point), and profit-oriented creativity (which a heavy-handed bureaucratic structure might stifle). "Tech culture," repeatedly instilled through both organizational rituals and everyday routines, produces employee commitment through normative control, which is an organizational "attempt to elicit and direct the required efforts of members by controlling the underlying experiences, thoughts, and feelings that guide their actions" (11). Normative control, in other words, is what any social group's dominant culture is usually about. This company's managers happen to be exceptionally aware of this fact and thus promote an organizational culture to serve the firm's interests. At the same time, organizations cannot simply impose a culture or set of meanings on their supine members. Organizational cultures are "negotiated orders" that emerge or fail as employees' perspectives interact with the organization's goals (Grant, Morales, and Sallaz 2009).

A third way managers motivate employees is by setting up models of thought and behavior in the form of exemplary actors and organizational stories. Model actors, like Lowenthal's "heroes of production," are both personally honored and presented as worthy of emulation. Hospital walls may display pictures of the "employee of the month," for example, just as real estate firms publicly honor those agents with the highest sales. The functions of honoring the exceptional and rewarding the faithful may contradict each other at times; in a grocery store where there are always several "employees of the week," the honor is devalued and its motivational capacity diminished because of its ubiquity. If it is not overdone, however, the model actor becomes a cultural object, simultaneously a model of good behavior and a model for other members of the organization (Geertz 1973).

The Chinese government has made conspicuous use of exemplary models. In 1963, Lin Biao, chosen by Mao to head the People's Liberation Army, initiated a campaign to remind the PLA's soldiers that their first obligation was service to the Chinese Communist Party (Spence 1990). The campaign centered on the *Diary of Lei Feng,* a posthumously discovered journal in which a young soldier recorded his loyalty to the CCP, Chairman Mao, and his duty. Lei Feng was an army truck driver whose peasant family had suffered cruelly under the pre-revolutionary landlords. Lei Feng's army career exemplified faithful service and sacrifice; he once declared, "I will be a screw that never rusts and will glitter anywhere I am placed." He died as he had lived, run over by a truck while he was helping a comrade. The diary became required reading in Chinese schools, promoted by Mao himself as a model of how the entire nation should "learn from the PLA." In reality, this model actor was a fiction. The fact that Lei Feng's diary had been concocted by the propaganda wing of the PLA did not seem to detract from its exemplary power, however, even if some Chinese suspected the truth. As late as 1987, as the CCP grew increasingly resistant to the pro-democracy movement, the party launched a new campaign honoring the "Lei Feng spirit."

Exemplary actors are one type of model; another comes from organizational stories. Some stories are aimed at outsiders; advertising would be the most familiar case. Organizations use stories to garner support from those upon whom they depend, as when firms that supply organs encourage donations from bereaved families through narratives extolling "the last best gift" (Healy 2006). Others are for organizational insiders. In orientation and training sessions, managers tell anecdotes that illustrate desired organizational values and practices. A well-known case in the sociology of organizations literature is that retold by Chester Barnard (1939) about the telephone operator who stayed at her switchboard even though she knew her mother was trapped in a burning house; Barnard, a former telephone company executive, hastened to point out that the mother survived. Such stories, managers assume, instill organizational loyalty and motivate desired behavior. But as we have seen in our discussion of worker subcultures, another type of story can emerge from interactions among the workers themselves, over and above the accounts sanctioned by management. We need to take a closer look now at how employees make their organizational lives meaningful.

Cultures of Solidarity and Ambiguity

When we hear "organizational culture," we assume an undifferentiated set of symbols and meanings that most of the organization's participants understand and accept. High schools have cultures in this sense, where students and teachers—regardless of their degree of loyalty or alienation—all understand the particular cultural characteristics of their schools. Organizations have such shared cultures as well. Diane Vaughan (1996) has shown, for example, how the culture of NASA (National Aeronautics and Space Administration) tolerated risk taking and cost cutting. Minor, organizationally legitimate decisions to cut corners cumulated, and the 1986 *Challenger* disaster, she suggests, was the result.

Organizational cultures are not necessarily unitary, however. Organizations have subcultures, different cultural worlds experienced by different levels and nodes of the organization—anyone who has ever seen *The Office* recognizes this—and these subcultures may be the basis for conflict. Like all cultures and subcultures, they organization maintain themselves through stories. From her study of Swedish public administration, Barbara Czarniawska (1997) concludes that members use stories to organize their experience, with the key genres being drama and autobiography. People interact with others and make sense of their own lives using these narrative resources. Gary Alan Fine has brilliantly analyzed diverse workplace cultures—from restaurant kitchens (1996) to the National Weather Service (2007)—and shown how professional norms, external audiences (clients, customers, reviewers, "the public"), and the concrete specifics of the job interplay to produce shared occupational micro-cultures.

Having raised the issue of solidarity within organizations, we have moved to a different type of organizational culture, one that emerges rather than one that is constructed more or less intentionally. Groups of people who work (or play) together produce their own subcultures or idiocultures, but this kind of cultural creation through interaction is not entirely independent of the larger social context. In other words, we must not forget the link on our cultural diamond between the social world and the creators of some cultural objects. In any organization, power matters, including symbolic power (Hallett 2003).

For example, even though race, ethnicity, or gender may not "matter" in performing a certain type of job, and although all such categories may be represented in a certain office or factory unit, these characteristics matter powerfully to the outside world. Moreover, members of these groups bring bits and pieces of different cultures with them to work; Puerto Ricans, on average, have knowledge of common friends, relatives, and institutions that Mexican Americans don't share. For this reason, worker subcultures may break down along ethnic or gender lines. Managers, who hold the symbolic power to "explain things" (Hallett 2003), try to discourage this form of partition because it works against functional equivalence. From a boss's point of view, a trained female African American should be the same as a trained male Samoan, and either one should be capable of task assignments without regard to ascribed characteristics. Cultural affinities are strongly felt, however, and people are drawn to other people who share their meaning systems. Organizational symbolic power can only go so far when it runs into other powerful symbols that come from outside the organization.

Perhaps the most influential division that affects the emergence of subgroups is that between labor and management. Here, most firms and organizations draw clear distinctions, as with soldiers and officers in the Army. Usually there are a few intermediate or bridging positions, such as the noncommissioned officers or foremen in a plant, and these positions may be unusually stressful because of divided loyalties; incumbents have often "risen from the ranks" yet no longer share solidarity with those whom they now supervise. The placement of most members of an organization, however, is unambiguous. Symbolism reinforces the divide: the officer's club, the executive cafeteria, the faculty lounge. Practical distinctions abound as well; workers are paid an hourly wage and management earns a monthly salary, for example, or workers are often unionized and managers rarely are.

How does the labor/management divide affect subcultures within an organization? On the one hand, the sharp class consciousness that Marx envisioned does not seem to apply in many places. In the United States, most working people view themselves as "middle class" regardless of their position, whereas in China a similarly placed person might well define himself as "a worker" or one of "the people." In a homogeneous society such as Japan, company unions and worker-manager socializing bridges the gap, whereas in a heterogeneous society such as Nigeria, ethnicity both bridges the gap and works against solidarity at either the labor or management level.

Because Marxian class consciousness seems to represent a nineteenth-century European model that has grown less relevant over time, some sociologists have concluded that class solidarities themselves are irrelevant to organizational analysis. In American firms, so the argument goes, workers are individualistic, seeking their own personal advancement and comfort. Subgroups may emerge to curb and channel individualism, but they are neither class based nor devoted to pursuing class interests. In his study of instances where worker solidarity did emerge in American firms, Rick Fantasia (1988) showed that class consciousness is neither irrelevant nor unproblematically given but instead is a cognitive frame that emerges during certain labor/management struggles. "Cultures of solidarity" arise in times of organizational crisis, such as a strike or layoff, when systems of meaning and action among the workers oppose the dominant regime within the organization. Not synonymous with unions, "cultures of solidarity are more or less bounded groupings that may or may not develop a clear organizational identity and structure, but represent the active expression of worker solidarity within an industrial system and a society hostile to it" (19). Although a high level of class consciousness is not always present, conflict and consciousness do emerge under certain specific conditions within an organization, and the workers' solidarities that result are likely to persist well after the conflict that initiated them.

Fantasia analyzed three emerging cultures of solidarity. One of his cases was the mobilization and collective action carried out by nurses and other women workers in a Vermont hospital. For a decade and more, nurses had labored under a contradiction: The greater need for them to acquire specialized technical skills had been offset by cost-cutting measures that appeared to denigrate these skills. The nurses experienced simultaneous professionalization and proletarianization, and many felt that the demand for greater technical skill, coupled with the demand that they care for an increasing number of patients, resulted in their inability to do their jobs properly. Other employees, such as housekeeping and cafeteria workers, were disgruntled over low pay levels and blocked opportunities. Conditions were ripe for unionization. Ironically, management recognized this fact and sought to ward off labor organization through a worker/management policy advisory committee. When a new hospital administrator, concerned that the committee was developing into a collective bargaining vehicle, abolished it, the workers were affronted, and the idea of some form of collective representation in opposition to the administration became firmly planted. In this promising context, representatives of the National Union of Hospital and Health Care Employees began working to organize the hospital in 1981.

The following months saw a series of actions and reactions as management and workers responded to one another with hardening lines of division and, at least on the workers' part, a growing solidarity that fed on its own successes and failures. Management initiated "one-on-ones" in which supervisors attempted to dissuade undecided workers from supporting the union;

pro-union workers responded by intruding on these conferences, thereby modifying the impact of the confrontation with authority. Union supporters tried to exhort fellow workers to join their side; management responded by keeping a close eye on pro-union leaders and preventing them from holding union-related discussions on the job. In such an atmosphere, class consciousness did indeed emerge and permeated not only the hospital (in the final election, the union was voted in) but also the homes of many workers, where traditional sexual divisions of labor often had to be modified in light of the long hours required by the wife's organizing activities. Husbands who were themselves union members proved especially supportive because they shared a common set of meanings with their wives.

Research like Fantasia's shows how a workers' culture can emerge. But what about a managerial culture? Do the upper echelons of an organization simply represent the dominant national culture, or is there a distinct culture of managers and owners representing the elite, the bourgeoisie? Max Weber suggested "both of the above." Attitudes toward the link between hard work and worldly success (the latter being a token of heavenly success) persisted long after their basis in religious belief had atrophied. Because these attitudes were held by the dominant middle class—and had, in fact, assisted in its rise—they tended toward cultural domination, as a perusal of nineteenth-century schoolbooks with their penny-saved-is-a-penny-earned maxims made clear. Until well into the twentieth century, the link between hard work and success, and between the success of a firm and the prosperity of the social order ("What's good for General Motors is good for the U.S.A."), was confidently upheld by the business class and was little questioned by everyone else.

No one believes in these links anymore, least of all managers in business, contends Robert Jackall (1988). Instead, managers attempt to negotiate their way through "moral mazes" where success is more a function of propitious alliances and avoiding blame than hard work or productivity and where managers take their ethical bearings not from an internal moral code but from what their boss wants and what influences seem to be currently ascendant— "looking up and looking around," Jackall calls it. In the upper levels of corporate culture, a bureaucratic ethic has replaced Weber's Protestant ethic, with the result that a firm's contribution to social welfare is a public relations problem. This managerial subculture upholds an increasing abstraction of organizational functions and a "psychic asceticism" whereby the manager's rationalized self becomes a tool for advancement in his work life that is increasingly removed from home or extra-work relationships.

So far we have looked at two models of organizational culture, one emphasizing consensus, the other cleavage. In the *consensus model,* shared goals and values within an organization are the norm, and dissidence is a problem requiring correction. This model, which assumes a single organizational culture, is essentially functionalist. In the *cleavage model,* groups within an organization have different interests; the classic fault line falls between labor and management, but gender, ethnicity, or organizational location (e.g., engineering vs. marketing) can give rise to comparable cultures of solidarity. These differing interests predictably generate intraorganization conflict. The cleavage model, rooted in Marxism and other conflict sociologies, sees apparent consensus as a problem because it constitutes the subordination of group interests under the dominant ideology of the capitalist class.

Joanne Martin (1992) has pointed out a third model, one she labels "fragmentation," that questions both the harmony of the consensus model ("integration," in Martin's terms) and the stability and predictability of the cleavage model ("differentiation"). In the fragmentation model, organizations are riddled with ambiguity, and people hold multiple perspectives. A single person in an organization is not so much an organizational actor (an IBM man) or a member of a salient group (an engineer) as he is a node of intersection of various groups, categories, and affinities (a male Korean American Presbyterian engineer who works for IBM, has a large family, and is politically liberal). Successive issues will activate different identities. A dispute over a new product introduction may find him allied with other engineers, all advocating moving slowly and getting all of the technological bugs worked out, against the marketing department's eagerness to get the product into the field; on the question of company-provided child care, on the other hand, he may be oriented according to his family interests and liberal leanings; and if IBM suddenly loses market share, he may hunker down as a loyal company man and accept a freeze in pay. This being the case, the organizational analyst, rather than looking for a single organizational culture or for conflicting subcultures, should look for the types of issues that call up different meaning systems. Indeed, Martin urges the analyst to adopt all three perspectives, at least provisionally, for a richer understanding of how cultural processes—people making meanings—influence organizational outcomes.

Organizations in Cultural Contexts

We have been looking at internal organizational cultures from the walls in, so to speak. Now let's look from the walls out. What is the relationship between an organization—a business firm, a school, a government bureaucracy—and the cultural context in which it operates?

In this area of research, the oscillating emphasis between culture and structure parallels the pattern we have seen before. Sociological theories of bureaucracy, especially that of Max Weber, posited that organizations in modern societies converge toward a single highly efficient model: a rationalized bureaucratic structure of positions having clear lines of authority, functional specialization, and a separation of the personal from the bureaucratic. In other words, from an employee's point of view, you know who your boss is, you know what your job is, and your private life is separate from your work life (e.g., you don't own your desk). This is the structure represented by the typical organizational chart of a firm or a government bureau (Weber himself used the Prussian army as his model).

During the 1950s and 1960s, people who studied organizations became increasingly impressed with the variations in this bureaucratic pattern from place to place. Accounting for such differences produced what we might call "national character" accounts, which had as their premise that different societies produced systematic deviations from the Weberian model even though such distinctive bureaucratic forms might impede organizational efficiency. Convergence toward a rationalized bureaucratic norm, what Weber referred to as the "iron cage," was not about to happen across cultures. In a classic study of this type, French sociologist Michel Crozier (1964) revealed that firms in his country proliferated formal rules and exquisite functional distinctions of the "tightening-that-screw-is-not-in-my-job-description" sort—a bureaucratic inflexibility that was often at odds with the organizational goal of getting the job done. Crozier argued that French culture was highly individualistic and that the French had an aversion to personal dependency relations on the job. Thus, the excessive rules and rigidities, although bureaucratically irrational, were culturally rational in minimizing managerial discretion and employee dependency. In other words, French culture valued autonomy over productivity, and French organizations reflected this value.

Such national culture studies never entirely went out of fashion, in part because Americans and Europeans continued to be fascinated by Japanese forms of business organization, so different and so infuriatingly successful. But the emphasis on structural analysis that generally prevailed from the late 1960s through the early 1980s combined with a certain unease over national culture models, which seemed both to imply that less-developed societies suffered from an inferior culture and to import Eurocentric assumptions where they didn't belong. Even though this line of research did not die out, for some time it was dormant.

By the mid-1980s, the interest in the relationship between organizations and their surrounding cultures came roaring back. The globalization of the economy was the principal reason for this development. Many companies that had formerly been exclusively American or European extended their reach globally, with respect to finance, production, and/or markets. This rapid expansion across national boundaries meant that individual firms, some for the first time, were concerned with understanding cultural differences. The continued success of Japan now was joined with the aggressive "Four Little Dragons" (Taiwan, South Korea, Singapore, and Hong Kong) and new players such as Mexico and Brazil in reshaping the global economy and the way Westerners conceived it. Finally, new theoretical moves within the social sciences were bridging the culture-structure gap, rendering work that explored their mutual influence both plausible and even fashionable.

James Lincoln and Arne Kalleberg's research (1990) offers a good example of the new interest in the interaction of structure and culture to produce organizational outcomes. Lincoln and Kalleberg began by observing that American business managers and scholars, intrigued by the success of Japanese management techniques, continue to wonder which of these techniques might be successfully imported. From surveys of matched firms in the United States and Japan, Lincoln and Kalleberg set out to compare structural versus cultural explanations for differences in worker commitment to firms and in job satisfaction. They labeled as "structural theory" the view that welfare corporatism, widely practiced by Japanese firms, accounts for differences in commitment and job satisfaction; welfare corporatism entailed job security, labor-management cooperation, decentralized decision making with a high degree of worker participation, and corporate sponsorship of employee welfare benefits and social activities. What they called "cultural theory," on the other hand, suggested that national differences in workers' values accounted for national differences in commitment and job satisfaction. The structuralist position implies that welfare corporatism increases worker commitment and satisfaction whenever it is applied; Japanese firms, especially those of the core industries, tend to have more of it, but the same principles would be beneficial anywhere. A strictly "culturalist" (their term) approach, on the other hand, would maintain that the Japanese organizational forms were suited to Japanese culture, which valued the collectivity over the individual, cooperation, and a dependent personal relationship between employees and supervisors (the exact opposite of French values, according to Crozier); according to this view, these forms would not be as successful if exported to other cultures.

Meticulous comparisons both supported the general thrust of the welfare corporatist hypothesis, which the authors initially favored, and suggested persistent cultural differences. As expected, work commitment was higher

among the Japanese workers than among the Americans, but—surprisingly—
actual job satisfaction was lower. As expected, the quality of the relationships
between workers and their coworkers and supervisors was positively associated with commitment and satisfaction, but friendships had no bearing on
these outcomes. (Quality of the relationship was measured by such questions
as "How satisfied are you with your supervisor?" whereas friendship was
measured by such questions as "How often do you get together with your
supervisor outside of work?") In the United States, this finding was not
surprising—outside get-togethers are not regarded as having much bearing
on organizational commitment but instead are considered matters of personal
choice. Japan, however, is noted for company social functions and the common pattern in which supervisors and employees go out drinking or to a
restaurant, all of which the company sponsors and encourages. Although we
might assume that such activities are assiduously cultivated by the Japanese
firms because they bind the employees to the organization, such is not the
case. It appears that expectations are different; Japanese worker-manager
social contacts are routine and therefore are regarded as no big deal, whereas
American workers and managers socialize within their own groups but not
with each other (so worker get-togethers could be occasions for bitching
about the boss!). In neither culture is the presence or absence of such friendships seen as affecting life on the job.

More generally, the two countries show distinct differences in work values.
The Japanese favor close relations with supervisors, working in groups, and a
variety of reciprocal ties; the Americans prefer independence in all of these
areas. These differences affect work attitudes, but they do not mediate the effect
of the job variables associated with the welfare corporatist hypothesis; such
things as employee participation in decision making raise commitment inde-
pendently of worker values. In other words, although distinct cultural differences affect workers' relations to the firm, at the same time the participatory
style of welfare corporatism can produce benefits of commitment and satisfaction in any cultural setting. Once again we see that posing the culture-versus-
structure explanation in either/or terms belies the complexities of real social
life.

New institutionalism directly addresses the interpenetration of culture
and structure (Powell and DiMaggio 1992). New institutionalist thinking
regards organizations not as tightly integrated bureaucracies mobilized to
pursue certain goals but as loosely connected assemblages of people, structures, and systems (Meyer and Rowan 1977). Moreover, instead of being
organized according to a single, rational efficiency principle, organizations
and their subunits tend to conform to their institutional contexts. For
example, American schools engage in certain symbolic rituals such as the

preparation of report cards (cultural objects) because, although learning and educational progress are notoriously hard to measure, the institutional context in which schools find themselves expects organizations to show a bottom line. Report cards or an emphasis on test scores are ways that the school establishes "institutional isomorphism" with its context; making up the report card represents a "ritual of good faith" prepared for the external audience (parents, school boards, politicians) and is a way of turning aside a more critical inspection of what might really be going on in the school. At the level of colleges and universities it is "the rankings," especially in *U.S. News and World Report,* that discipline the system toward a reactive conformity (Espeland and Sauder 2007).

Another type of institutional fit, this one internal, is that between an organizations ideology and its structure. Wilde (2007) examines Vatican II as a social movement in order to explain its progressive results, results such as changing the Mass from Latin to spoken languages and having priests face the congregation, that were unexpected by everyone. She found that the progressives did not have much in terms of resources or power, but they did have an organizational model of "collegiality" whereby their inclusive, egalitarian ideology supported the horizontal Episcopal Conferences that allowed them to communicate and operate effectively, while the conservatives' model of hierarchical top-down authority, parallel to their theology of "God orders and humans obey," paralyzed them in struggles over church practices.

Given a certain plasticity of structure, organizations and organizational relationships match and mirror their institutional contexts. This may be particularly true of such organizations as school, church, and government bureaucracies, for which there is no clear "bottom line," but it applies to business firms as well. Moreover, cross-cultural organizational comparisons can readily benefit from a new institutionalist approach. A team of organizational sociologists (Orrù, Biggart, and Hamilton 1991) compared the structures of business enterprise groups (stable aggregates of firms related by shared ownership or management, mutual financial transactions, and/or other forms of interdependency) in Japan and two of the "Little Dragons"—Taiwan and South Korea. All three countries featured stable enterprise groups having no exact counterparts in the United States. But the structures of enterprise groups differ among the three countries. Japan's groups involve stable, noncompeting horizontal links, "a community of equals" intersected by some vertical, hierarchical links. South Korea, in contrast, has fewer horizontal links; its enterprise groups are centralized outgrowths of a founding patriarch's firm and exhibit "vertical domination." Taiwan is different still; its enterprise groups are small, less central, and both controlled and financed by single families. These different organizational patterns, the authors contended, are isomorphic with other enterprise groups and other institutions within the same society. They represent different cultural principles—communitarianism in Japan, patrimonialism in South Korea, and familialism in Taiwan—that are manifest in a variety of institutional settings. This kind of comparison suggests how new institutionalist thinking can reveal connections between national or local culture on the one hand and organizational structure on the other.

Given the global orientation of this book, it is appropriate that we have been considering work that compares organizational operations cross-nationally. At the same time, we need to remember that all organizations must operate in an external cultural context, and the relationship between organization and context is never simple.

Consider the connection between church and community. Most people assume that churches are "good for" their communities. In the poor areas of American cities, the presence of churches—storefront churches and the more substantial kind—suggests stability, a bulwark against chaos, and a source of resources and positive role models for the church's neighbors. Omar McRoberts (2003), who has studied inner-city churches in Boston, finds this popular conception to be inaccurate. The churches he studied, mainly African American and West Indian, moved around a lot, finding storefronts and halls in buildings that could no longer attract commercial tenants. Their congregations commuted to wherever the church happened to be located. Often the parishioners were very loyal to their church, its pastor, or its ethnic complexion. What they weren't loyal to was the neighborhood, for they just passed through, coming to services but having virtually no other contact with the community. Nor were the pastors or church officials focused on the neighborhood and its needs; they tended to think in universal terms (bringing all people to the word of God) and/or in terms of the needs of the parishioners. So most of these churches made little effort to adapt to, or improve, their communities.

Many organizations don't have this option of simply ignoring the context in which they operate. For profit-oriented firms or NGOs, such adaptation is essential to their missions. Organizations have to figure out their external contexts, and the more these differ from the cultural assumptions built into the organization, the trickier this can get. In the next section we will look at some of the ways organizations try to fit into their cultural contexts.

Working Across Cultures

It is one thing to recognize that cultural differences have some effect on "getting it done" and that planners or business managers must employ different organizational forms and incentives in Accra than they do in Los Angeles. Comparative research can enable the manager or program implementer trying to transact business in a foreign culture to proceed circumspectly and effectively. To an ever-increasing extent, however, organizational goals involve actively synchronizing operations within a variety of cultures. This is as true for the firm in Los Angeles trying to set up incentives for its multilingual workforce as for the transnational firm trying to coordinate its production flow in six different countries. Such transactions involve recognition of and negotiation with multiple cultural systems.

One way of working in various cultural contexts is to hold on to your main mission while adapting on the minor issues. McDonald's' pattern of quick in-and-out customers might seem inviolable, but since the company's goal is to sell food and not to shuffle people, it can adjust to the local culture so long as its mission is not jeopardized. In Chinese cities, McDonald's offers a safe and clean place for grandmothers to spend the day while waiting for their grandchildren to get out of school (Watson 1997). They sit in McDonald's, chatting and nursing cups of tea. Though this is not especially profitable, McDonald's managers recognize that allowing these women to sit for hours means that hoards of hungry kids—consumers of the future as well as the present—will pour in at the end of the school day. It's both culturally sensitive and shrewd from a business standpoint to let the grandmothers alone.

While selling Big Macs in China is a one-way cultural adaptation where an American firm adjusts its practices to the local context, sometimes the adaptation is two-way and ongoing. In a remarkable study that asks how Israelis and Arabs can work together at a multinational production site where the managers are both colleagues and, at times, enemies, Mizrachi, Drori, and Anspach (2007) conducted two years of ethnographic study—in Arabic, English, and Hebrew—of an Israeli textile company's Israeli and Jordanian managers running three plants in Jordan. The study constituted a natural experiment in that it occurred during both a period of normalization of relations between Israel and the Arab world (1998 to 2000) and a period of conflict (late 2000 following the Intifada El-Aqsa [Palestinian Uprising]). They found that during the normalization period, "Jordanian managers relied on normative modes of trust [I trust this guy because I know him], whereas Israelis used paternalistic and calculative strategies [I trust this guy insofar as he is following the rules]" (156). During the phase of political unrest this pattern reversed, with Israelis turning to normative trust relations (as one Israeli manager put it when talking about his Jordanian colleagues, "I trust them on the basis of our personal friendship, and I know that they won't let me down") while the Jordanians turned to calculative trust (as one put it, "We are working now according to the book"). Mizrachi, Drori, and Anspach argue that trust has three dimensions: (1) agency (the managers were active manipulators of the forms and symbols of trust), (2) culture (the managers drew from complex repertoires rather than being bound by any strict set of cultural schemas), and (3) political context (the political meaning of trust relations changed according to the context, and managers adjusted their behavior in light of the shifting situation).

The pitfalls for organizations attempting to juggle cultural multiplicity are legion. Everyone has heard, for example, of the disastrous General Motors promotion of its Chevy Nova in Mexico, in which no one had pointed out that, in Spanish, *No va* means "It doesn't go." The problems involved go deeper than understanding a simple relationship between words and what they refer to, however. If culture involves shared meanings, moving in different cultures requires understanding different systems of meaning and the assumptions, principles, and nuances that any particular cultural object may evoke in these systems.

In his aptly titled book *Cultures in Conflict,* Stanley Heginbotham (1975) set out a memorable case of how lack of cultural coordination can undermine the most rationally conceived program. His subject was the implementation of the agricultural Green Revolution, specifically a high-yield variety of rice, in India. The plan was simple: Trained village workers called *Gram Sevaks*, under central coordination from New Delhi, were to serve as onsite agricultural extension officers whose job was to convince the local farmers to try the new rice, along with new fertilizers and other farming techniques promoted by Green Revolution advocates. The problems came from the fact that four cultures and, hence, four distinct ways of thinking were engaged in the plan's implementation. Many of the higher-level agricultural extension officers (AEOs) had been trained at such places as the University of Iowa and were aglow with American theories of community development and local empowerment. A Gandhian culture of individual responsibility animated some of the local extension workers. The Indian bureaucracy, however, still followed the British colonial model of tight central control and elaborated paper passing, without much concern for the end results as long as the proper routines were carried out. The peasant farmers, meanwhile, operated under yet a fourth cultural model, that of traditional dharma, which emphasized doing one's duty and submitting to one's fate. Thus, the people responsible for implementing the program held four cognitive models—community development, Gandhian, colonial bureaucratic, and dharmaic. The first two models emphasized change and flexibility in order to meet specific goals; the second two stressed stability and following the correct procedure regardless of the consequences.

The results were predictably disastrous. Extension agents gave enthusiastic speeches about crop rotation to patient farmers who smiled and paid no attention, assuming the agents were simply performing some obscure duty. Bureaucrats sought to meet quotas on seed distribution without expressing any great interest in whether the seeds were actually planted. And the Gram Sevaks and extension officers improvised like crazy. In the case of "green manure"—a fast-growing, high-foliage crop that farmers were to plant when the fields would otherwise be fallow and then plow under to enrich the soil—most farmers were not persuaded by the scientific rationale of soil improvement. To them, "green manure" sounded like a waste of time and energy. The extension officers had quotas of green manure seed distribution to fill, however—quotas established by the bureaucrats in New Delhi. So, the AEOs and the Gram Sevaks induced the farmers to take the green manure seeds, which they did not want, in return for being able to buy cheap fertilizer, which they did. Heginbotham reported,

> As a result of such a quid pro quo, a farmer might count himself fortunate to have obtained a permit to buy fertilizer at a subsidized rate and an AEO would be relieved to have made progress toward fulfilling his target for the sale of green manure seeds nobody wanted. Neither would be particularly disturbed by the fact that the farmer would simply throw out the seeds. (169)

Given the pitfalls of cultures in conflict, and given the increasing necessity for individuals and organizations to work in and with a variety of cultures, what help can cultural sociology offer? At the most basic level, it can focus attention on the fact that even a tangible, physical "thing" like fertilizer is a cultural object. As such, it is a bearer of meaning, but its meanings vary with the human beings—producers and recipients—who interact with it. Although everyone agrees that green manure is a seed for a type of plant, they most definitely do not agree about what it represents as a cultural object. Green manure was produced by Western scientists, to whom it meant one shot fired in a revolution in Third World agriculture. But it also meant low-cost organic fertilizers to the Gram Sevaks, more work to the farmer, and a means of furthering his civil service career to the bureaucrat. Once more we are reminded that meanings are not implanted in a cultural object; they are constructed by those human beings who interact with the object. An astute, culturally aware member of the implementation team might have anticipated some of these different meaning constructions and made provision for them.

The need to be alert to multiple meanings and culturally based nuances carries over to intangible cultural objects such as words. Considerable intercultural confusion comes from translations that, though accurate on a word-to-word basis, do not capture the nimbus of implications with which a culture surrounds a word. For example, President Clinton once complained that the Japanese say yes when they mean no. A writer familiar with both cultures pointed out that *hai,* the Japanese equivalent of yes, can mean that the speaker has heard you and is weighing a reply or that the speaker understands your request and would like to accommodate you but unfortunately cannot (Hatsumi 1993). A Japanese speaker is not intending to be deceitful in such "yes" responses, merely polite. Nigerians behave similarly when they have bad news to report. Because breaking bad news too abruptly is considered insensitive, if a Nigerian has news that the other party wants—the answer to a question such as "Is he dead?" or "Did the deal go through?"—he will often equivocate for some time, saying, "Things are well" or "The story is a complicated one," before telling the painful truth. Outsiders who understand such cultural patterns can avoid either misinterpreting the response or drawing the mistaken conclusion that the party with whom they are interacting is a liar.

The multiple interpretations of intangible cultural objects can be understood through the cultural diamond framework. A Japanese produces a *hai* as a cultural object; his period eye, his collective consciousness, imbues his *hai* with a set of meanings and implications. A Japanese recipient, coming from the same social world, would have no trouble comprehending his meaning. But an American, coming from a social world that overlaps but is not identical to that of the Japanese, has a different horizon of expectations. She constructs different meanings out of the cultural object *hai,* especially if it has been translated as a simple yes. A general rule might be this: In any situation wherein the creator of a cultural object and its receiver come from different cultures, an individual or organization must be alert at all times to the possibility of different meaning constructions, for these nonequivalent meanings may have significant consequences for "getting things done."

SUMMARY

The international flows of people, goods, images, and information mean that virtually every organization must contend with cultural multiplicity. From the viewpoint of a business firm, a government agency, or another organization trying to get something done, multiple cultures are always potentially cultures in conflict. A sociological understanding of cultures and how they operate will help predict areas of conflict, reduce the conflict if possible, and manage it when it does arise. In this chapter, we have considered the impact of culture on organizations at a number of levels:

1. *Culture and motivation.* Organizations need to motivate their employees to behave in ways beneficial to the organization's goals. Both internal subcultures of work groups and external cultural influences can interfere with this process by motivating different types of behavior. Management needs to create an organizational culture using some combination of structural means, recruitment, socialization, rituals, model actors, and illuminating stories so that the desired behavior becomes meaningful and satisfying to the employees.

2. *Organizational subcultures.* In spite of managerial efforts to exert normative control by creating an organizational culture, subcultures emerge that to some extent resist the dominant culture. Such subcultures and the stories they tell often reproduce social cleavages of class, ethnicity, and gender. Within a particular organization, each subculture is both a meaning-making unit, such as Fantasia's nurses, and a medium through which meanings from the external culture find expression and enactment. If we consider a new product, program, or policy as a cultural object, we can anticipate some of the different meanings that object will have for different groups and their implications for attitudes and behavior.

3. *Cross-cultural differences.* People's ways of thinking and acting vary enormously from place to place, and much scholarly ink has been spilled trying to assess the impact these variations have on organizational effectiveness. In the past, a culturalist model, which claimed that national or local cultural values explained organizational differences, opposed a structuralist model, which contended that similar organizational structures produced similar consequences regardless of culture. Recent thinking has moved beyond the either/or terms of these two models to explain how culture influences structure and how structures are interpreted through cultures.

4. *Organizations in multicultural environments.* Organizations that operate in more than one country or involve several cultural groups in a single country face multiple systems of meaning creation. Although managers cannot control the cognitive frames that will make their organization's products and programs meaningful in different cultures, they can first recognize this lack of control rather than assume that the characteristics and meanings of something like a Big Mac are transparent and unitary. Second, managers can anticipate when meaning construction will seriously challenge the goals of the organization and act in light of this understanding.

All such levels of cultural contention suggest that success in a firm, an NGO, or a government bureaucracy may rest as much on cultural sensitivity and flexibility as it does on the mastery of finance and law.

QUESTIONS FOR STUDY AND DISCUSSION

1. Describe the culture of an organization where you have worked. What are the stories and symbols that everyone who works there knows? What are the subcultures, and what forms of conflict take place between them? How do the heads of the organization use symbolic power to motivate people?

2. Discuss the question of how culture does and does not cross organizational boundaries. If people come into an organization with certain values and beliefs based on their external identities and networks, to what extent can an organization modify these to meet its goals? To what extent *should* it?

3. Imagine that you represent a Western firm that is doing business in a non-Western country that has very different cultural assumptions. Some of these assumptions involve forms of discrimination (e.g., against women or religious minorities) that would not be tolerated in the firm's home country. Local managers say that in order not to alienate local suppliers and customers, these local customs must be followed. Drawing on your knowledge of the relationship between organizations and culture, how would you handle this situation?

RECOMMENDED FOR FURTHER READING

Fantasia, Rick. 1988. *Cultures of Solidarity: Consciousness, Action, and Contemporary American Workers.* Berkeley: University of California Press. Fantasia presents rich case studies of the creation and reception of the image of worker solidarity as a cultural object.

Fine, Gary Alan. 2007. *Authors of the Storm: Meteorologists and the Culture of Prediction.* Chicago: University of Chicago Press. Fine shows how weather forecasters occupy a series of intermediary positions—for example, between science and the public—and how the tensions that come from being pulled in multiple directions plus the inherent ambiguity of their work shape an occupational culture.

Hochschild, Arlie Russell. 1983. *The Managed Heart: Commercialization of Human Feeling.* Berkeley: University of California Press. This book discusses how organizations control what Geertz calls the moods and motivations of its employees. Hochschild studied airlines, which train flight attendants to be nice, and collection agencies, which use similar techniques to train their employees to be mean.

Kunda, Gideon. 1992. *Engineering Culture: Control and Commitment in a High Tech Organization*. Philadelphia: Temple University Press. From ethnographic fieldwork, Kunda depicts an organization that is highly aware of its organizational culture and highly skilled at manipulating it.

Ogasawara, Yuko. 1998. *Office Ladies and Salaried Men: Power, Gender, and Work in Japanese Companies*. Berkeley: University of California Press. Ogasawara shows how "office ladies," disadvantaged by their gender and their exclusion from lifetime employment, develop cultural repertoires to resist the male domination and exert control despite their lowly official status.

7

Culture and Connection

People have become linked together at an accelerating rate—economically, politically, socially, and culturally—throughout the twentieth century and into the twenty-first. Today, only a few isolated groups, deep in the disappearing rain forests or concealed in increasingly accessible mountain strongholds, are unaware of their connections with the rest of humanity. And even they are profoundly affected by these unseen connections. Pollution reaches them; national governments claim them; diseases jump geographic barriers to infect them; concerned citizens of the developed world—connected with one another through social media, texting, e-mail, frequent flying, Skype, conferences real or virtual, online forums—debate issues relating to their preservation and survival. Geographically remote people become the cultural objects of strangers from another world.

If the world is becoming increasingly interconnected, are we moving toward a single homogeneous culture, what Marshall McLuhan once called a "global village"? Or does greater connection magnify the differences among societies? Like a cable television system that is accessible to every household but has a different channel for every conceivable taste, does the universal reach of the electronic media also generate a proliferation of fine distinctions and particularized local cultures? Paradoxically, both seem to be happening. Globalization is exerting simultaneous pressures toward unity and fragmentation. In fact, the image of cultural unity versus diversity may be wrong in the Internet age when social action takes place not though fixed groups but through mutable, shifting networks.

In this chapter, we consider the implications the new information technology and its offspring globalization are having for culture and cultural meanings. We look at the relationship between culture, technology, and community in an effort to identify how changes in communication technologies have changed the nature of culture and how different cultural technologies have affected human communities and the very idea of community. We move from oral storytelling around the fire to literacy and then to the present era of electronic communications. Finally, returning to culture as the bearer of meanings, we consider the future of meaning in a global culture.

Media Revolutions and Cultural Communities

Like culture, the word *community* has a number of meanings for sociologists, but two are paramount: *community as a territorial concept* and *community as a relational concept*. In the first sense, a community is something we can locate on a map. It has spatial properties: borders, a center, and outskirts. It also has a name and a set of symbols associated with it. Residents of Chicago know where the South Side, Lincoln Park, and Andersonville are; they know the borders, the landmarks, and the sorts of people found in each. Communities are meaningful cultural objects to their residents and to many outsiders as well.

Community in its second, relational sense refers to people who are tied together by webs of communication, friendship, association, or mutual support. They may be scattered geographically, and they may not even know one another, but they constitute a meaningful, self-aware collectivity. Thus, it makes sense to speak of the Jewish community, the gay community, or the academic community. In the past, of course, there was considerable overlap between territorial and relational types of community. People who lived in the same town or village were also linked with one another through friendship, kinship, trade, shared beliefs, and a common set of symbols. But in an increasingly mobile and highly differentiated society, there is less and less identity between the two. Moreover, the boundaries are blurry. Facebook. com "friends" are linked through a network, and they may know a great deal about one another, but their actual interactions may be few and their shared culture minimal. Such a social network constitutes a relationship, to be sure, but just barely a community.

Whether a community is bound by geography or network links, members are united, at least to some extent, by culture. This does not imply that all community members share in an undifferentiated collective consciousness but simply that some considerable numbers of shared meanings are recognized by the members of any collectivity we would call a community. A group of people waiting for a light to change does not constitute a community; these people share some signs (they all know that red means stop) but not necessarily much else. Members of the gay community, the Jewish community, or the South Side community, on the other hand, share experiences, meanings, ways of thinking and acting, beliefs, and cultural objects. Vaisey (2007) finds this shared moral order to be fundamental for producing people's sense of belonging to a community; structural factors (interaction, authority, investments) are not enough to produce a sense of what he calls the "we-feeling." Culture can bind a community for centuries even when social forces have scattered or suppressed its members; the history of the Jews or the Gypsies or the ethnic minorities under the Soviet Union gives strong evidence of this.

If we accept this Durkheimian argument that culture is the tie that binds, we must ask: What happens to community in times of cultural revolution? This question is particularly pressing today, for we are in the midst of such a revolution: the explosive growth in global electronic information and communication technologies (ICTs for short). This is the third major media revolution, with the phonetic alphabet being the first and printing the second. Like the ICT revolution now under way, each of these earlier revolutions profoundly affected human communities.

Let us trace briefly the evolution of communications media and their impact. To do this, we must start at the beginning, before the technologies of literacy appeared, when culture was transmitted largely by people talking with one another.

Oral Cultures

For most of its history, humankind has lived in a strictly oral culture. Oral cultures, in which communication depends on face-to-face interaction, are characterized by widely shared knowledge throughout the community. Such cultures demand prodigious feats of memorization from a few memory specialists, who serve as repositories of group history and genealogy, but most knowledge is held in common and constantly reiterated. From this comes two more characteristics of oral cultures: first, the widespread use of proverbs (a residual is still found in African literature); second, the flourishing of epic poetry, for shared wisdom can be encoded in poetic rhythms and figures of speech as an aid to memory.

In oral cultures, vocabularies tended toward the concrete. They were elaborate where, and only where, they needed to be; because there were no dictionaries to "store" words, infrequently used words would simply drop out of the discourse. Similarly, history—as stored in human memory—would be modified to serve present needs. Early in the twentieth century, British colonialists wrote down that the Gonja of northern Ghana had seven chiefdoms; the Gonja said this was a legacy of Ndewura Jakpa, the founder of their state, who had seven sons. Sixty years later, when two of the political divisions had disappeared, the Gonja reported that Jakpa had five sons. In oral societies, "myth and history merge into one" (Goody and Watt 1963:311).

What type of community does oral culture support? Durkheim described it well: a small-scale, undifferentiated social order in which people think, do, and believe much the same things. In such communities, the overlap between an individual's consciousness and the collective consciousness is nearly total. Having little basis for comparing their own group's thinking with any other's, members of such a community would find their own way of life both stable and profoundly normal (as suggested by the common practice premodern groups had of simply calling themselves "the people"). Oral cultural communities are filled with magic, enchanted with mysterious forces and spirits. Because facts and histories lack fixity, the boundaries between reality and unreality are fluid, easily crossed.

Despite the profound changes literacy would bring to human communities, it did not simply sweep away oral culture. To a considerable extent, we still live in an oral world. The cultures of families, friendships, and neighborhoods are primarily oral, which may be why we place such value on letters, photographs, and other documentary traces of these cultures. Because these cultures are in what Cooley (1956) called "primary groups" in which the self is shaped, we can see the continuing power of orality. Moreover, much of the culture of institutions and organizations is oral. Nevertheless, writing and literacy produced revolutionary upheavals in human culture and the communities from which people took their identities. Let's turn now to this first revolution in communications technology.

Written Cultures

Although phonetic writing systems developed in the Near East some 3,000 years ago (Goody and Watt 1963), other and earlier forms of writing had effected their own social consequences. A number of non-phonetic writing systems—the Sumerian, the Egyptian, the Chinese—had already emerged in the ancient world in which signs stood for particular words, more or less on a one-to-one basis. Such systems are extremely complex, for literate people in these cultures must know thousands of signs in order to have a reading capacity that matches their spoken vocabulary. Classical Chinese, for example, has some 50,000 characters and takes about twenty years to learn. The result was that only a very small group of specialists, the religious or governmental elite, were literate in that society.

Phonetic alphabets, in which characters represent sounds rather than words or concepts, are far simpler and thus far easier to learn. In Western Europe and the United States, most three-year-olds can rattle off the 26 letters of our Roman alphabet. Such ease in learning encourages the general adoption of writing, especially among commercial classes. Popular literacy may be something of a misnomer—it was first established among the Greeks, but women and slaves were much less likely to be literate than free men—but nevertheless alphabetic scripts made possible a widespread participation in written culture. Literacy on this scale is generally taken as distinguishing modern from premodern societies and, traditionally, sociology from anthropology.

Print Cultures

The second communications revolution occurred in the fifteenth century, when a German printer named Johann Gutenberg invented movable type, which facilitated written communication on a totally different scale from that which handwritten manuscripts could support. The shift from manuscript to print culture democratized literacy in the West and allowed for transmission and comparison of knowledge. In Europe, printing laid the technical basis for the Renaissance (print made classical texts widely available), the Reformation (now people could have and read their own Bibles, rather than having to depend on the interpretations of priests), and the rise of rationalized science (Eisenstein 1979). Print made modernity itself possible. Two intellectual consequences of literacy were the separation of history from myth and the increased individualism based on highly specialized knowledge (Goody and Watt 1963). In literate cultures, people are stratified on the basis of what they have read; academic disciplines and college majors are an obvious example of this kind of specialization.

What was the impact of print and widespread literacy on connections among people? First, literacy made relational communities possible as they had not been before. Because members of relational communities are not in regular face-to-face contact, they need some medium through which they can develop and preserve their sense of connection. The written word was that medium. Clearly, relational communities existed before printing—commercial traders exchanging goods and correspondence along a particular trading route, for example, and political or religious leaders communicating through manuscripts, letters (the Apostle Paul didn't have a printing press but managed to put together a far-flung relational community with impressive staying power), and oral messengers—but printing and the proliferation of written materials allowed ordinary people to be members of any number of relational communities.

Second, printing brought forth an entirely new kind of territorial community, that of the nation. Benedict Anderson ([1983] 1991) showed how national consciousness emerged in Western Europe from the seventeenth-century spread of vernacular languages in printed form, supplanting the former use of Latin as a common language for business and legal, as well as religious, matters. Now it became possible for people to conceive of other people, unseen and unknown, who read the same materials, knew the same things, and shared the same cultural objects. A language community would not have to be territorially connected, of course, but most vernacular languages were; hence, the nation took on a territorial, as well as a linguistic, specificity. New print genres, especially the newspaper and the novel, were both cause and consequence of the spread of nationalism as an idea and of particular national identities.

So the print revolution gave rise to relational communities connected by the written, and especially the published, word, and it gave rise to that very modern form of territorial human organization, the nation-state. Of course, print helped establish and bind together smaller communities as well, for example with local newspapers for territorial communities and mailed newsletters for relational communities. All of this is familiar to us, for print culture has shaped the world in which we live. But what will happen to this familiar world if print is superseded?

ICT Cultures

Electronic communications, including broadcasting, mark the third great revolution in human communications and move us from the modern into the postmodern era. This revolution includes two-way transmission (telegraph, telephone, fax, the Internet), one-way transmission (broadcasting—radio, television; audio- and videocassettes, CDs, MP3s), and participatory new media (the proliferation of social media like Facebook, YouTube, Ratemyprofessor, Yelp, Linkedin, etc., as well as older forms like blogging, chatrooms, and talk shows). All of these technologies have a number of common attributes:

1. They connect people in separate locations, often with no lapse in time. They can reach far greater numbers of people than was feasible with print; e-mail spam, for example, is global in its distribution, with virtually no increased costs for increased numbers of people reached.

2. They allow the raw expression of ideas and emotions, making possible the immediacy and intimacy that had previously occurred only in face-to-face communication. In some respects they exceed what can be conveyed face-to-face, as when the most private acts like sexual activity or giving birth are broadcast over the Internet.

3. They democratize cultural access in spatial and temporal terms. A cultural event such as a concert is no longer fixed to one time and one location; when it is recorded on tape, the receiver can select when and where to listen.

4. They democratize cultural access based on education. Whereas written communications require mastery of a set of skills, many forms of electronic communication—especially television and telephone—require far fewer skills. A two-year-old can "follow" her favorite television program; a functional illiterate can get the news on the radio; an unschooled man can make his views known over the telephone, on a talk show, or through a website.

5. They have a strong impact on language. Print stabilized and nationalized languages; for example the Tuscan dialect, spoken by only a few people, became the foundation of formal Italian because of Dante's *The Divine Comedy*. ICTs both stabilize and destabilize language, spreading certain idioms around the globe while introducing words and shortcuts (e.g., txtng) that abruptly enter the common discourse (Crystal 2008; Menchik and Tian 2008).

The social consequences of electronic media flow from these attributes, often in rather unexpected ways. Because of the breadth of the electronic audience and the speed with which messages may be sent, influencing public opinion through the media has become a key objective of those promoting a certain political or social program. Exiled political leaders use media to encourage and rally their supporters, as Ayatollah Khomeini did with tapes of his addresses. Government officials use the media to sell and justify their actions. The political revolutions in Eastern Europe in which country after country threw off Communist governments were linked by television and fax machines; Lech Walesa, when asked what had caused the collapse of Communism, pointed to a television set (Lippman 1992). Civil rights movement leaders in the late 1950s and 1960s recognized and made effective use of television's capacity to awaken revulsion in viewers, who were moved by images of police dogs attacking unarmed marchers in a way they had not been by years of printed newspaper reports of lynchings and other racial atrocities. As Todd Gitlin (1980) said about the televised anti–Vietnam War movement, "The whole world is watching."

Electronic media increase not only the immediacy of human contacts but also their intimacy. This effect was unanticipated. Claude Fischer's (1992) history of the telephone in America showed that the Bell System initially assumed that its product would be used primarily by firms to conduct business. To everyone's surprise, the fastest growth of telephone subscribers came from private households, especially those of rural women eager to be in touch with relatives and friends. In this sense, the telephone contributed to the preservation of relational communities; social networks, blogs, and e-mail do the same today.

The possibility of immediate and intimate communications has broken down a number of long-standing social barriers (Meyrowitz 1985). Now it is common for lifestyles that were formerly hidden from mainstream view, the subject of rumor but little knowledge, to parade openly and loquaciously on talk shows and the Internet. Now raw, unedited human responses—the politician snarling at reporters after his bill has been defeated, the parents sobbing when their child has been killed in a gang shoot-out—are shared with millions of total strangers. Such direct contact with the personal lives of strangers has contributed to an increasing informality of human relations. Whether or not it has led to greater tolerance, as Matthew Arnold dreamed, is another question, however. Human emotions have become entertainment, as in reality television, and as mass culture theorists predicted, the continued spectacle of suffering may have dulled our sensitivity to it.

The visual representation of starvation offers an example. Probably the first effective use of what might be called the public relations of hunger was mounted by Biafran government officials during the Nigerian civil war of the late 1960s. Pictures of children with the bloated stomachs caused by kwashiorkor, a disease caused by a deficiency in protein, aroused concern and some considerable support for Biafra in Europe and the United States. However, in the 1970s and 1980s, when Africa experienced a series of droughts and war-created famines, images of starving children became common. Advocates for humanitarian interventions like the Save Darfur Coalition (savedarfur.org) must fight against such desensitization.

The third and fourth attributes, the democratizing impact of media, also have had profound social effects. Print tends to segment audiences: Different groups of people read different books. Similarly, the traditional concentration of intellectuals, universities, theaters, cathedrals, and other cultural institutions in a few cities formerly meant that there were cultural centers and peripheries. This is now changing. Huge, widespread, and undifferentiated audiences see the same television programs and YouTube videos.

The flow of new images and ideas is hard to stop, even in a police state or theocracy. Of course, not all electronic messages are directly political or critical, but authoritarian regimes take any images of democracy or gender equality as potentially threatening. Such regimes find it increasingly difficult to intercept foreign cultural messages and control the online communications of their own people—recall the Mubarak government's frantic efforts to shut down the Internet during Egypt's 2011 Arab Spring revolution—though that doesn't stop them from trying, with China being particularly aggressive in this regard (Yang 2009). If communities are bound by cultures, and if national cultures are increasingly penetrated from outside, "global culture" displaces "national culture" to an ever-greater extent. Does this mean the world will soon be one happy community? The Internet, which is regarded by many as the most profound development in the wired world, seems to offer a promise of not community but communities.

The Cultural Impact of the Internet

In Estonia, young men carry swords. Student fraternities use swords in their rituals, and their members can wear these swords in public spaces. Sword carrying may seem like a tradition, invented or otherwise, an odd residual from the past. True enough, but young-men-with-swords is also one of the fruits of the Internet. Estonia has one of the most advanced information systems in the world; some call it E-Stonia. Estonians who never had checkbooks now bank online. Estonians who never had telephones—and most didn't when Soviet control ended in 1991—now use cell phones. And the government set up a website called "Today, I'm Deciding," where citizens voice their views, suggest ideas, and chat. One suggestion that generated online support and eventually succeeded was that the government ease its restrictions on carrying swords in public (Tarm 2003). In this case at least, far from demolishing tradition, the Internet has facilitated it.

So far, this seems to be the common pattern: ICTs have not so much changed cultural practices as reproduced and facilitated them. Groups and nations become networks, and in doing so, they reiterate their cultures and re-forge their connections. Estonians rediscover swords, and dispersed communities rediscover each other. Emigrants from Newfoundland, one study shows, use the Internet to offset the social fragmentation of their diaspora, as they develop new ties, nourish old ties, and rediscover lost ties to confirm their Newfoundland identities when far from home (Hiller and Franz 2004). In some cases the Internet creates a virtual community where one did not exist before; perhaps more often it extends and enables a pre-existing core of like-minded people (Chayko 2008).

A decade ago in their introduction to *The Internet in Everyday Life,* Barry Wellman and Caroline Haythornthwaite (2002) reviewed the research on Internet use in the opening years of the twenty-first century and found the following:

- *Increasing access.* More people—some two thirds of American adults, according to one study—are going online. The digital divide between more affluent and less affluent members of Western countries is closing. Globally there is still considerable unevenness, with leaders like the Nordic and Baltic nations and laggards like sub-Saharan Africa, but the trend is toward ever-greater access.
- *Increasing commitment.* People are spending more time online and doing more things while they're there. While new users may at first confine their activities to e-mail, the more experienced people become, the greater their variety of online activities.
- *Domestication.* No longer just a workplace tool, the Internet has followed people home.
- *Longer work hours.* Since the Internet has entered the domestic space, it has also facilitated bringing work into the home, which is no longer "a haven in a heartless world."
- *Schoolwork.* Schools have been the institutional link between the home and the Internet. Not only do students use the Internet more, but also the presence of school-aged children dramatically increases the likelihood that the household will have Internet access.
- *Keeping up.* Non-Internet users, a vanishing breed, report that they would like to have Internet access to "keep up."
- *A networked society.* Networks, not bounded groups, are the most socially meaningful formation in the Internet age.

Their list—formulated before Facebook, texting, and Twitter—has stood the test of time and technological change remarkably well. The Internet has penetrated everyday life in the developed world and, increasingly, in the developing world as well, as in the One Laptop Per Child project that aims to put $100 computers in the hands of rural children everywhere. Of its many ramifications and implications, we want to focus here on its impact on cultural practices. Has the Internet been as revolutionary as print was five centuries ago? We can start by thinking about the actual relationship between the Internet and print. When electronic media in general and the Internet in particular were new on the horizon, many commentators feared that this would be the death of reading. People would entertain themselves by surfing the net or downloading music and videos rather than curling up with a good book. One such pessimistic view even bore the title *The Gutenberg Elegies.*

It hasn't worked out that way, at least not so far. It appears the people who use the Internet the most also read the most (Griswold and Wright 2004). In part this is due to education, and in part to the way the Internet facilitates finding out about and buying books. The Internet has not had the negative impact on reading that many feared; in fact, there seems to be a positive association between the two activities (Robinson et al. 2002). In some ways this should not be surprising, for despite its capacities in other media forms, the Internet itself remains a text-based medium, with little to offer for non-readers. The same is true for listening to music. Although music downloading is having enormous impact on the structuring of the music industry, the Internet doesn't compete with but facilitates people enjoying music. The same seems to be the case for attending social and cultural events. What the Internet *did* decrease in the early years was television viewing (UCLA Center for Communication Policy 2003; Robinson et al. 2002), although now with streaming video, Hulu.com, BitTorrent, and similar sites, it is becoming difficult to distinguish watching TV from being online in general. Overall, and despite some contradictory evidence, it seems that Internet use is not displacing desirable leisure activities like reading, sports, and cultural participation.

Religion shows the same pattern. About one quarter of all Americans are "religion surfers," in that they have gone online to get religious materials (Larsen 2004). Religion surfers are more intensely devout than most Americans, but aside from that they are demographically comparable to religiously active people in general. They go online for reference materials (e.g., information about their own faiths), social contexts (e.g., religious chat groups), devotional materials, and advice and support. Religious organizations also try to increase their outreach through websites. Going online helps those who are already devout; the Internet is a great resource for the religiously active. While most often this augments rather than changes current practices and beliefs, Turner (2007) has argued that new media in general produce a breakdown of traditional religious authority in favor of scattered, competing "micro intellectuals" who attempt to outdo each other in terms of their strictness. A similar phenomenon is apparent in politics, where political extremists from MoveOn.org on the left to the Tea Party movement on the right use new media to polarizing effect.

Nor is the Internet having a revolutionary impact on social gender inequality. So far, political forums and candidate websites largely reach people already disposed to favor a particular position or party. Eszter Hargittai's research (2003) suggests that although the digital divide in terms of access to the Internet may be diminishing, the skill divide—how effective people are in getting the information they seek online—remains large even for young adult "digital natives" who have grown up with the Internet (Hargittai 2010) and is related to other forms of social inequality. Gender roles are reproduced over the Internet, sometimes in the vilest ways, as in pornography, trafficking in women, or sexual harassment (see Walsh [2007] for discussion of a particularly vicious example), sometimes in routine ways like males dominating the conversations in chat rooms. Lori Kendall's study of "online masculinities" leads her to conclude that there is no basis for the

> technologically determinist view, expressed by both participants and research-
> ers, that online interaction significantly changes either participants' experi-
> ences and understandings of identity or the power structures based on
> identities such as race, gender, and class. . . . [Internet forums] provide a new
> kind of meeting place, but far from solving some of the problems of the offline
> world, they may in fact intensify those problems by providing a forum in
> which the relatively privileged can escape to an arena where their privilege
> remains relatively hidden. . . . (2002:224)

So far the picture is this: The Internet enables people to do what they did before, from reading to sexual harassment, only more efficiently. Even suicide is an ICT-mediated activity. In South Korea and Japan, people considering doing away with themselves contact like-minded people online to share information (which pesticides are most lethal) and support, through blogs with names like "Let's Die Together" (Choe 2007). "[T]he Internet has become a lethally efficient means of bringing together people with suicide on their minds." ICTs are connecting more people via networks, if not changing their intentions or practices. What might these network formations mean in terms of the production and reception of culture?

Old Diamonds, New Media[1]

Returning to the cultural diamond, we begin by noting that any particular cultural diamond is static, a snapshot. While all of the elements and links have histories that reward exploration, the diamond represents the relationship among them at a single moment in time. One could examine changes over time, the diamond for some cultural object at Time 1, Time 2, and so forth; this creates a more complex model—a cultural parallelepiped—but the analysis required would be the same.

However, the advent of the ICTs and new media forces reconsideration. What is most distinctive of new media is not their speed (there has been a general progression of the speed at which complex messages travel from sender to receiver, and instant messaging between two people is no faster then talking on the telephone) or their technologically enhanced virtual quality (a prayer or performance is similarly immaterial and time-dependent) but their participatory nature. In older media like an encyclopedia, an expert (creator) produces an entry (cultural object) that is made available in a volume (one link between entry and receiver) and is read by a passive recipient. In new media—blogs, Wikipedia, instant messaging, photoblogs, videoblogs (vlogs), podcasts—the recipient can add to the entry or compose it from multiple sources. With minimal or no vetting from a central authority, every one can participate. While a posting, an encyclopedia entry, a playlist, or a string of messages may still be considered a cultural object, the distinction between creator and receiver all but disappears.

Can the diamond model represent this change? The simplest way is for the cultural analyst to impose a moment of stability. After all, the diamond was always a snapshot of a dynamic system whereby recipients become creators (the audience for dance and poetry is largely made up of dancers and poets), so while new media broaden the interchange of roles, the necessary analytic move of a somewhat artificial stabilization—making things hold still for examination—is quite comparable. But this obscures the fundamental difference involved in the emerging media culture, that of widespread participation.

Shifting the analytic focus, and the research question, from the vertical to the horizontal axis of the cultural diamond accommodates this change. The diamond responded to simplistic reflection models of either the Marxian (culture reflects social world) or the functionalist (social world reflects cultural values) type by drawing attention to people (i.e., agency), people's groups and categories, and the institutions through which people operate. Thus it broadened and elaborated the research necessary to make claims about the vertical axis, the connection between the social world and culture, but that axis remained the primary focus of interest.

With new media, agency and interactions become primary. The diamond remains the same, but attention now shifts to the horizontal axis representing the relationships among people (Figure 7.1). Instead of people producing and consuming culture, it is better to conceptualize the situation as people using cultural objects to communicate, network, learn, persuade, influence, and celebrate their sociability. (Instant messaging and texting among teenagers, with its dearth of substantive content, is the very essence of what Georg Simmel meant when he described sociability as a playful form of association removed from utilitarian objectives or individuality.) People use culture to be who they are and develop into whom they might become, to link up with other people who are like-minded (political parties, activist groups), attractive (online dating), or necessary (work groups, information providers) or

Figure 7.1 Cultural Diamond for New Media

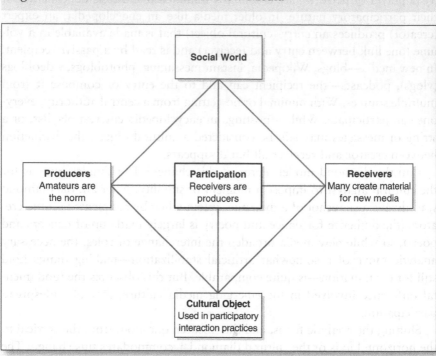

with whom they already have a structural connection (friends, family members). Culture in this view becomes less a matter of objects and more a matter of practices.

Regional cuisine can serve to illustrate the interplay of the two axes. Analysis according to the first diamond might set the social world as that of Turin, in the Piedmont region of northwestern Italy. One may set the cultural object at any level, from Piedmonte cuisine in general to some specific food in particular, or one might identify the cultural object as an individual recipe, a book of recipes, a memoir, a travel guide, a city promotion, a restaurant, a television cooking program, and so forth. Thinking in terms of old media, we could regard the creators of the cuisine as chefs, housewives, travel writers, editors, farmers, or people in the food business; the receivers would be cooks, diners, family members, readers, television viewers, or travelers.

The impact of new media prompts a shift in focus to the interaction between producers and consumers of regional cuisine and how the same cuisine facilitates specific kinds of participation. Now the social world might be global in scale—for example, followers of the Slow Food movement or more broadly the movement favoring local, authentic, unaltered foods. Such a movement encourages culinary regionalism, whatever the region, for it by definition uses local foods in traditional ways. In the case of Turin, Slow Food members and food-industry professionals might have come together in the Salone del Gusto, held in Turin every two years. Non-professional enthusiasts of Turin cuisine might meet in restaurants, read the same recipe books and magazines, do parallel cooking in their own homes without ever meeting, and thereby become producers themselves. Such people communicate online, sharing recipes, blogs, tips on food producers and restaurants, photos of markets, or mass alerts about the dangers of genetically modified foods or agribusiness. Culinary authenticity, its virtues and its specific characteristics in any one place like Turin, become known through participation via new media.

Old media and new media (OM and NM for short) are all mixed together in real life. For example, the March 21, 2007, print edition of the *Chicago Tribune* (OM) featured local chef and restaurateur, John Bubala (of Irish and Slovak descent, not Italian), who visited Turin for the Salone del Gusto; the article includes recipes and tempting photographs—piles of olives and pears, a street scene ("The flags of the ancient novel houses of Turin flutter over the Medieval streets"). The article stayed available online (NM), and people could e-mail it to their friends. In the article the chef raves about the diversity of Turin's cuisine and how it might be brought to American consumers. Now he is the producer, more accurately the re-producer and re-creator of the cultural object (Turin's cuisine); in fact, the article goes on to say, he is opening a new restaurant in Chicago devoted to this form of regional cooking. Bubala focuses on a specific example of the cuisine: *lardo*. "It's one if the 10 best things I've ever eaten. But it's cured fatback! Nobody's going to eat that!"

He means that his American customers may have a terror of fat that their European cousins do not share. Yet Bubala set about curing his first batch of *lardo* almost as soon as he arrived home from the trip. "The first thing I did when I got back was jump on the Internet and Google '*lardo*' to find out how to make it," he said.

According to the older version of the cultural diamond, *lardo* has some relationship to the social world that produced it (a peasant food, related to the agricultural tradition of the region); according to the newer version, *lardo* is a way people can participate in an ideological movement, make money in the upscale restaurant business, feed and amuse their guests, or display their ethnic identity or affinities. Cured pork fat and the meanings attached to this unlikely delicacy move through old and new media to old and new audiences. This is the world created by ICTs, where the most traditional of cultural objects become both intensified locally and available globally.

Communities of Meaning in a Global Culture

Rhacel Parreñas (2001) has studied the Filipinas—caregivers, cleaners, nannies—who serve families in Rome and Los Angeles while their own families wait back home. She sees them as living in three different spaces. First is the global, where workers circulate worldwide following the demand for their labor. Second is the transnational, where the women live, simultaneously, in two different societies, that of their home in the Philippines and that of the Western country in which they are working. And third is local, as Filipinas create meeting places and hangouts where they can commiserate and share stories, even though they are spatially isolated in both the city and their employers' homes. Her analysis raises interesting questions about the relationship between place and culture. What is the culture of these women? What do they need to know more, the Roman bus system or the tastiest way of preparing chicken adobo? In some respects, the Filipinas in Los Angeles or Rome constitute an enclave, though it is a very fragile one. Parreñas shows how these domestic workers use Philippine magazines and cassettes to preserve their cultural participation in the island culture, even as they navigate the cultural landscape in which they currently find themselves.

Robert Bellah and his colleagues (1984) used the expression "lifestyle enclaves" to describe the places where people can choose to live with others just like them. They point out that, formerly, people lived and interacted with different types of people (in age, occupation, and family form) in their communities. Now, if people elect to live in communities where only retired people who like golf live or where only young, childless professionals live, they can do so. Bellah sees this development as a failure of the Durkheimian organic exchange that should take place in modern communities. Parreñas's example forces us to extend the enclave idea: Many live where they must, not where they choose, yet still endeavor to form lifestyle enclaves to whatever degree they are able. Similarly, people can now live within what we might call "cultural enclaves." Individuals with very different meaning systems—from cyberpunks to fundamentalist Muslims—can create and receive their own distinct cultural objects and confine their interactions to others who share their meaning systems. These interacting cultural groups may be labeled communities, and they may and do cross political and geographical boundaries, but they are built around sameness rather than around diversity. Their tendency is not to increase tolerance—the stated goal of multiculturalism—but to diminish it. Electronic communication facilitates this. Bellah's lifestyle enclaves were geographical, but the process of separation is even more pronounced for relational communities. Mexican soccer fans can watch Spanish-language soccer games twenty-four hours a day.

They can contact other soccer aficionados on computer networks to share information and debate fine points of the game. Through developments in virtual reality, they soon may be able to amuse themselves by simulations that allow them to experience actually playing the game. Such individuals could maintain this cultural enclave, a tight relational community (or self-designed ghetto) anywhere in the world they happen to live.

Once again, the paradox: Just as electronic globalization seems to unite people geographically, it also seems to separate them relationally — on the one hand, a global village; on the other, the self-absorbed worlds of the soccer fans and other cultural enclaves. Both are communities, but both seem to lack depth. And this—say theorists of postmodernity much taken with these developments—is the whole point.

Postmodernity and Community

Global electronic communications, with their infinite capacity for the reproduction and dissemination of signs, are the foundation of postmodernism. Postmodern culture is a culture of surfaces, a play of images denying depth, history, or meaning. It has been characterized as having the following attributes (Harvey 1989; Jameson 1984):

- *Depthlessness, a self-aware superficiality.* Depth has been replaced by multiple surfaces. There are no hidden meanings, for indeed there is nothing beneath the glittering surfaces that the culture presents. The mirrored sunglasses or the mirrored surface of a building are exemplary postmodern cultural objects, denying depth or meaning within, stopping visual penetration at the surface, throwing back the image of the beholder.
- *The rejection of meta-narratives* (which we discuss in Chapter 2). One aspect of this is a weakened sense of national history or destiny. To speak of a concept such as American destiny or the inevitable triumph of socialism today would be to sound embarrassingly naive. Frederick Jameson (1984) described it: "The advanced capitalist countries today are now a field of stylistic and discursive heterogeneity without a norm. Faceless masters continue to inflect the economic strategies which constrain our existences, but they no longer need to impose their speech (or are henceforth unable to): and the postliteracy of the late capitalist world reflects not only the absence of any great collective project but also the unavailability of the older national language itself" (17).
- *Fragmentation, the breakdown of connections.* Postmodern culture embraces the fragmentary, the ephemeral, and the discontinuous. Pastiche, the splicing together of cultural elements from different times and places, is a convention of postmodernist art and literature. This technique holds echoes of the cultural bricoleur discussed in Chapter 4, but the bricoleur is trying to accomplish something with the jerry-rigged construction. Postmodern pastiche has no such end in mind.

Now a culture that denies depth and history, a culture that rejects any larger story of its past and future, a culture wherein anything can be combined with anything else—such a culture, to put it mildly, does not sound promising as a foundation around which community can be built. What can we conclude about the relationship between electronic media and global postmodern culture on the one hand and the possibility for community on the other? The question is not an idle one for sociology. A century ago, men who worried about the corrosive effects that modernity—rationalization, capitalism, anomie—would have on human community were the founders of the discipline. In their various social theories, they envisioned the type of ties that could bind people and give their lives meaning in the contemporary world. For Marx, it was class-consciousness; for Weber, it was systems of ideas; for Durkheim, it was some embodiment of the collective conscience. All of these thinkers proposed cultural meaning-producing systems that might offer a defense against the individualistic, dog-eat-dog world of their society.

These founders of sociology looked ahead to the twentieth century; we embark upon the twenty-first. Electronic media have made it possible to put human beings in touch with one another as never before. The global circulation of money and people has been accompanied, and even preceded, by a circulation of cultural objects trailing shreds of meanings behind them. Will this course have a unifying effect? Will cultural sharing at last achieve Matthew Arnold's dream of a tolerant and reasonable human community?

The cultural theories we have discussed give basis for both optimism and pessimism. On the optimistic side, community and a sense of solidarity come from interaction, for it is through interactions with others that we, like Fine's Little Leaguers, build up shared meaning systems. Charles Cooley (1956) wrote that primary groups, those groups such as the family and neighborhood where we have our earliest and most intimate interactions, form people's sense of who they are and with whom they are identified. Extending Cooley's reasoning, if electronic communications make intimate interactions possible for more and more people regardless of where they are physically located, it may lead to a greater communion among them, a greater sense of what they have in common as people. Recall that when Americans and Europeans watched the CNN reports of the Gulf War in 1991, they shared a heightened sense of all being "in this together." Could communications foster a global sense of "all being in this together"?

Perhaps. Sociology counters its own optimism with darker views, however. Durkheim pointed out the paradox that in a society with a highly advanced division of labor, the only thing people have in common is their individualism. Today, we have the technological means to give rich cultural expression to that individualism. In fact, recent years have produced an explosion of cultural forms serving highly specialized groups and interests: desktop publishing, computer networks, 'zines, cable television channels, the decline of "top 40" radio stations in favor of segmented stations for hip-hop, soft rock, contemporary country, rap, and salsa. Plugged into their iPods, selecting their own videos, and interacting with their special Internet networks, people can increasingly dwell in cultural ghettos of their own choosing. These ghettos may be continental in size. When Americans and Europeans saw the 2003 war in Iraq on their televisions and Internet screens, Americans watched and felt more American, whereas Europeans—who generally opposed the war—watched and felt more European.

Some sociologists have suggested that the need to erect and emphasize cultural boundaries is a response to pressure on other boundaries. The general idea is that external pressure on a society will bring about a greater emphasis on internal hierarchies, as well as on defending the distinctions perceived to be threatened. Christie Davies (1982) showed this to be true for deviant sexuality. There are always rules and laws against tabooed sexual behavior such as homosexuality, bestiality, or cross-dressing, but these laws are not always enforced. His historical analysis shows that it is precisely when groups come under pressure from outside that they become obsessed with purifying internal categories, such as the distinctions between male and female or human and animal, and one sign of this obsession is a stepped-up enforcement of sex codes. A more general statement of Davies's point would be that when institutions and meaning systems are threatened or disrupted, it may not be the case that entirely new ones will be created; one response may simply be a greater emphasis on preexisting cultural traits and distinctions. Even something as globally disruptive and seemingly univocal as McDonald's gets reinterpreted according to the social mind of the receiving culture (Watson 1997). Thus, Wuthnow's (1987) "breakdowns in the moral order" may not produce new ideologies; it may reinvigorate old ones, including old hatreds that were assumed to have vanished from the modern world. The increasing fragmentation and resurgent ethnicity of the former Eastern bloc gives evidence of this. The concept of "ethnic cleansing" represents community with a vengeance.

But it may be that we have posed the issue incorrectly. Spatial and relational communities are nothing new, and the fact that electronic communications have multiplied the latter does not necessarily mean the eclipse of the former; community is not a zero-sum game, nor is meaning. Theorists of postmodernity may have missed something: We may, in fact, witness a proliferation of both surfaces and depths. Human beings—like the Filipina nannies—may well learn to operate simultaneously in global, relational communities and in local, spatial ones. Each community will have its own culture. Let us conclude by considering what such a world would look like.

Mediated Transnationals

Picking up from an earlier book on "transnational villagers," which argued that today's migrants have a foot in both worlds, Peggy Levitt (2007) argues that the popular term *globalization* emphasizes integration too much and downplays the diversity and contradictions of the contemporary world. She prefers the term *transnational* to indicate the complex layers and the new boundaries and borders that get created in a borderless world. While the "global" suggests the absence of a center, "transnational" suggests how migrants may well be firmly "anchored" in more than one place. They may participate in the political, social, and cultural life of both their communities of origin and their communities of residence. This is increasingly possible because of ICTs. Turks in Denmark can watch Turkish television; they can e-mail their friends back home, get online help studying the Qur'an, and keep connected with the Turkish diaspora through MySpace.com. At the same time they go to Danish schools, purchase the consumer goods available in the European Union, and speak Danish. They can travel back and forth far more easily than was the case for immigrants of generations past. Such people participate quite intensively in two worlds.

Levitt studied transnational families now living in Massachusetts who migrated from Valadares, Brazil (Protestant town founded by German Lutherans), Gujarat State in India (ISSO or Swaminarayan, a Hindu denomination), Pakistan (Muslim, some strict and others not), and Inishowen Peninsula, Ireland. She focused in particular on their religious practices and beliefs. Having spent years interviewing people both in Massachusetts and in the four places of origin, she found a wide variety of ties, supports, and contacts back and forth between the United States and the countries of origin. Some migrants responded to transnational realities by being nationals, either American or oriented to their homeland or a mix of both. Some are cosmopolitans, with either weak ties to a place or highly selective ties to specific locales. And some are "religious global citizens," members of "communities of faith composed of fellow believers around the globe."

Carolyn Chen (2006) tells a similar story about Taiwanese immigrants to the United States who convert to evangelical Christianity. Sociologists have usually regarded religion as a way for immigrant communities to maintain ethnic solidarity, for example by giving them a place to use their native language and to establish social and business connections with others from the home country. Chen shows a different pattern whereby the immigrants use their faith to challenge traditional relationships between parents and children and between the sexes, thereby reconstructing family relationships along less hierarchical lines.

Levitt's and Chen's migrants may be representative of a more general situation, that whereby people have a hitherto unheard of flexibility in picking and choosing their cultural affinities and commitments. New media and ICTs make it easy to find new communities, stay in touch with old ones, confirm old identities, and shape new ones. The South African fan downloading kung fu films from Hong Kong, the lonely Senegalese girl in Dakar e-mailing her boyfriend who is studying in Paris, the American trading MP3s with friends around the world—these are cultural transnationals even if they have never left their country of birth. They are experiencing new forms of connection for which the sociological terminology—groups, communities, networks—is inadequate. Producing and receiving cultural objects, both they and the objects themselves are shaped by the speed of their transmission. The cultural worlds they are creating mount a major conceptual challenge for new sociological thinking.

NOTE

1. This discussion is adapted from "Diamanti, Civette e (Nuovi) Media: Ovvero Come Mettersi d'Accordo Sull'Analisi Culturale", in Marco Santoro (ed.), *Cultura in Italia, vol. 1, Media vecchi, media nuovi*, Bologna: Il Mulino 2008.

QUESTIONS FOR STUDY AND DISCUSSION

1. Interview someone who attended college before the Internet was in widespread use. Find out how his or her college experience was different from yours in terms of staying in touch with friends, doing research and studying, entertaining him- or herself, and coordinating class and extracurricular schedules. Then discuss in class the question of whether the culture of college life has been changed by the coming of the Internet.

2. Christianity, Judaism, and Islam are known to be "religions of the book," for each is based on a foundational text. Consider the extent to which new media are having an impact on religious life in these faith communities. Do you expect the numbers of believers to increase or decrease in the ICT era, and why?

3. Given the global circulation of cultural objects, is the world coming together or falling apart? Are human societies becoming more and more alike or just more and more aware of their differences? Should we be optimistic or pessimistic about the emergence of a world culture?

RECOMMENDED FOR FURTHER READING

Anderson, Benedict. [1983] 1991. *Imagined Communities: Reflections on the Origin and Spread of Nationalism*. Rev. ed. London: Verso. Anderson offers a masterly historical account of the rise of the nation as a cultural object, paying particular attention to the role of print and newspapers.

Chayko, Mary. 2008. *Portable Communities: The Social Dynamics of Online and Mobile Connectedness*. Albany: State University of New York Press. The relationship between technology and community in the twenty-first century.

Crystal, David. 2008. *Txtng: The Gr8 Db8*. Oxford: Oxford University Press. Crystal gives a breezy, well-informed portrait of a communications revolution. Previous communication innovations were managed over a number of years by adult experts. "But texting is different. Here we have a set of linguistic adaptations being introduced by youngsters, on their own, spontaneously, rapidly, and without professional tuition. I have, quite frankly, never seen anything like it" (148).

Fischer, Claude S. 1992. *America Calling: A Social History of the Telephone to 1940*. Berkeley: University of California Press. The relationship between technology and community in the early twentieth century.

Parreñas, Rhacel Salazar. 2001. *Servants of Globalization: Women, Migration and Domestic Work*. Stanford, CA: Stanford University Press. Parreñas studies the multiple levels and cultural networks that constitute the lived experience of Filipinas working in Western cities. Far from the "frequent fliers" that the globalization model often connotes, these women and the cultures they create and respond to represent the far more common inhabitants of what Appadurai called the global ethnoscape.

Yang, Guobin. 2009. *The Power of the Internet in China: Citizen Activism Online*. New York: Columbia University Press. Yang takes a close look at online collective action in an authoritarian state and how the Internet can partially compensate for the absence of civil society. This is a timely discussion that will provoke debate and comparisons with online practices and assumptions in the West.

8

Culture and Power

P ower—having it, getting it, and keeping it—is a primordial human desire. In its pursuit, people actively deploy cultural resources. More basic still, culture defines the arena in which the struggle for power takes place, who are the combatants, what is at issue and for whom, what should be accepted and what should be resisted, and what are the consequences of compliance or rebellion. Given the high stakes in power relationships at any level, a consideration of culture and power bring together many of the conceptions and processes we have seen previously.

This chapter investigates the way in which culture shapes power. It begins with a consideration of what power actually is and why powerful actors and institutions need cultural resources and schemas in the first place. It then considers power at different levels of human interactions, from the micro level of the couple or family all the way to the national and global levels. Finally it zeroes in on politics, the institutionalization of power, by looking at the role of culture in elections, spectacles, and cognitive and emotional responses—from patriotic sentiments to revolution—toward political regimes.

Power: What Is It, Who Has It, and Why Do People Submit to It?

Power is the ability to get one's own way. Whether the "one" is an individual, a group, a category, or a nation, when we say one has power, we mean that he can do what he wants and get what he desires, regardless of whether other people agree or disagree. For example, most people are able to cross a room to get a glass of water—they have the power to do so—but a bedridden person in a nursing home cannot. He lacks the capacity to satisfy this simple desire, and some other person must assist. If a country has power vis-à-vis another country, it can go in and take the resources, and the second country will be helpless to prevent it.

Let's call one unit, anything from an individual to a country, A and a second unit B. Then we can express a series of questions formally: What role, if any, does culture play in the ability of A to dominate B? What role, if any, does culture play in the ability of B to resist being dominated by A? Now let's introduce a third unit, C, and ask, What role, if any, does culture play in C's interpretation of and response to what has taken place between A and B?

We may address these questions starting with the social scientific definition of culture set out in the first chapter. Recall Clifford Geertz's (1973:89) definition of culture: "an historically transmitted pattern of meanings embodied in symbols, a system of inherited conceptions expressed in symbolic forms by means of which men communicate, perpetuate, and develop their knowledge about and attitudes toward life." From this definition it follows that people's culturally instilled knowledge and attitudes would prompt them to accept certain power arrangements and reject others.

Power is when A can get B to do something that B would not do otherwise. For example, A says to B, "Give me your money" or "Plow my fields" or "Have sex with me." If B does it, A has some sort of power over B. And C, the witness, may regard this exercise of power as legitimate or as an abuse.

What are the ways in which people exert power? First would be sheer force. A says, "Give me your money or I'll shoot you," A whips B if B doesn't plow the field, A rapes B because A is physically strong enough to overcome B's resistance, or A physically restrains B. The observer C would usually interpret this as an abuse unless (1) it were in the context of play (i.e., sports or a contest with clearly specified rules), or (2) the powerful A has the authority to keep order through force, as with the police and justice system or with parents who might use force to make a child stop doing something dangerous. Designating something as "play" (boxing vs. a street fight) or as a permissible use of force (parents may spank their children, but unrelated adults may not) is a case of drawing cultural boundaries.

A second kind of power comes through exchange. Here A buys B's compliance. A gives B something in return for B's money or buys B's sexual favors or pays wages for work done. In a market economy C would probably see this as legitimate, although such questions might be raised as, Why does A have more money? or Why is B forced to sell the goods or labor?

Neither force nor exchange necessarily requires cultural support. Indeed conquest and colonialism show us that A can extract compliance from B by force or exchange even if there is virtually no common cultural ground. But both force and exchange are costly for A in that they require energy (e.g., using physical force) or resources (e.g., buying something). This is where culture comes in. In some situations B submits to A's wishes because the "historically transmitted pattern of meanings embodied in symbols" makes B think and feel ("knowledge about and attitudes toward") that A's demand is legitimate and/or that complying with A's demand is desirable and proper. And C, the witness, may share in this cultural interpretation or may recoil from it.

How would this cultural support for the exercise of power come about? As we have seen, culture provides models of and for behavior. It defines what is legitimate, proper, and normal. It sets out a moral code. And it shapes our common sense, our all-but-unconscious understanding of how things are and should be.

Legitimacy, morality, and common sense might illuminate the power relationship between professors and students, for example. Say a professor demands that a student give her his jacket. Most students would feel that, according to the institutional rules and norms of college, it is legitimate that professors ask students to write papers but illegitimate that they ask for students' property. However, in some instances the moral code might say otherwise, as in the case of traditional Japanese respect and obedience toward teachers or of the Christian instruction that if someone asks for your cloak, you give it to him and more. And common sense might suggest that the demand is appropriate to the situation—for example, that the teacher needs the jacket to put over another student who has fainted.

So culture influences behavior, in this case B's compliance with A's demands, through defining what is legitimate, setting out a moral code guiding behavior, and shaping the common sense through which we interpret situations.

Next, we have a series of questions about the relationship between culture and the social world. How binding is culture? How does it work? Do the operations of culture—legitimacy, moral codes, and common sense—systematically advantage one group or type of person over another, or are they neutral?

On the question of how binding culture is, a question that is particularly important when we are thinking about the cultural legitimation of power, we may identify two extreme positions. The first is free agency: People, individually or collectively, are free agents in control of their own destiny. Culture provides resources for resistance as well as for domination, and people can draw on these resources to pursue their ends. The second is cultural "dopes": People are programmed by their culture to such an extent that they fail to recognize their own interests. Harold Garfinkel (1967) used the term *dopes* in his critique of functionalism, but the same image applies to strong hegemony theories, which similarly regard people as having limited freedom or even awareness. Some theories are politically neutral, and others follow Marx's assumption that the "ruling ideas are the ideas of the ruling class" and that these ideas rule by shaping knowledge and attitudes. Now we have already seen that people both create and are directed by meanings. Neither extreme—complete freedom or robotic control—is persuasive. We need to take a closer look at how culture actually works to produce or challenge power.

Power in Face-to-Face Interactions

Power exists in any group that involves two or more people. If the woman in a dating couple always decides what the couple will do, she holds the power in the relationship. If certain popular or simply aggressive teenagers can lead their friends into risky behavior, they are powerful within the group. Sometimes such power is legitimated by rules, as when the professor has the power to ask students to write papers, and sometimes the power is legitimated through the force of personality. And sometimes, although there are no explicit rules, certain categories of people have more power.

There may be no rhyme or reason to why people accord power to certain categories of people. Tall people, for example, have an advantage that does not seem related to any historical causes.

> Of 43 American presidents, only five have been more than a smidgeon below average height, and the last of those was Benjamin Harrison, elected in 1888. (Another three, most recently Jimmy Carter, were just a hair below average.) Most presidents have been several inches above the norm for their times, with the five tallest being Abraham Lincoln, Lyndon Johnson, Bill Clinton, Thomas Jefferson, and Franklin Roosevelt. (Landsburg 2002; for similar benefits of height to earnings, see Judge and Cable 2004)

But some categorical power and powerlessness has deep historical roots. Consider ethnicity, for example: Disadvantaged minorities—Dalits (untouchables) in India, Roma (gypsies) in Eastern Europe—lack power, and they may be socially discriminated against long after legal discrimination has ended.

Gender in face-to-face interactions seems to exert an independent effect. A considerable body of research on how conversations work, for example, suggests that women talk less than men and are more likely to be interrupted. Theory explains this is because gender shapes performance expectations; group members do not expect women to make as important a contribution as men, so women hold less power in the conversation. At the same time the internal development of the conversation itself may be more important than gender in determining who can change the topic. Early participants accumulate more power to direct the conversation than those who hold back at the beginning. In this sense the group develops its own micro-culture of power (Okamoto and Smith-Lovin 2001). Either can be seen as an issue of legitimacy: The group regards men and/or early participants as having a legitimate right to initiate topics or cut other people off—in other words, to get their own way in the discussion.

Although we usually assume that even small groups must have a strong leader to work, egalitarian cultures may be even more effective. Some political movements have internal cultures that encourage sharing power, working toward consensus, and bottom-up decision making. Francesca Polletta (2002) has shown that social movements from the 1950s and 1960s advocated and practiced such "participatory democracy." Instead of this diffusion of power producing paralysis or anarchy, she found that such micro-cultures enabled civil rights and antiwar groups to strengthen their solidarity even as they nimbly adjusted to local circumstances.

> The sheer diversity of input into tactical choice that participatory democracy makes possible has enabled activists to outpace their opponents in generating novel tactics. In the Southern civil rights movement, organizers used participatory democracy to school local residents in the practice of politics. . . . Far from opposed to leadership, they aimed to create political leaders—and to create the mechanisms that would keep leaders accountable to their constituents. (2)

On the other hand, some groups skirt political conversation altogether in the interests of peace as they pursue other, non-political goals (Eliasoph 1998). Although this type of consensus through not talking about contentious issues may allow the group to function, such a non-confrontational local culture discourages reflection on the power relationships within the group itself. Becker's (1999) study of the local cultures in American church congregations suggests something along this line. Some churches were "families," and like families, their conflicts were passionate and personal. One church's conflict over reporting procedures became "a matter of trust and caring, not accounting practices" (93). These churches were subject to upheavals and either dramatic change or the highly visible reassertion of power, which often rested in the hands of the pastor as patriarch. Other churches were emotionally cooler "houses of worship," where offices and committees held the power and made the decisions. In these, conflicts were rare, and issues seldom unsettled the bureaucratic arrangements whereby power rested in duly elected officials. An appropriate exercise of pastoral power in the church as family would be an improper procedural violation in the house of worship.

Identity Politics

We have seen some of the mechanisms whereby culture serves the interests of power, including making something legitimate, moral, or common sense. One of the critical and most common ways this process takes place is in the construction of a group's past and its implications for future action. History, in particular a group's or a nation's collective memory, makes some actions seem legitimate, moral, or common sense but not others. Yet history is a cultural construct, subject to individual and institutional manipulation, revision, and selective emphasis and forgetting.

We begin with the social basis of cognition and its consequences. As we saw in Chapter 4, Eviatar Zerubavel (1997), who looks at the structuring of time and other forms of collective cognition, argues that in between cognitive universalism of neuroscience and the cognitive individualism of romantic ideology and psychoanalysis lies the social mind. This defines the field of cognitive sociology, which requires a comparative approach to cognition that would "highlight our cognitive diversity as members of different thought communities" (11). Zerubavel urges us to examine the cognitive division of labor within a society, as well as the differences among societies. He draws attention to the social influences on perception (what people notice), attention and concern (what people care about), classification (how people categorize things, meanings, memories—what to remember, what to forget, how to feel about it), and time (how people place things in the past or future). For example, many African Americans regard slavery as a relatively recent "cultural trauma" having pressing contemporary meaning, while many white Americans see it as a long past institution having little current relevance (Eyerman 2002). Such group differences in the salience of past events are true at the level of nations as well; old wounds are commemorated by some and conveniently forgotten by others.

While we may say that the shared understanding of the past and future shapes our "worlds" in a phenomenological sense, such "worlds" do not necessarily lead to specific behavioral outcomes, nor do they necessarily influence other people's worlds. Culture gains power only when it combines with resources. Ideologies about gender, for example, only work in combination with resource advantages. If a society believes that girls are not as good at math as boys are (ideology), the girls may prove this to be wrong if equal opportunities in the classroom (resource); if the boys are channeled into science classes, however, the ideology will combine with the educational resources to result in a self-fulfilling prophesy: more boys will succeed in science (Charles and Bradley 2009). Here Sewell's (1992) theory of structure, mentioned in Chapter 2, will help. Recall Sewell's discussion of cultural schemas, the general presuppositions underlying more explicit rules that can be transferred and applied to new situations. Schemas were only part of structure, however. The other half consists of resources, both human and material. Sewell puts resources and schemas together in his definition of social structure, which is "composed simultaneously of schemas, which are virtual, and of resources, which are actual." Schemas are the effects of resources, and resources are the effects of schemas.

It is easy to see where power comes into such a conception. The powerful control more resources than the less powerful. We usually think of this at the level of nations or large groups, but it can operate at the small group level as well. When a family watches television together, the person holding the remote has the power; in the British working-class family, that person is usually the father (Morley 1986). Power gets legitimated through schemas; if there is an underlying schema that says that men are more decisive than women, this schema will structure new situations in which men get to make the decisions, often accumulating resources by doing so, and thus will reproduce male power.

But what about change? Wouldn't any given structure of power just reproduce itself: Dad always gets the remote, Mom is always seen as not very capable outside the home sphere, and on and on forever? It is certainly the case that power structures tend to reproduce themselves. Educational systems, as Pierre Bourdieu and many others have pointed out, tend to take children who already have social advantages and pile on more advantages, putting them in more powerful positions when they become adults (Bourdieu 1984; Gaztambide-Fernandez 2009; Lareau 2003). Yet things obviously do change, and to account for this, Sewell modifies Bourdieu's (1984) idea of the habitus, those underlying transposable dispositions that reproduce structure even in improvised action in totally new contexts. Although the habitus is basic to his conception of schemas, Sewell stresses that we need a less rigid conception, a more "multiple, contingent, and fractured conception of society—and of structure" (16). With multiple structures, various schemas that may conflict, and unpredictable resource shifts, change happens. Mom enters the labor force, accumulating new resources and new domestic power. Or second-wave feminism changes the schemas about men's and women's capacities to make decisions. And next thing you know, Mom is holding the remote—or will be until technological change, another unpredictable factor, makes the remote itself obsolete.

Powerful schemas include those of gender and race, as in the above examples, but one that may be less obvious is that of collective memory. Groups differ sharply in what they remember and how they feel about it— Zerubavel's "social mind" at work—and when a memory acquires resources, it becomes history. We saw this in Chapter 4 in Binder's (2001) study of local school conflicts where proponents of Afrocentrism or creationism struggled to control curricular decisions that could institutionalize their version of history. The former found support from a widely shared memory of discrimination against African Americans, where there was no general collective memory of discrimination against evangelicals. At an international level, the ongoing conflict between Japanese and Chinese interpretation of the events of the 1930s and World War II is an example of a clash of collective memories institutionalized in textbooks, museums, and commemoration.

More generally we can say that history is a documented account of the past, institutionally supported (e.g., in books and through education). History is complex, with levels of detail; it must be taught and may not be known by all members of the group. Collective memory, on the other hand, is known by definition, for it is an account of the past shared by a group. Often such memories are perpetuated orally, informally, and sometimes secretly if the memory goes against the history as promoted by the dominant group. History and collective memory may or may not coincide. Commemorations, monuments, and museums are typical ways states try to make them coincide. Documentaries, eyewitness accounts, stories, rumors, and photos are typical ways people resist.

A recent example comes from the tenth anniversary of the massacre of Bosnian Muslims in Srebrenica, at which time the different ways the Bosnian Muslims and Serbians commemorated the event were in sharp conflict. In 1995 during the Bosnian War in former Yugoslavia, Bosnian Serb forces advanced on Srebrenica as part of the "ethnic cleansing" campaign. Thousands of Bosnian Muslims fled their homes and sought help from the small contingent of Dutch UN peacekeepers, for the UN had designated Srebrenica as a "safe area." But Serb forces attacked, killing the men and boys, while the peacekeepers stood by helplessly. About 8,000 men and boys died in Europe's worst atrocity since World War II.

In the summer of 2005 tens of thousands of people held ceremonies marking the tenth anniversary of the massacre of Bosnian Muslims in

Srebrenica. Grieving relatives buried more than 600 newly identified dead, after prayers and words of support from international and local officials. Serbian officials led by President Tadic paid respects for the first time. Muslim prayers echoed through the valley of the memorial site at Potocari, the site of the slaughter, as women in white headscarves wept beside the remains of their loved ones. The green coffins were then passed from hand to hand through the crowd to the freshly dug gravesites, as announcers called out one by one the names of the 610 dead. Each family buried its own dead, by hand or using shovels and buckets.

Serbia's parliament, on the other hand, observed a minute of silence for all victims of violence in and around Srebrenica *and* of the previous week's London subway bombing by Islamists. It failed to make specific reference to the Srebrenica massacre. Even the parliament's diluted commemoration was boycotted by the ultranationalist Serbian Radical Party. Here we have a striking contrast, with the Muslims trying to concentrate the focus on the massacre, limiting the attention in terms of time and space, and the Serbs trying to broaden it, referring to other atrocities (London bombings, times when Bosnian Muslims killed Serbs) or, in the case of the Nationalist Party and many Serbs (according to news accounts based on interviews), ignoring and denying it altogether.

The collective memory of the Bosnian Muslims differs from that of the Serbs. The many books and historical accounts written by outsiders, for example, Dutch peacekeepers, U.N. records, generally supports the Bosnian Muslim version, but that is irrelevant to the Serbs. This matters, of course, because past grievances justify—make legitimate, make moral, make common sense—future actions.

Historian David Lowenthal (1985) describes how collective memory and history intertwine, pointing out that for many people the past has become fragile and elusive, something cherished as "heritage" to be "preserved." We know the past—and shape our schemas about it—through memory, history, and relics but also through imagination. With such aids, memory organizes consciousness, transforming welter of actual experience into desirable or meaningful events, and these become institutionalized as history. "Just as memory validates personal identity, history perpetuates collective self-awareness" (213). The past can be changed in many ways (e.g., through museum exhibits, artifacts, textbooks, or reenactments). Sometimes it is cleaned up. Typically this happens when myths of national origins conveniently lose sight of the atrocities that took place at the country's founding. Lowenthal discusses a more amusing example of how hyperrealistic reenactments at Nova Scotia's Louisbourg fortress had to be prettied up when too many tourists were disconcerted by the bored soldiers and "syphilitic whores" taking tickets.

Who has the power to reshape the past? While oral accounts associated with collective memory have the capacity to change the past, as in Goody and Watt's (1963) account of the revised tribal history discussed in the previous chapter, those with control over institutions that can fix "history" have the most power. In the United States, museums and history textbooks for over a century presented a progressive view of history, but in the late twentieth century they replaced this with a relativistic one that gives more weight to the costs (for Native Americans, African slaves, and immigrant laborers) of nation building. Even relativism has its costs, as when critics charge that the Smithsonian's monumental Museum of the American Indian homogenizes Native American experiences, making all Indians seem alike.

The Aesthetics of Power

Identities are the key to political thought and action. If cultural creators can frame their message so it resonates with a frame that the audience already possesses, they are more likely to persuade that audience to "buy" the message. Political propaganda operates this way quite overtly. Barry Schwartz (1996) has shown how Franklin Delano Roosevelt's administration, working to mobilize support for American involvement in World War II, keyed its pro-war message to the Lincoln frame from the past. Counting on the collective memory that honored Abraham Lincoln's resolve in the face of war, the administration legitimated American military action by fitting it to the public's "horizon of expectations" that included the sacred place that Lincoln held. This succeeded in orienting Americans toward the necessity and nobility of going to war.

Political framing is hard to accomplish. Debate over whether or not the Darfur conflict should be called genocide is an example where using the past (holocaust) to frame the present (the Janjaweed's slaughter of Darfur villagers) is hotly contested. Some want to use the genocide to organize the political response to Darfur, focusing attention and ascribing meaning. But there are various historical discourses at play—not just genocide but memories of Western interference, African tribalism, and Muslim grievances—and so far there has been no agreed-upon frame.

Power holders as well as seekers of power work to legitimate their chosen frames through rituals and symbols. We saw earlier that this is in part a matter of efficiency: It is cheaper to organize a parade that whips up enthusiasm for the regime than it is to operate a police state. But how do such aesthetic claims about power actually work?

Paul DiMaggio (1997) has looked at the interaction between cognition and social life. He notes that under everyday circumstances, people organize information via automatic cognition, using "culturally available schemata—knowledge structures that represent objects of events and provide default assumptions about their characteristics, relationships, and entailments under conditions of incomplete information" (269). But sometimes there is the need to employ deliberative cognition, which is slow, deliberate, reflexive, and critical. One can think of this in Zerubavel's terms as the social mind on autopilot versus the social mind aware of itself.

DiMaggio sees culture operating through the interaction of three forms: information, distributed unevenly through a population; schematic representations that shape the way we perceive, interpret, remember, and feel about the information we encounter; and culture as external symbol systems. Culture is not any one of the three but the interaction among them. For example, think of the schemas of the Bosnian Muslims versus those of the Serbs. Such schemas become activated by external cues, as in Srebrenica anniversary commemoration. Enacting their different schemas through institutional venues (e.g., the Serbian parliament, the international media), the two groups offered jarringly different interpretations of the recent past, and these interpretations then were available as information that could confirm or challenge future understanding of that past.

While power gets embodied in parliamentary speeches and commemorative rituals, it also impresses itself on human bodies. Susan Bordo (1993) has taken as her cultural object the female body as cultural image and biological organism. Everyone is aware of the fashion industry's and the media's celebration of an unnatural thinness, and this is often linked to the rise of eating disorders like anorexia among both celebrities and the population at large. Bordo maintains that contrary to the medical establishment's view of such eating disorders as pathological, in fact the anorexics' attitudes toward eating is not some "bizarre" cognitive disorder but an accurate representation of, and appropriate response to, cultural messages about desirable weight. Starvation constitutes a reasonable plan of action whereby the anorexic as creator produces a body as cultural object that reflects the ideal embedded in the receivers' horizon of expectations. The plan makes cultural sense, in other words, even though it may prove fatal. In Bordo's contrarian account, it is not the anorexic who is sick; it is the culture itself with its objectification and commodification of women's bodies. Beauty both confers and is defined by power, and the anorexic is just trying to grab some power back.

Probably the most familiar form of power through aesthetics is at the national level—parades, holidays, spectacular celebrations—but even nationalism can be enacted on and through bodily aesthetics. Falesca-Zamponi (1997) describes how, during the Fascist period, Mussolini demanded that Italians greet one another with a Roman salute (stiff arm, right hand perpendicular) rather than a handshake, which according to the regime signified bourgeois decadence. Mussolini said the salute was "more hygienic, more aesthetic and shorter." The salute was mandatory in schools and when subordinates greeted superiors, but it was also used between equals, for it became a sign of loyalty and fit a regime that promoted itself as dynamic and efficient. Since it showed "decisive spirit, firmness, seriousness, and acknowledgment and acceptance of the regime's hierarchical structure," therefore proof of fascist character, the theory was that practicing the salute itself could actually change character. Today on the other side of the globe Korea—the mass games of the North, the March 1 parades linking patriotism and Protestantism of the South—offers vivid examples of the corporal expression of nationalism (Kane and Park 2009; Myers 2010;).

People tend to distinguish between states and nations with respect to the culture/power relationship along the following lines: States deploy culture to legitimate themselves and their power over citizens, and they often meet resistance. Nations, on the other hand, are primordial, based on pre-existing cultures; they too deploy culture, but it meets no resistance. Ever since Benedict Anderson's ([1983] 1991) "imagined community" thesis discussed in the previous chapter, however, which itself built on earlier work on "the invention of tradition," sociologists have been aware that nations are not "natural" but constructed. States make their claims to legitimacy on the basis of this myth of a nation, a myth elaborated in cultural symbols.

The Baltic nation of Latvia, under Soviet control until 1991, exemplifies the political potency of national culture. Diana Eglitis (2002) locates the founding national myth in the Bearslayer epic about a heroic defender of his nation's freedom. The epic features love of nature, ambivalence of Christianity, mistrust of cities, centrality of song, and suspicion of foreigners. Latvia's "singing revolution" (1986–1991) voiced antipathy toward Soviets and the desire for return to "normality," the nation's "natural" state that preceded the Soviet takeover. In other words, the goal was a return to the Bearslayer nation. The revolution began on June 14, 1987, when a massive demonstration took place at the Freedom Monument in downtown Riga. The Freedom Monument, created by Kârlis Zâle in 1935, features a Liberty Statue—a woman with three stars symbolizing regional parts of Latvia—and allegorical and historical carvings, including one of the Bearslayer in action. The monument came to symbolize the anti-Soviet resistance of the late 1980s and today is a shrine to national independence, decorated with flowers each day by the city's residents. The Latvian nation-state is a political entity founded on epic poetry, sculpture, and floral tributes.

Even statues and salutes have trouble molding a nation in the face of sharp group divisions. Multicultural societies prove especially challenging. Nation builders can use schemas, resources, and aesthetics to support a number of approaches:

- Suppress multiculturalism through removal, ethnic cleansing, or denial. Examples include pre-1995 Bosnia, the Darfur region of the Sudan, and Iraq under Saddam Hussein. Such suppression is typically a tactic of authoritarian regimes but may also be a choice made by separatist movements themselves, as in the Kurdish independence movement or the back-to-Africa movements of the early-twentieth-century United States.
- Deny multiculturalism. Such a denial characterized the United States during the late nineteenth and early twentieth centuries, when assimilation and a melting pot were the shared assumptions. Japan to this day largely ignores its ethnic minorities and their problems. France and the Netherlands are similarly seen as denying the fundamental differences represented by their Muslim minorities under an illusion that time will transform them into simply being French or Dutch.
- Marginalize or create a separate space for minority cultures. This has been the policy toward Native Americans in Canada and the United States, Aboriginals in Australia, and the Sami in Norway and Finland. Marginalized groups are often excluded from the nation's political discourse and/or forcefully assimilated, as in the case of China's policy toward Tibetans.
- Admit the existence of multiculturalism but create an overarching, pan-cultural identity. This was the policy of the Soviet Union. It was also the policy of Nigeria in 1970s, where the intractable differences among 250 different tribes were papered over by the cosmopolitan image of the "New Nigerian." More recently, New Nigerian has given way to a tenuous balance among the competing ethnic and religious interests.
- Celebrate multiculturalism as part of their national identity. This has become the United States' policy, though imperfectly and not without struggle, of the late twentieth and twenty-first centuries. Many expect it to become European policy as well, though it is meeting strong resistance in Europe.

One thing a nation cannot do with multiculturalism is ignore it. The Netherlands offers a cautionary example here. For decades the Dutch welcomed immigrants but paid little attention to their cultural worlds, assuming that the Netherlands' easygoing, tolerant, rational way of life would absorb the newcomers and shape their values along European lines. For some immigrants it worked that way, but others were appalled by what they regarded as the licentiousness and godlessness of Dutch life. When Ayaan Hirsi Ali, a Somali-born feminist critical of Islam's treatment of women, and Theo van Gogh, an avant-garde filmmaker, made a provocative film relating the abuse of women to the Qur'an, a radical Islamist named Mohammed Bouyeri responded in November 2004 by stabbing van Gogh to death (Buruma 2006). Bouyeri, born in Amsterdam and holding both Moroccan and Dutch passports, might seem an exemplar of the cosmopolitan, global citizen, but instead he epitomizes those fundamentalists who reject modernity in favor of a narrow and intolerant worldview. He pinned a note to van Gogh's body excoriating the West, Jews, feminists, and secularized Muslims. Immigrant leaders and Dutch officials, while decrying the murder itself, became increasingly engaged in wrestling with the complexities of a multicultural society. A statue, erected in 2007 at the site of the murder, that honors free speech is one symbolic response. More significant is the widespread recognition that while different cultures need not produce perpetual conflict, their co-presence has real consequences—witness the struggle over the "Ground Zero mosque" in New York—that cannot be dismissed in some complacent fantasy of the Enlightenment.

Political Acts as Cultural Objects

Culture's role in political life goes well beyond spectacles of power and group membership. Elected and unelected office holders use aesthetic means to shore up their claims to legitimacy. Rituals seem especially pertinent to the assurance of orderly transitions, continuity despite change, as when European countries proclaim at the accession of a new monarch with "The King is dead. Long live the King." Barack Obama's 2008 Election Night rally in Chicago's Grant Park—the media coverage, the giant high-definition screens, the stage, the flags, the victory speech, and the crowd itself both making history and witnessing itself witnessing history—is a recent case of the ritualized aesthetics of power.

Americans are familiar with the symbols that attend a president: The band plays "Hail to the Chief," everyone stands when the president enters the room, and important speeches are delivered against a carefully studied background of flags, portraits of Lincoln, and other sacred symbols of the American polity. Candidates for office and their advisors ponder how to dress, what photo opportunities to arrange, and how to project both leadership and the common touch required in a democracy. Impressions matter, and the specter of Richard Nixon visibly sweating during his debate with

John Kennedy in 1960 haunts candidates, as the media zoom in. At the inauguration of the president, Washington witnesses a round of balls—there were nine official inaugural balls in 2005—with the president making an appearance to dance briefly at each. Through the media, the whole world is indeed watching, and the rituals do not just ornament the political transition but in some respects actually make it happen.

In Britain the queen opens Parliament each autumn in an elaborate performance that seems straight out of a fairy tale. First is the ceremonial search of the cellars of Westminster Palace, reenacting the danger posed by the Gunpowder Plot of 1605. Next a member of the House of Commons is taken hostage at Buckingham Palace to guarantee the sovereign's safe return. The queen travels to Westminster in a horse-drawn coach, where she puts on the Robes and Crown of State. She delivers the Speech from the Throne (written not by her, of course, but by the Cabinet) outlining the government's agenda for the coming session. Finally she withdraws, having ensured by this ritual that the business of government can commence.

It might seem from such panoply of tradition that when it comes to impression management, more is always better, but this is not the case. Not only does the substance of impression management differ from place to place—black tie and cowboy boots versus the Crown of State—but the style does as well. Jean-Pascal Daloz (2003) has studied displays of ostentation by political elites in various countries. Ostentation in politics is "a sharp contrast with regard to the common lot . . . expressed through the appropriation of the rarest goods but also through the ceremonial, and the most refined manners" (38–39). Ostentation can legitimate power in some contexts but not others (in terms of the cultural diamond, it all depends on the receivers' expectations). Daloz shows that in Nigeria, the leaders' extravagant show of wealth in expensive cars, luxurious dress, and bevies of retainers reassures the clients in a patronage system that the Big Man continues to be in a position to provide for them. At the opposite extreme are the Scandinavian countries, where ostentation is rejected. There, politicians work hard to maintain the profile of being very ordinary and somewhat boring. France falls in between, with leaders wavering between exhibiting aristocratic refinement and the common touch.

Of course, such political rituals often don't succeed. When the electorate perceives politicians to be working too hard on their images, it is distinctly unimpressed. If not altogether cynical, voters are sophisticated in the marketing and media manipulation—spin—done by political candidates, thus making it harder than ever to impress them. New technologies help, so in the early twenty-first century political websites and blogs were fertile arenas for managing impressions and garnering support (Howard Dean's candidacy in 2004 was initially an Internet phenomenon), but such novelty is hard to maintain. Even rituals with some tradition behind them can lose their ability to legitimate power.

This may be a function of the limited capacity of ritual itself in today's complex and media-saturated world. Jeffrey Alexander (2004) has defined rituals as "episodes of repeated and simplified cultural communication in which the direct partners to a social interaction, and those observing it, share a mutual belief in the descriptive and prescriptive validity of the communication's symbolic contents and accept the authenticity of one another's intentions" (527). An effective ritual "energizes the participants and attaches them to each other" (527). This surely captures what every political leader would like to achieve. Formal rituals as such are less central in complex, rationalized societies, but social performances—like those of political leaders—have the same structures and goals (to legitimate power, to make a transition from one social state to another). Such performances and rituals fail when they seem artificial and inauthentic. As always, much depends on the perceptions of those in the position of receiving the cultural object. This is why every four years Americans watch their presidential candidates go through their performances in early primary states—shaking hands in New Hampshire, touring hog farms and ethanol plants in Iowa—but are more amused than persuaded by these mandatory performances.

The slightly silly spectacle of a suit-and-tie candidate making the rounds of hog farms and maple sugar houses is not just an American political quirk. French candidates get photographed on horseback; Japanese politicians protect inefficient rice farmers through tariffs; Nigerian presidents visit chicken farms. "In the South Korean National Assembly, rural voters are 'overrepresented' by a margin of three to one. This disproportionate influence of farm voters has led to high tariffs on food imports, forcing Korean consumers to pay some of the world's highest prices for beef, fruits, and vegetables" (Stokes 2007). Around the ever-more-urban world, the farm is a meaningful cultural object that bespeaks the native soil and homely virtues at the root of national pride. The cultural object is universal, but the particularities—hog farms, rice farms, chicken farms—fit the social world in which the politician is operating. Or at least that is the producer's (the political advisor's, the media specialist's, the party leader's) intention. The recipients (the voters, the onlookers, the media), however, may find the object meaningless, or they may attach a more cynical meaning to it, viewing the image of man-looking-thoughtfully-at-cow not as a signifier of the candidate's rural sympathies but as one more obligatory photo-op as he trolls for votes.

Cultures Without Centers

National myths and politicians' efforts to embody them are fighting against the tide of a de-centered world. At the dawn of the twentieth century, William Butler Yeats made the double prediction that bears repeating: "Things fall apart, the centre cannot hold." Now, at the dawn of a new century, we realize he was half right. Cultural centers did not hold. We have gone from a bipolar to a polycentric world, from a world of cultural hierarchies to a world of multiple and parallel meaning systems, from a world where specialists controlled access to information to a world where "the best that has been thought and known," and the worst too, is accessible to anyone who goes online.

Cultural purity is gone from the face of the earth; it was probably always a myth, but now few even pretend to believe in it. We are all hybrids now (Ang 2001; Bhabha 1994). Even the popular image of multiculturalism as a mosaic, a salad bowl in which different cultures mix but keep their integrity, is misleading (Hannerz 1993). Cultures are more like soups, flavored with many ingredients, some unidentifiable.

At the same time, however, things did not fall apart. Human beings continue to ward off chaos through cultural objects; the embrace of chaos tends to be a temporary and highly stylized posture of youth, like the jackets embroidered with "Live fast, die young." People continue to produce and perpetuate their cultures through interaction and socialization. Our original cultural definitions still work. People may exist in multiple communities through multiple networks, but along these networks they still share meanings with one another. Communities, whether relational or spatial, still collectively represent themselves through patterns of meanings embodied in symbols, meanings that shape attitudes and actions.

In a de-centered world, understanding the connections among cultures and societies may require a handful of cultural diamonds, but the familiar questions still apply. To understand any cultural phenomenon, from the traditional to the postmodern, one needs to ask: What are the characteristics of this specific cultural object? What does it mean, and for whom? Who are its creators? Who are its receivers, and how do they interpret it? From what social world does it come, and into what social world is it sent? One can ask these questions about an MTV video or an idea sent through the Internet just as one can ask them about a Chinese poem or a Nigerian masquerade. Their answers will continue to be revealing about the relevant social world. And those people who can come up with the answers will be those best equipped to navigate in this still new century.

QUESTIONS FOR STUDY AND DISCUSSION

1. Think of the micro-politics, the power struggles and attempts to get one's own way, of a very small group: a dating couple. In the case of a conflict, how does each person use culture to support his or her own position? Develop an example of how the conflict might play out.

2. What makes the various forms of reconstructing the past work politically, and what makes them fail? Consider how a contemporary leader or candidate refers to some historical figure or past event to justify a line of action. Is this move successful? Why or why not?

3. How does your own country, or a country with which you are familiar, deploy culture to create nationalism? What succeeds and what fails? Why are some attempts to do this more successful than others? Is this form of nation building ultimately divisive and destructive, or is it a necessary part of building a collective identity?

4. Can a visual spectacle like a parade or convention have any impact on political life today? What about a website? If you were running for office, what type of political aesthetics would you invest in, and why?

RECOMMENDED FOR FURTHER READING

Howard, Phil. 2006. *New Media Campaigns and the Managed Citizen.* Cambridge, UK: Cambridge University Press. Howard gives a partly appalling, partly amusing account of the impact of the Internet and ICTs on American political life during the first presidential election in which it played a major role. He also portrays the inside-the-beltway geek culture that produces the techno-politics.

Ikegami, Eiko. 2006. *Bonds of Civility: Aesthetic Networks and the Political Origins of Japanese Culture.* Cambridge, UK: Cambridge University Press. In this rich cultural history by a sociologist, Ikegami locates the aesthetic foundation of Japanese collective identity and political practices.

Straughn, Jeremy Brooke. 2005. "Taking the State at Its Word": The Arts of Consentful Contention in the German Democratic Republic. *American Journal of Sociology* 110:1598–1650. Straughn shows how even in a repressive political context, the powerless can fight back by seeming to take the ideals of the powerful with utmost seriousness, thereby justifying their resistance.

References

Adut, Ari. 2008. *On Scandal: Moral Disturbances in Society, Politics, and Art*. Cambridge and New York: Cambridge University Press.

Alexander, Jeffrey C. 2004. "Cultural Pragmatics: Social Performance Between Ritual and Strategy." *Sociological Theory* 22:527–662.

Anderson, Benedict. [1983] 1991. *Imagined Communities: Reflections on the Origin and Spread of Nationalism*. Rev. ed. London: Verso.

Anderson, Elijah. 1990. *Streetwise: Race, Class, and Change in an Urban Community*. Chicago: University of Chicago Press.

Anderson, Elijah. 2011. *The Cosmopolitan Canopy: Race and Civility in Everyday Life*. New York: Norton.

Anderson, Eric. 2009. *Inclusive Masculinity: The Changing Nature of Masculinities*. New York: Routledge.

Ang, Ien. 2001. *On Not Speaking Chinese: Living Between Asia and the West*. London and New York: Routledge.

Appadurai, Arjun. 1990. "Disjuncture and Difference in the Global Cultural Economy." *Public Culture* 2:1–24.

Armstrong, Elizabeth. 2002. *Forging Gay Identities: Organizing Sexuality in San Francisco, 1950–1994*. Chicago: University of Chicago Press.

Arnold, Matthew. [1869] 1949. "Culture and Anarchy." In *The Portable Matthew Arnold*, edited by Lionel Trilling. New York: Viking.

Auyero, Javier and Debora Swistun. 2008. "The Social Production of Toxic Uncertainty." *American Sociological Review* 73:357–379.

Barnard, Chester A. 1939. *The Functions of the Executive*. Cambridge, MA: Harvard University Press.

Barnes, Sandra L. 2005. "Black Church Culture and Community Action." *Social Forces* 84:967–994.

Bastian, Misty L. 1992. "The Lure of the Roads." Pp. 199–254 in *The World as Marketplace: Historical, Cosmological, and Popular Constructions of the Onitsha Market System*. Unpublished doctoral dissertation, University of Chicago.

Bauman, Zygmunt. 2000. *Liquid Modernity*. Cambridge, UK: Polity.

Baumann, Shyon. 2007. *Hollywood Highbrow: From Entertainment to Art.* Princeton, NJ: Princeton University Press.

Baxandall, Michael. 1972. *Painting and Experience in Fifteenth-Century Italy.* New York: Oxford University Press.

Becker, Howard S. 1953. "Becoming a Marihuana User." *American Journal of Sociology* 59:235–242.

Becker, Howard S. 1982. *Art Worlds.* Berkeley: University of California Press.

Becker, Penny. 1999. *Congregations in Conflict: Cultural Models of Local Religious Life.* New York: Cambridge University Press.

Beisel, Nicola. 1990. "Class, Culture, and Campaigns Against Vice in Three American Cities, 1872–1892." *American Sociological Review* 55:44–62.

Bellah, Robert N., Richard Madsen, William M. Sullivan, Ann Swidler, and Steven M. Tipton. 1984. *Habits of the Heart: Individualism and Commitment in American Life.* Berkeley: University of California Press.

Benford, Robert D. and David A. Snow. 2000. "Framing Processes and Social Movements: An Overview and Assessment." *Annual Review of Sociology* 26:611–639.

Benson, Susan Porter. 1986. *Counter Cultures: Saleswomen, Managers, and Customers in American Department Stores, 1890–1940.* Urbana: University of Illinois Press.

Berger, Peter L. 1969. *The Sacred Canopy: Elements of a Sociological Theory of Religion.* New York: Author.

Bhabha, Homi K. 1994. *The Location of Culture.* London and New York: Routledge.

Bielby, William T. and Denise D. Bielby. 1994. "'All Hits Are Flukes': Institutionalized Decision-Making and the Rhetoric of Network Prime-Time Television Program Development." *American Journal of Sociology* 99:1287–1313.

Bijker, Wiebe E. 1995. *Of Bicycles, Bakelites, and Bulbs: Toward a Theory of Sociotechnical Change.* Cambridge: MIT Press.

Binder, Amy J. 2001. *Contentious Curricula: Afrocentrism and Creationism in American Public Schools.* Princeton, NJ: Princeton University Press.

Bordo, Susan. 1993. *Unbearable Weight: Feminism, Western Culture, and the Body.* Berkeley: University of California Press.

Bourdieu, Pierre. 1984. *Distinction: A Social Critique of the Judgment of Taste.* Translated by Richard Nice. Cambridge, MA: Harvard University Press.

Burns, Tom and G. M. Stalker. 1961. *The Management of Innovation.* London: Tavistock.

Buruma, Ian. 2006. *Murder in Amsterdam: The Death of Theo van Gogh and the Limits of Tolerance.* New York: Penguin Press.

Carey, James W. 1989. *Communication as Culture: Essays on Media and Society.* Boston: Unwin Hyman.

Cerulo, Karen. 2006. *Never Saw It Coming: Cultural Challenges to Envisioning the Worst.* Chicago: University of Chicago Press.

Chan, Cheris Shun-ching. 2009. "Invigorating the Content in Social Embeddedness: An Ethnography of Life Insurance Transactions in China." *American Journal of Sociology* 115:712–754.

Chan, Tak Wing and John H. Goldthorpe. 2007. "Social Status and Newspaper Readership." *American Journal of Sociology* 112:1095–1134.

Charles, Maria and Karen Bradley. 2009. "Indulging Our Gendered Selves?: Sex Segregation by Field of Study in 44 Countries." *American Journal of Sociology* 114:924–976.

Chayko, Mary. 2008. *Portable Communities: The Social Dynamics of Online and Mobile Connectedness*. Albany: State University of New York Press.

Chen, Carolyn. 2006. "From Filial Piety to Religious Piety; Evangelical Christianity Reconstructing Taiwanese Immigrant Families in the United States." *International Migration Review* 40:573–602.

Choe, Sang-Hun. 2007. "South Koreans Follow Online Path to Suicide." *International Herald Tribune*, May 21.

Cooley, Charles Horton. [1902] 1964. *Human Nature and the Social Order*. New York: Schocken.

Cooley, Charles Horton. 1956. *Social Organization*. Glencoe, IL: Free Press.

Cornell, Stephen. 1988. *The Return of the Native: American Indian Political Resurgence*. New York: Oxford University Press.

Crozier, Michel. 1964. *The Bureaucratic Phenomenon*. Chicago: University of Chicago Press.

Crystal, David. 2008. *Txtng: The Gr8 Db8*. Oxford, UK: Oxford University Press.

Czarniawska, Barbara. 1997. *Narrating the Organization: Dramas of Institutional Identity*. Chicago: University of Chicago Press.

Daloz, Jean-Pascal. 2003. "Ostentation in Comparative Perspective: Culture and Elite Legitimation." *Comparative Social Research* 21:29–62.

Davies, Christie. 1982. "Sexual Taboos and Social Boundaries." *American Journal of Sociology* 87:1031–1063.

DeSoucey, Michaela. 2010. "Gastronationalism: Food Traditions and Authenticity Politics in the European Union." *American Sociological Review* 75:432–455.

DiMaggio, Paul. 1987. "Classification in Art." *American Sociological Review* 52:440–455.

DiMaggio, Paul. 1997. "Culture and Cognition." *Annual Review of Sociology* 23:263–287.

DiMaggio, Paul and John Mohr. 1985. "Cultural Capital, Educational Attainment, and Marital Selection." *American Journal of Sociology* 90:1231–1261.

Durkheim, Émile. [1915] 1965. *The Elementary Forms of the Religious Life*. Translated by Joseph Ward Swain. New York: Free Press.

Dworkin, Shari L. and Faye Linda Wachs. 2009. *Body Panic: Gender, Health, and the Selling of Fitness*. New York and London: New York University Press.

Eglitis, Daina Stukuls. 2002. *Imagining the Nation: History, Modernity, and Revolution in Latvia*. University Park: Pennsylvania State University Press.

Eisenstein, Elizabeth A. 1979. *The Printing Press as an Agent of Change: Communications and Cultural Transformations in Early-Modern Europe*. Cambridge, UK: Cambridge University Press.

Eliasoph, Nina. 1998. *Avoiding Politics: How Americans Produce Apathy in Everyday Life*. Cambridge, UK, and New York: Cambridge University Press.

Emerson, Michael O. and David Hartman. 2006. "The Rise of Religious Fundamentalism." *Annual Review of Sociology* 32:127–144.

Erickson, Bonnie H. 1996. "Culture, Class, and Connections." *American Journal of Sociology* 102:217–251.

Esherick, Joseph W. 1987. *The Origins of the Boxer Uprising*. Berkeley: University of California Press.

Espeland, Wendy Nelson and Michael Sauder. 2007. "Rankings and Reactivity: How Public Measures Recreate Social Worlds." *American Journal of Sociology* 113:1–40.

Eyerman, Ron. 2002. *Cultural Trauma: Slavery and African-American Identity*. Cambridge, UK: Cambridge University Press.

Eyerman, Ron and Andrew Jamison. 1998. *Music and Social Movements: Mobilizing Traditions in the Twentieth Century*. Cambridge, UK: Cambridge University Press.

Fabricant, Florence. 1992. "Fresh From the Baker, a New Staff of Life." *New York Times*, November 11.

Falasca-Zamponi, Simonetta. 1997. *Fascist Spectacle: The Aesthetics of Power in Mussolini's Italy*. Berkeley: University of California Press.

Fantasia, Rick. 1988. *Cultures of Solidarity: Consciousness, Action, and Contemporary American Workers*. Berkeley: University of California Press.

Faulkner, Robert R. and Andy B. Anderson. 1987. "Short-Term Projects and Emergent Careers: Evidence From Hollywood." *American Journal of Sociology* 92:879–909.

Fine, Gary Alan. 1987. *With the Boys: Little League Baseball and Preadolescent Culture*. Chicago: University of Chicago Press.

Fine, Gary Alan. 1996. *Kitchens: The Culture of Restaurant Work*. Berkeley: University of California Press.

Fine, Gary Alan. 2007. *Authors of the Storm: Meteorologists and the Culture of Prediction*. Chicago: University of Chicago Press.

Fischer, Claude S. 1992. *America Calling: A Social History of the Telephone to 1940*. Berkeley: University of California Press.

Fiske, John. 1989. *Understanding Popular Culture*. Boston: Unwin Hyman.

Gamson, Joshua. 1994. *Claims to Fame: Celebrity in Contemporary America*. Chicago: University of Chicago Press.

Gamson, William A. 1995. "Constructing Social Protest." In *Social Movements and Culture*, edited by Hank Johnston and Bert Klandermans. Minneapolis: University of Minnesota Press.

Garfinkel, Harold. 1967. *Studies in Ethnomethodology*. Englewood Cliffs, NJ: Prentice Hall.

Gaztambide-Fernandez, Rubén A. 2009. *The Best of the Best: Becoming Elite at an American Boarding School*. Cambridge, MA: Harvard University Press.

Geertz, Clifford. 1973. "Religion as a Cultural System." In *The Interpretation of Cultures*. New York: Basic Books.

Gitlin, Todd. 1980. *The Whole World Is Watching: Mass Media in the Making and Unmaking of the New Left.* Berkeley: University of California Press.

Goffman, Erving. 1959. *The Presentation of Self in Everyday Life.* New York: Doubleday.

Goffman, Erving. 1974. *Frame Analysis.* Cambridge, MA: Harvard University Press.

Goldstone, Jack A. 1991. *Revolution and Rebellion in the Early Modern World.* Berkeley: University of California Press.

Goody, Jack and Ian Watt. 1963. "The Consequences of Literacy." *Comparative Studies in Society and History* 5:304–345.

Grant, Don, Alfonso Morales, and Jeffrey J. Sallaz. 2009. "Pathways to Meaning: A New Approach to Studying Emotions at Work." *American Journal of Sociology* 115:327–364.

Grayburn, Nelson H. 1967. "The Eskimos and 'Airport Art.'" *Transaction* (October):28–33.

Grazian, David. 2003. *Blue Chicago: The Search for Authenticity in Urban Blues Clubs.* Chicago: University of Chicago Press.

Griswold, Wendy. 1981. "American Character and the American Novel." *American Journal of Sociology* 86:740–765.

Griswold, Wendy. 1986. *Renaissance Revivals: City Comedy and Revenge Tragedy in the London Theatre 1576–1980.* Chicago: University of Chicago Press.

Griswold, Wendy. 1987. "The Fabrication of Meaning: Literary Interpretation in the United States, Great Britain, and the West Indies." *American Journal of Sociology* 92:1077–1117.

Griswold, Wendy and Nathan Wright. 2004. "Wired and Well Read." In *Society Online: The Internet in Context*, edited by Philip N. Howard and Steve Jones. Thousand Oaks, CA: Sage.

Gusfield, Joseph R. 1981. *The Culture of Public Problems: Drinking-Driving and the Symbolic Order.* Chicago: University of Chicago Press.

Hall, Stuart, Dorothy Hobson, Andrew Lowe, and Paul Willis. 1980. *Culture, Media, Language.* London: Hutchinson.

Hallett, Tim. 2003. "Symbolic Power and Organizational Culture." *Sociological Theory* 21:128–149.

Hannerz, Ulf. 1993. *Cultural Complexity.* New York: Columbia University Press.

Hargittai, Eszter. 2003. "How Wide a Web? Inequalities in Accessing Information Online." Ph.D. dissertation, Department of Sociology, Princeton University.

Hargittai, Eszter. 2010. "Digital Na(t)ives: Variation in Internet Skills and Uses among Members of the 'New Generation'." *Sociological Inquiry* 80:92–113.

Harrison, J. Richard and Glenn R. Carroll. 1991. "Keeping the Faith: A Model of Cultural Transmission in Formal Organizations." *Administrative Science Quarterly* 36:552–582.

Harrison, Lawrence E. and Samuel P. Huntington, eds. 2001. *Culture Matters: How Values Shape Human Progress.* New York: Basic Books.

Harvey, David. 1989. *The Condition of Postmodernity: An Enquiry Into the Origins of Cultural Change.* Oxford, UK: Basil Blackwell.

Hatsumi, Reiko. 1993. "A Simple 'Hai' Won't Do." *New York Times*, April 15.

Hebdige, Dick. 1979. *Subculture: The Meaning of Style*. London and New York: Methuen.

Healy, Kieran. 2006. *Last Best Gifts: Altruism and the Market of Human Blood and Organs*. Chicago: University of Chicago Press.

Heginbotham, Stanley J. 1975. *Cultures in Conflict: The Four Faces of Indian Bureaucracy*. New York: Columbia University Press.

Hilgartner, Stephen and Charles L. Bosk. 1988. "The Rise and Fall of Social Problems: A Public Arenas Model." *American Journal of Sociology* 94:53–78.

Hiller, Harry H. and Tara M. Franz. 2004. "New Ties, Old Ties and Lost Ties: The Use of the Internet in Diaspora." *New Media & Society* 6:731–752.

Hirsch, Paul M. 1972. "Processing Fads and Fashions: An Organization Set Analysis of Culture Industry Systems." *American Journal of Sociology* 77:639–659.

Hochschild, Arlie Russell. 1983. *The Managed Heart: Commercialization of Human Feeling*. Berkeley: University of California Press.

Homans, George C. 1950. *The Human Group*. New York: Harcourt, Brace & World.

Huntington, Samuel P. 1996. *The Clash of Civilizations and the Remaking of World Order*. New York: Simon & Schuster.

Inglis, David, Andrew Blaikie, and Robin Wagner-Pacifici. 2007. "Sociology, Culture and the 21st Century." *Cultural Sociology* 1:5–22.

Jackall, Robert. 1988. *Moral Mazes: The World of Corporate Managers*. New York: Oxford University Press.

Jackall, Robert. 1997. *Wild Cowboys: Urban Marauders & the Forces of Order*. Cambridge, MA: Harvard University Press.

Jacobson, Matthew Frye. 2006. *Roots Too: White Ethnic Revival in Post-Civil Rights America*. Cambridge, MA: Harvard University Press.

Jaeger, Gertrude and Philip Selznick. 1964. "A Normative Theory of Culture." *American Sociological Review* 29:653–669.

Jameson, Frederick. 1984. "Postmodernism, or the Cultural Logic of Late Capitalism." *New Left Review* 146:53–92.

Jauss, Hans Robert. 1982. *Toward an Aesthetic of Reception*. Minneapolis: University of Minnesota Press.

Johnson, Victoria. 2008. *Backstage at the Revolution: How the Paris Opera Survived the End of the Old Regime*. Chicago: University of Chicago Press.

Jones, James Howard. 1992. *Bad Blood: The Tuskegee Syphilis Experiment*. New York: Free Press.

Judge, Timothy A. and Daniel Cable. 2004. "The Effect of Physical Height on Workplace Success and Income: Preliminary Test of a Theoretical Model." *Journal of Applied Psychology* 89:428–441.

Kane, Danielle and Jung Mee Park. 2009. "The Puzzle of Korean Christianity: Geopolitical Newtorks and Religious Conversion in Early Twentieth-Century East Asia." *American Journal of Sociology* 115:365–404.

Kefalas, Maria. 2003. *Working-Class Heroes: Protecting Home, Community, and Nation in a Chicago Neighborhood*. Berkeley: University of California Press.

Keister, Lisa A. 2007. "Upward Wealth Mobility: Exploring the Roman Catholic Advantage." *Social Forces* 85:1195–1225.

Keister, Lisa A. 2008. "Conservative Protestants and Wealth: How Religion Perpetuates Asset Poverty." *American Journal of Sociology* 113:1237–1271.

Kendall, Lori. 2002. *Hanging Out in the Virtual Pub: Masculinities and Relationships Online*. Berkeley: University of California Press.

Kroeber, Alfred L. and Clyde Kluckhohn. 1952. *Culture: A Critical Review of Concepts and Definitions*. Cambridge, MA: Harvard University Peabody Museum of American Archeology and Ethnology.

Kunda, Gideon. 1992. *Engineering Culture: Control and Commitment in a High Tech Organization*. Philadelphia: Temple University Press.

Lamont, Michèle. 1992. *Money, Morals, and Manners: The Culture of the French and the American Upper-Middle Class*. Chicago: University of Chicago Press.

Lamont, Michèle. 2000. *The Dignity of Working Men: Morality and the Boundaries of Race, Class, and Immigration*. New York: Russell Sage.

Landsburg, Steven E. 2002. "Short Changed: Why Do Tall People Make More Money?" Posted on Slate.com, *Everyday Economics*. http://www.slate .com/?id=2063439 (accessed May 29, 2007).

Lareau, Annette. 2003. *Unequal Childhoods: Class, Race, and Family Life*. Berkeley: University of California Press.

Larsen, Elena. 2004. "Deeper Understanding, Deeper Ties: Taking Faith Online." In *Online: The Internet and American Life*, edited by Philip E. N. Howard and Steve Jones. Thousand Oaks, CA: Sage.

Lee, Jennifer and Frank D. Bean. 2007. "Reinventing the Color Line: Immigration and America's New Racial/Ethnic Divide." *Social Forces* 86:561–586.

Lee, Leo Ou-fan and Andrew J. Nathan. 1985. "The Beginnings of Mass Culture: Journalism and Fiction in the Late Ch'ing and Beyond." Pp. 360–395 in *Popular Culture in Late Imperial China*, edited by David Johnson, Andrew J. Nathan, and Evelyn S. Rawski. Berkeley: University of California Press.

Lévi-Strauss, Claude. 1966. *The Savage Mind*. Chicago: University of Chicago Press.

Levine, Lawrence W. 1988. *Highbrow/Lowbrow: The Emergence of Cultural Hierarchy in America*. Cambridge, MA: Harvard University Press.

Levitt, Peggy. 2007. *God Needs No Passport: Immigrants and the Changing American Religious Landscape*. New York: The New Press.

Liebes, Tamar and Elihu Katz. 1990. *The Export of Meaning: Cross-Cultural Readings of Dallas*. New York: Oxford University Press.

Lincoln, James R. and Arne L. Kalleberg. 1990. *Culture, Control, and Commitment: A Study of Work Organizations and Work Attitudes in the United States and Japan*. Cambridge, UK: Cambridge University Press.

Link, Perry. 1981. *Mandarin Ducks and Butterflies: Popular Fiction in Early Twentieth-Century China*. Berkeley: University of California Press.

Lippman, John. 1992. "Tuning in the Global Village." *Los Angeles Times*, October 20.

Lizardo, Omar. 2006. "How Cultural Tastes Shape Personal Networks." *American Sociological Review* 71:778–807.

Loseke, Donileen R. 1999. *Thinking About Social Problems: An Introduction to Constructionist Perspectives*. New York: Aldine de Gruyter.

Lowenthal, David. 1985. *The Past Is a Foreign Country*. Cambridge, UK: Cambridge University Press.

Löwenthal, Leo. [1944] 1968. "The Triumph of Mass Idols." Pp. 109–140 in *Literature, Popular Culture, and Society*. Palo Alto, CA: Pacific.

Luker, Kristen. 1991. "Dubious Conceptions: The Controversy Over Teen Pregnancy." *The American Prospect* 5:73–83.

Martin, Joanne. 1992. *Cultures in Organizations: Three Perspectives*. New York: Oxford University Press.

Marx, Karl. 1977. "Preface to A Contribution to the Critique of Political Economy." Pp. 388–392 in *Karl Marx: Selected Writings*, edited by David McLellan. Oxford, UK: Oxford University Press.

Marx, Karl and Friedrich Engels. 1970. *The German Ideology*. Edited by C. J. Arthur. New York: International Publishers.

Maslow, Abraham H. 1962. *Toward a Psychology of Being*. New York: Van Nostrand.

McGreal, Chris. 2006. "McDonald's Changes Its Brand to Suit Kosher Appetites." *The Guardian*, Monday, March 13. http://www.guardian.co.uk/israel/Story/0,,1729492,00.html (accessed June 3, 2007).

McRoberts, Omar Maurice. 2003. *Streets of Glory: Church and Community in a Black Urban Neighborhood*. Chicago: University of Chicago Press.

Mead, George H. 1934. *Mind, Self, and Society From the Standpoint of a Social Behaviorist*. Chicago: University of Chicago Press.

Melucci, Alberto. 1989. *Nomads of the Present: Social Movements and Individual Needs in Contemporary Society*. Edited by John Keane and Paul Mier. London: Century Hutchinson.

Menchik, Daniel A. and Xiaoli Tian. 2008. "Putting Social Context into Text: The Semiotics of E-mail Interaction." *American Journal of Sociology* 114:332–370.

Merton, Robert K. 1938. "Social Structure and Anomie." *American Sociological Review* 3:672–682.

Meyer, John W. and Brian Rowan. 1977. "Institutionalized Organizations: Formal Structure as Myth and Ceremony." *American Journal of Sociology* 83:340–363.

Meyrowitz, Joshua. 1985. *No Sense of Place: The Impact of Electronic Media on Social Behavior*. New York: Oxford University Press.

Mizrachi, Nissim, Israel Drori, and Renee R. Anspach. 2007. "Repertoires of Trust: The Practice of Trust in a Multinational Organization Amid Political Conflict." *American Sociological Review* 72:143–165.

Modleski, Tania. [1982] 1984. *Loving With a Vengeance: Mass-Produced Fantasies for Women*. New York: Methuen.

Morley, David. 1986. *Family Television: Cultural Power and Domestic Leisure*. London: Comedia Publishing Group.

Morning, Ann. 2009. "Toward a Sociology of Racial Conceptualization for the 21st Century." *Social Forces* 87:1167–1192.

Mukerji, Chandra. 1997. *Territorial Ambitions and the Gardens of Versailles*. Cambridge, UK, and New York: Cambridge University Press.

Mukerji, Chandra. 2009. *Impossible Engineering: Technology and Territoriality on the Canal du Midi*. Princeton, NJ: Princeton University Press.

Myers, B. R. 2010. *The Cleanest Race: How North Koreans See Themselves—and Why It Matters*. Brooklyn, NY: Melville House.

Nagel, Joane. 1995. "American Indian Ethnic Renewal: Politics and the Resurgence of Identity." *American Sociological Review* 60:947–965.

Ogburn, William Fielding. [1922] 1936. *Social Change With Respect to Culture and Original Nature*. New York: Viking.

Okamoto, Dina G. and Lynn Smith-Lovin. 2001. "Changing the Subject: Gender, Status, and the Dynamics of Topic Change." *American Sociological Review* 66:852–873.

Okri, Ben. 1991. *The Famished Road*. London: Jonathan Cape.

Orrù, Marco, Nicole Woolsey Biggart, and Gary G. Hamilton. 1991. "Organizational Isomorphism in East Asia." Pp. 361–389 in *The New Institutionalism in Organizational Analysis*, edited by Walter W. Powell and Paul J. DiMaggio. Chicago: University of Chicago Press.

Parreñas, Rhacel Salazar. 2001. *Servants of Globalization: Women, Migration and Domestic Work*. Stanford, CA: Stanford University Press.

Peterson, Richard A. 1978. "The Production of Cultural Change: The Case of Contemporary Country Music." *Social Forces* 45:292–314.

Peterson, Richard A. 1979. "Revitalizing the Culture Concept." *Annual Review of Sociology* 5:137–166.

Peterson, Richard A. 1992. "Understanding Audience Segmentation: From Elite and Mass to Omnivore and Univore." *Poetics* 21:243–258.

Peterson, Richard A. and N. Anand. 2004. "The Production of Culture Perspective." *Annual Review of Sociology* 30:311–334.

Polletta, Francesca. 2002. *Freedom in an Endless Meeting: Democracy in American Social Movements*. Chicago: University of Chicago Press.

Polletta, Francesca. 2006. *It Was Like a Fever: Storytelling in Protest and Politics*. Chicago: University of Chicago Press.

Powell, Walter W. and Paul J. DiMaggio. 1992. *The New Institutionalism in Organizational Analysis*. Chicago: University of Chicago Press.

Radway, Janice A. 1984. *Reading the Romance: Women, Patriarchy, and Popular Literature*. Chapel Hill: University of North Carolina Press.

Rajagopal, Arvind. 2001. *Politics After Television: Hindu Nationalism and the Reshaping of the Public in India*. Cambridge, UK: Cambridge University Press.

Robinson, John P., Meyer Kestnbaum, Alan Neustadtl, and Anthony Alvarez. 2002. "The Internet and Other Uses of Time." Pp. 244–262 in *The Internet in Everyday Life*, edited by Barry Wellman and Caroline Haythornthwaite. Malden, MA: Blackwell.

Saguy, Abigail C. 2003. *What Is Sexual Harassment?* Berkeley: University of California Press.

Sahlins, Marshall. 1985. *Islands of History*. Chicago: University of Chicago Press.

Scheper-Hughes, Nancy. 1992. *Death Without Weeping: The Violence of Everyday Life in Brazil*. Berkeley: University of California Press.

Schilt, Kristen and Laurel Westbrook. 2009. "Doing Gender, Doing Heteronormativity: 'Gender Normals,' Transgender People, and the Social Maintenance of Heterosexuality." *Gender & Society* 23:440–464.

Schwartz, Barry. 1996. "Memory as a Cultural System: Abraham Lincoln in World War II." *American Sociological Review* 61:908–927.

Sewell, William. 1992. "A Theory of Structure: Duality, Agency, and Transformation." *American Journal of Sociology* 98:1–29.

Shilts, Randy. 1987. *And the Band Played On: Politics, People, and the AIDS Epidemic*. New York: St. Martin's.

Silva, Jennifer M. 2008. "A New Generation of Women?: How Female ROTC Cadets Negotiate the Tension Between Masculine Military Culture and Traditional Femininity." *Social Forces* 87:937–960.

Snow, David A., E. Burke Rochford Jr., Steven K. Worden, and Robert D. Benford. 1986. "Frame Alignment Processes, Micromobilization, and Movement Participation." *American Sociological Review* 51:464–481.

Snow, David A., and Leon Anderson. 1993. *Down on Their Luck: A Study of Homeless Street People*. Berkeley: University of California Press.

Spence, Jonathan D. 1990. *The Search for Modern China*. New York: Norton.

Steensland, Brian. 2007. *The Failed Welfare Revolution: America's Struggle Over Guaranteed Income Policy*. Princeton, NJ: Princeton University Press.

Stendhal (Marie Henri Beyle). [1830] 1958. *The Red and the Black*. Translated by Lowell Bair. New York: Bantam.

Stevens, Wallace. [1936] 1954. "The Man With the Blue Guitar." P. 165 in *The Collected Poems of Wallace Stevens*. New York: Alfred A. Knopf.

Stokes, Bruce. 2007. "Protectionism and Politics." *International Information Programs eJournal USA: An Electronic Journal of the U.S. Department of State* (January). http://usinfo.state.gov/journals/ites/0107/ijee/stokes.htm (accessed May 31, 2007).

Swidler, Ann. 1986. "Culture in Action: Symbols and Strategies." *American Sociological Review* 51:273–286.

Swidler, Ann. 2001. *Talk of Love: How Culture Matters*. Chicago: University of Chicago Press.

Tannahill, Reay. 1973. *Food in History*. New York: Stein & Day.

Tarm, Michael. 2003. "Small Baltic Nation Blazes Internet Trail." Associated Press, April 20.

Thomas, W. I. 1966. *W. I. Thomas on Social Organization and Social Personality: Selected Papers*. Edited and with an Introduction by Morris Janowitz. Chicago: University of Chicago Press.

Thomas, William I. and Florian Znaniecki. 1918–1920. *The Polish Peasant in Europe and America: Monograph of an Immigrant Group*. Chicago: University of Chicago Press.

Thrasher, Frederic Milton. 1927. *The Gang: A Study of 1,313 Gangs in Chicago*. Chicago: University of Chicago Press.

Turner, Bryan S. 2007. "Religious Authority and the New Media." *Theory, Culture & Society* 24:117–134.

Tylor, Edward B. [1871] 1958. *Primitive Culture: Researches Into the Development of Mythology, Philosophy, Religion, Art, and Custom.* Gloucester, MA: Smith.

UCLA Center for Communication Policy. 2003. "The UCLA Internet Report: Surveying the Digital Future: Year Three." Available online at www.ccp.ucla.edu

Vaisey, Stephen. 2007. "Structure, Culture, and Community: The Search for Belonging in 50 Urban Communes." *American Sociological Review* 72:851–873.

Vaughan, Diane. 1996. *The Challenger Launch Decision: Risky Technology, Culture, and Deviance at NASA.* Chicago: University of Chicago Press.

Walsh, Joan. 2007. "Men Who Hate Women on the Web." http://www.salon.com/opinion/feature/2007/03/31/sierra/ (posted March 31, 2007; accessed June 1, 2007).

Watson, J. L., ed. 1997. *Golden Arches East: McDonald's in East Asia.* Stanford, CA: Stanford University Press.

Weber, Max. (1904–1905) 1985. *The Protestant Ethic and the Spirit of Capitalism.* Translated by Talcott Parsons; introduction by Anthony Giddens. London and Boston: Unwin Paperbacks.

Weber, Max. 1946. From *Max Weber: Essays in Sociology*, edited by H. H. Gerth and C. Wright Mills. New York: Oxford University Press.

Wellman, Barry and Caroline Haythornthwaite, eds. 2002. *The Internet in Everyday Life.* Malden, MA: Blackwell.

Wertham, Frederic. 1954. *Seduction of the Innocent.* New York: Rinehart.

Wherry, Frederick F. 2008. *Global Markets and Local Crafts: Thailand and Costa Rica Compared.* Baltimore, MD: Johns Hopkins University Press.

White, Harrison C. and Cynthia A. White. 1965. *Canvases and Careers: Institutional Change in the French Painting World.* New York: John Wiley.

Wilde, Melissa J. 2007. *Vatican II: A Sociological Analysis of Religious Change.* Princeton, NJ: Princeton University Press.

Wilkins, Amy C. 2008. *Wannabes, Goths and Christians: The Boundaries of Sex, Style, and Status.* Chicago: University of Chicago Press.

Williams, Raymond. [1973] 1980. "Base and Superstructure in Marxist Cultural Theory." Pp. 31–49 in *Problems in Materialism and Culture.* London: Verso.

Williams, Raymond. 1976. *Keywords: A Vocabulary of Culture and Society.* New York: Oxford University Press.

Wilson, William Julius. 1987. *The Truly Disadvantaged: The Inner City, the Underclass, and Public Policy.* Chicago: University of Chicago Press.

Wray, Matt. 2006. *Not Quite White: White Trash and the Boundaries of Whiteness.* Durham, NC: Duke University Press.

Wright, Lawrence. 2006. *The Looming Tower: Al-Qaeda and the Road to 9/11.* New York: Alfred A. Knopf.

Wuthnow, Robert. 1985. "State Structures and Ideological Outcomes." *American Sociological Review* 50:799–821.

Wuthnow, Robert. 1987. *Meaning and Moral Order: Explorations in Cultural Analysis.* Berkeley: University of California Press.

Wuthnow, Robert and Marsha Witten. 1988. "New Directions in the Study of Culture." *Annual Review of Sociology* 14:49–67.

Yang, Guobin. 2009. *The Power of the Internet in China: Citizen Activism Online.* New York: Columbia University Press.

Yeats, William Butler. 1956. "The Second Coming." P. 184 in *The Collected Poems of W. B. Yeats.* New York: Macmillan.

Zerubavel, Eviatar. 1997. *Social Mindscapes.* Cambridge, MA: Harvard University Press.

Index

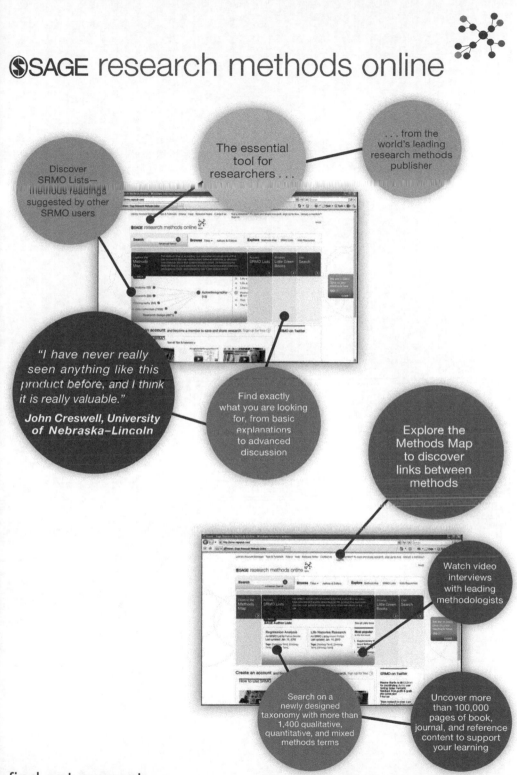

$SAGE research methods online

Discover SRMO Lists—methods readings suggested by other SRMO users

The essential tool for researchers . . .

. . . from the world's leading research methods publisher

"I have never really seen anything like this product before, and I think it is really valuable."
John Creswell, University of Nebraska–Lincoln

Find exactly what you are looking for, from basic explanations to advanced discussion

Explore the Methods Map to discover links between methods

Watch video interviews with leading methodologists

Search on a newly designed taxonomy with more than 1,400 qualitative, quantitative, and mixed methods terms

Uncover more than 100,000 pages of book, journal, and reference content to support your learning

find out more at
www.srmo.sagepub.com